A Pattern of Rulers

By the same author

GENERAL

War By Revolution
Ten Angels Swearing
Democracy's Last Battle
The Triple Challenge
Ernest Bevin—Portrait of an Englishman
A Prime Minister Remembers
(*with Earl Attlee*)
Press, Parliament and People
Dangerous Estate: The Anatomy of Newspapers
The American Invasion

FICTION

No Man Is An Island
A Provincial Affair
The Richardson Story

Francis Williams

A PATTERN OF
RULERS

Longmans

LONGMANS, GREEN AND CO. LTD
48 Grosvenor Street, London W1

*Associated companies, branches and representatives
throughout the world*

*Printed in Great Britain by
The Camelot Press Ltd, London and Southampton*

To Jess — As always

Contents

Foreword to a Puzzle   1

Stanley Baldwin

1. *Reluctantly to Business*   5
2. *Struggle with the Devil*   12
3. *The Man Who Understood the English*   25
4. *Rise and Fall of an Idol of the People*   42

Ramsay MacDonald

1. *Young Man on the Outside*   61
2. *The Doors Swing Open*   73
3. *Survival of a Myth*   80
4. *The Appearance of Leadership*   97
5. *Palladium of the People*   109
6. *Death of a Wraith*   125

Neville Chamberlain

1. *Solitary in Andros*   135
2. *Businessman in Politics*   144
3. *Diplomacy by Bigamy*   152
4. *The Age of the Old Men*   159
5. *Peace Not in Our Time*   182

Montagu Norman

1. *Lame Duck in Hell*   195
2. *Autocrat on the Gold Standard*   205

Lord Halifax

1. *Saint in Anger*   223
2. *Patrician over Politics*   228
3. *The Indestructible Man*   238

The Age of Myth   251

Select Bibliography   261

Index   263

Illustrations

Baldwin
New Statesman, 4 November 1933
PAGE 47

Tramsay
Evening Standard, 10 February 1930
PAGE 103

Would you oblige me with a match please?
Evening Standard, 25 February 1938
PAGE 164

Here we go round the mulberry bush
Evening Standard, 24 October 1932
PAGE 220

Nazi Hunting Exhibition
Evening Standard, 19 November 1937
PAGE 233

We are indebted to the executors of the late
Sir David Low and to the *New Statesman* and
Evening Standard for permission to reproduce
these cartoons

Foreword to a Puzzle

THERE have been few periods in our history when so unfortunate a hash of affairs was made in so many directions in so short a time as in the twenty years from 1919 to 1939. In retrospect appeasement and the consequences that flowed from it tend to push into the background the rest of those two disastrous decades. But before consigning their country to a war that earlier prudence and courage might have made unnecessary, the small group of people who passed power from hand to hand in Britain at this time also embroiled their country in the only General Strike in its history, helped to put more of its people out of work than ever before or since, evoked a run on the pound and the crash of the gold standard and produced a mutiny in the Royal Navy. For good measure they also got rid of a king. But that was, perhaps, not their fault.

In these two decades Britain came nearer to one-party government than at any time since modern parties began. The disintegration of the Liberal Party, the weakness of the Labour Party which found itself thrust prematurely into major parliamentary place and office without the electoral backing or political cohesion to support its condition, produced a situation where the challenge and counter-challenge of political interests on which the parliamentary system depends virtually ceased to exist as an effective force. In 1931 it was openly abandoned with the formation of the National Government. Thenceforward Britain had its own respectable version of single-party rule.

The theme of this book is the part played by personality in these events. One must not overestimate the significance of the individual in politics. There are tides of history beyond personal or national control: political, social and economic movements that even the most powerful individuals cannot halt or deflect. But equally one must not underestimate what Professor Trevor-Roper has rightly called 'the huge consequence of personality in politics'. The room for manoeuvre open to individual British statesmen at decisive stages in the two decades between the wars was considerable – certainly greater in international affairs than it is ever likely to be again. Of those who directed our affairs in these years it can properly be said, as Sir Pierson Dixon has written of the rulers of sixth-century Constantinople, that they 'shaped and marred history in a very individual way at a turning point in human affairs'.

From this remarkable period the personalities of five men emerge with particular emphasis, forming a subtle and intricate pattern of high-mindedness and disaster: Stanley Baldwin, Ramsay MacDonald, Neville Chamberlain, Montagu Norman and Lord Halifax; three Prime Ministers, a banker and an ecclesiastically-minded peer. They were not the greatest men of their time. Foreshortened by distance they seem, indeed, in many ways extraordinarily small to have played so large a part in so great a drama. But individually and as a group they exercised effective power and influence longer and more decisively than any others. Nor did they seem small to most, though not all, of their contempories. They were admired more than most men. Each achieved a pinnacle of public adulation rare indeed in our public life – only, in the case of four of them, to fall from it to depths of public contempt as much below their true deserts as their earlier eminence had been above. There is about all their careers an almost classical symmetry of triumph and disaster.

They were not guilty men. Or if they were their guilt was of innocence, not intent. Yet coming to power after what had been until then the greatest war in history each became in some degree an impresario of the next, which was to be even greater. Moreover, although at the end of the first world war all were of an age at which those likely to establish themselves in positions of power have normally reached at least the middle peaks of fame, none at that time seemed likely candidates for authority. Neither character nor attainment distinguished them. Unnoticed or little esteemed, they waited in the wings for the astonishing moment when destiny called them. One of the most puzzling features of those puzzling decades is surely that of all those available the British people accepted these men to control their affairs and having accepted them approved them so long.

What kind of men were they and how far did the kind of men they were determine events? In seeking an answer one needs to remember that, as that most perceptive of modern parliamentary reporters, the late Harry Boardman, once observed, 'there is always a great possibility of error in inferring the real from the public character of a statesman'. The possibility is not less when the inference is drawn the other way round. In these frankly personal portraits of five men, all of whom I knew and whom I had the opportunity to observe closely at several important stages in their careers, I have done my best to bear this in mind. The private personalities of public men are one element only in their public personalities which are constantly affected by the movement of events and the response of audiences. But they are an important element. The private life of an artist, as W. H. Auden has observed, is irrelevant to a study of his work but 'a man of action, a ruler, a statesman, a general, is identical with his biography ... we can distinguish between his private personal life and his public life but both are lives of action and therefore capable of affecting each other'. Although one must not, of course, wholly identify the private with the public man, the successes and failures of a public man's non-public self, the moral demands that move or fail to move him, the durability of his nervous system and the temper of his mind, are all relevant to a consideration of why he acted the way he did. A statesman must be measured against a background. But what he himself is helps to determine the shape of the shadow he throws. These five men have thrown long shadows. It is the thesis of this book that there are elements in their personalities – sometimes bizarre, sometimes tragic – that compose an oddly similar pattern and that this pattern is of significance still.

Yet although they are here considered as public men, components in a pattern that greatly affected the history of the twentieth century, I would not have it thought that this is their only interest. Lytton Strachey observed in his introduction to *Eminent Victorians* that 'Human beings are too important to be treated as mere symptoms of the past'. If it is as symptoms of the past, a past so near as to be still almost a part of our present, shaping it and our future also, that these five have their public importance it is as human beings that they intrigue. They have fascinated me for some thirty-five years or more, ever since as a very young writer on political and economic matters I first became acquainted with them and found myself irresistibly drawn to trying to understand what had made them the kind of people they were. It may be that part of their interest for me was that they were almost the first public men I knew. Familiarity had not yet dulled the palate. But I think there was more to it than this. There was, as one observed them, the difference in so many respects between the private man and the

3

public one. And not only this, but the unexpected vistas of personality one kept stumbling on, mysteries round corners. They seemed to me at that time to be very rum people indeed to be in the positions they were and to command such adulation as they did. They still do.

Let us begin with Stanley Baldwin.

Stanley Baldwin

Born 1867; son of Alfred Baldwin, M.P., ironmaster; educated at Harrow and Trinity, Cambridge; Unionist M.P. for Bewdley, Worcestershire, 1908-37; Financial Secretary to the Treasury 1917-21; President of the Board of Trade 1921-22; Chancellor of the Exchequer 1922-23; Prime Minister 1923-24, 1924-29; Chancellor of Cambridge University 1930; Lord President of the Council 1931-35; Lord Privy Seal 1932-34; Prime Minister 1935-37; created Earl Baldwin of Bewdley 1937; died 1947.

1. Reluctantly to Business

ONE June day in the summer of 1883 the Headmaster of Harrow School, Dr Montagu Butler, found himself confronted with a troublesome moral problem, although not, it might be thought, a very exceptional one in a schoolmaster's career. A boy of fifteen in the Lower Sixth, a member of his own House, had been caught in possession of 'a piece of pornography'. It was of a nature greatly to shock his Headmaster, who found it hard to credit that one under his own moral influence could stoop so low, especially as the boy concerned, the sandy haired son of a prosperous and godly ironmaster of Wilden in Worcestershire, had previously been known as a model student, indeed in some ways a brilliant one: the previous term he had not only won his form prizes for classics, history and mathematics but a Headmaster's prize also. Dr Butler was shocked almost as much by the hypocrisy as by the sin.

A telegram was at once dispatched to the boy's father, the Worcestershire ironmaster. It reached him as he completed an entry in his journal on his forty-second birthday: 'I have many things to be thankful for ... but I cannot feel too lighthearted when I remember past years. God be merciful to me and my boy.' A long letter in Dr Butler's own hand followed. It gave further details of the dreadful business and asked for attendance at Harrow without delay.

Meanwhile, Dr Butler wrestled with his conscience. His duty to the school – to society as a whole indeed – seemed to point to expulsion before contamination could spread. But was there no case for clemency? If the boy showed true penitence, might not a flogging and public disgrace be sufficient to save his soul and convey adequate warning to others? Could he be believed if he did profess repentance?

It was only after a long interview between Dr Butler and the shaken father who expressed a manly faith in his boy's fundamental goodness that clemency won the day. The moral needs of the closing decade of Victoria's reign were satisfied by a flogging. Stanley Baldwin was reprieved.

Looked at retrospectively this affair, whatever it meant to Dr Butler, is hardly likely to impress the modern observer as having much intrinsic importance. Yet it cannot help but seem a bizarre incident in the boyhood of a future Prime Minister – particularly such a Prime Minister as Mr Baldwin. But if bizarre it was also characteristic. The young Baldwin's fall from grace was, it would appear, due rather to indolence than sin. He lacked the interest or the energy to pass on what had been passed to him.

Upon his scholastic career, and perhaps upon his character, the incident had an effect altogether disproportionate to the offence. Although reprieved Baldwin was not forgiven. The formidable Dr Butler did not forget. Henceforth the light of his countenance was withdrawn from the once promising pupil and Baldwin was allowed to enjoy none of those honours and offices which normally accrue to the bright boy on his way through school. Alone among his contemporaries he was never promoted to be a monitor.

In later years although he could never quite bring himself to wear his old school tie but liked, according to his son, to wear instead the red, yellow and black of I Zingari, he was to boast of packing more old Harrovians into his Cabinet than any Prime Minister has ever done before and declare (at the age of fifty-six): 'As a son of the Hill I will run straight: I will bear my share of the burden. If I fail I will not whine and, if success is mine, I shall not be puffed up but I will try in all things to follow in the footsteps of those who have trodden this same difficult path before me; and I will, with God's help, do nothing in the course of an arduous and difficult career which shall cause any Harrovian to say of me that I have failed to do my best to live up to the highest ideals of the school.' In the circumstances this speech indicates a nostalgia for the days of youth more than usually masochistic, for

6

after the incident in the Lower Sixth Baldwin tried for no more prizes, achieved no more distinctions, did no work that he could avoid. Conscious of injustice, he neither rebelled nor sought to rehabilitate himself, retreating – the pattern was to repeat itself in later life – into nonactivity until the time of escape should come. On the evidence of his first few terms he had expected to leave Harrow in, at the very least, a modest glow of academic glory. Instead he left it with a reputation as a docile but mediocre student: 'A nice enough boy', said one of his masters, 'but without the brains to do anything big.'

By what must have seemed a particularly unfair stroke of fate, when he did finally escape to the university the consequences of the unfortunate affair at Harrow followed him. He arrived at Cambridge to find that a new Master of his college, Trinity, had just been installed – Dr Butler. The suspicious, disapproving eye stayed on him – not to soften until another thirty years had passed and the reputation of the statesman could be thrown into the scales to outbalance the misdemeanour of the boy.

It was an unhappy background to a university career. Baldwin abandoned classics for history, where he was less likely to come up against his old headmaster, and retreated into the negative somnolence that was to become his habitual defence in moments of nervous crisis. Such ambitions as he had brought with him were allowed to wither. He had at one time hoped for an academic career – he remained something of an academic *manqué* all his life – but came down with a poor third. 'I hope', said his father, 'this does not mean you are to be third class all your life.'

In later life Baldwin liked to be thought of as the most English of Prime Ministers, 'English of the English … not Scottish or Welsh', as one admirer, D. C. Somervell, wrote. In fact, although Worcestershire born, he was wholly Celt on his mother's side, a Macdonald with a strong clash of Welsh, and even some Irish, blood along with that of the Highlands. In him the war of Saxon and Celt of which A. E. Housman wrote from the neighbouring county of Shropshire (from which indeed the Baldwins themselves originally came) was never quite stilled.

> In my heart it has not died,
> The war that sleeps on Severn side;
> They cease not fighting, east and west,
> On the marches of my breast.

7

He was an only child. His mother was the youngest but one of the clever and lively daughters of the distinguished Methodist preacher and writer of popular fairy stories, George Macdonald. All but one of her sisters made some stir in the world; one married Edward Burne-Jones, the pre-Raphaelite painter, another Edward Poynter, later President of the Royal Academy, a third was the mother of Rudyard Kipling. She herself was well known to the Victorian lending library public as the successful author of romantic melodramas of the Worcestershire countryside in whose simple tales, so unlike the political life, virtue after an adequate number of vicissitudes always triumphed and villainy after transitory success suffered a proper penalty.

Baldwin was deeply attached to his mother. No doubt it was from her that he inherited that touch of literary sentiment that later won him such popular success as an orator: the various collections of his speeches under such titles as *On England* and *Service of Our Lives* sold in almost as large numbers as the novels of Mary Webb, whom he made into a best-seller when he referred to her in one of them: surely a truly staggering demonstration of his hold on the British people.

Louisa Baldwin was a confirmed invalid. Her days were spent concocting her romantic melodramas on a couch in a curtained room. She left it rarely and then always in an invalid chair, a brave and un-complaining martyr to motherhood, for her invalidism dated from her son's birth and made it dangerous, so her doctors said, for her to con-template having another child. It is possible that modern medical science might have diagnosed her complaint as psychosomatic. At any rate when her son was fifteen a visit to a doctor in Westphalia produced a cure. When Baldwin saw her descend from her carriage and walk towards him on the lawn he turned deathly white and those with him thought he would fall to the ground in a faint.

His father, a successful ironmaster and local M.P., was a man of great energy and commercial shrewdness, but sombre of temperament and much tortured by nerves – he had a severe facial tic and was so terrified of physical violence that he would fling himself prostrate on the floor during a thunderstorm. Originally a Dissenter, he had turned High Churchman and communed constantly with God in his private diaries. The success of the firm of E. P. and W. Baldwin Ltd, origin-ally founded by his father, was due entirely to him, for he had taken it over when it had been brought to the verge of bankruptcy by the wildness of two half-brothers and turned it into a flourishing industrial enterprise and one of the largest and most benevolent employers of labour in the country. This success he achieved only at the cost of an iron self-control in the day-to-day business of living that precluded any demonstration of private feeling, lest emotion, if once allowed to show itself, should break all bounds. This fear of the show of emotion he passed, along with much else, to his son, who, when he himself was grown up and married, was so disturbed by seeing his wife enact a love scene on the stage that she had to agree never again to take part in the amateur theatricals in which she delighted.

Morally upright and austere in habit, paternalistic in his business dealings and frugal in his personal life, Alfred Baldwin set standards it was not always easy for a boy to follow. He had never known his own father, who died before he was born, and his relationship with his son if affectionate was never intimate. Even in later years Baldwin remained deeply in awe of him, finding ordinary communication difficult. When some time after his son's marriage the elder Baldwin offered to meet the cost of alterations to his house to make it more suitable for a growing family and then overlooked the account in his preoccupation with other matters, his son could not bring himself to remind him of it, although what would have meant little or nothing to the older man placed the younger one in grave difficulties.

It was a strange, inhibited childhood for a man whom the British people were later to take to their hearts as a simple, placid countryman. The nervous strains it imposed left their mark in a twitching of the facial muscles very similar to the tic from which his father suffered, and a habit of involuntarily snapping his fingers which conveyed to the observant a revealing comment on the public image he managed to impose on his followers. His maternal relations, the Burne-Joneses, the Poynters and the Kiplings, brought him, it is true, glimpses of a more spacious and genial world – although one, in the case of the Kiplings, not without its own undertones of darkness. But the Baldwin family was tightly knit and possessive. It was the life at Wilden, and, above all, the example of the austere and god-like, although often emotionally tortured, figure of his father that fixed the mould in which Baldwin grew to maturity.

In his political life later he often spoke of the virtues of that industrial paternalism, already passing by the time he came to know it, of which his father was the epitome. It had, however, few attractions for him as a young man. He was a conscript to the family business, not a volunteer, doomed to a fate he loathed by the unhappy consequences of that trivial affair in the Lower Sixth of Harrow School and its effects on his subsequent career at school and university. When his hopes of an academic life had to be abandoned he wrote to his father from Cambridge asking to be allowed to take Holy Orders. But it was not a proposal that recommended itself to the elder Baldwin who wished his son to follow him in the family business, and was soon forgotten. With a better degree Baldwin might have found the courage to stand out against his father's plans. With no more than a Third he lacked, or felt he lacked, the munitions to oppose so formidable a force. He acquiesced.

Henceforth for the rest of his father's life he devoted himself to a career for which he had neither aptitude nor liking, finding particularly unsympathetic the Midland businessmen with whom he was sent to consort on the Birmingham metal exchange.

'He hates it cordially but, of course, as a sensible man, will stick to it and do his level best', his cousin Harold Baldwin, who had been his closest personal friend at Cambridge, noted in his diary after one talk. And on another occasion '... he's evidently awfully depressed by this damnably dull business life and he hates it as cordially as I do: poor old chap, it is terrible for him, and as one looks forward the view is gloomier still'. And on a third occasion: 'The way in which he has settled down to business amazes one ... and at the same time from the bottom of his heart he detests it.' Harold Baldwin was an epileptic. His first totally unexpected attack had taken place at Cambridge in the presence of his shocked and horrified cousin who picked him up bleeding after a fall from a window. The progressive deterioration in his condition thereafter forced him to abandon all hopes of a career for himself. But he seems to have spent much of his time sympathising with his cousin's lot.

Over the next twenty years such relief as there was from the uncongenial life of business, in which Baldwin made the progress to be expected of the only son of the head of the firm, came out of working hours in the minor preoccupations of a country gentleman. He liked to spend his time ruminating in his library (he would amble from shelf to shelf picking up first one book and then another and putting them to his nose to sniff in the same way as later he would often be seen sniffing papers on the Front Bench), or strumming on a mechanical piano player.

He married when he was twenty-five: a marriage, according to his chosen official biographer, G. M. Young, of affection rather than passion – although not all the secrets of the human heart are known, of course, to official biographers, even those who, as happened with Young, find that they do not like their subjects very much. His wife, Lucy Ridsdale, was a neighbour of his Burne-Jones relations at Rottingdean and, according to report, first touched his heart when he watched her score half a century in a ladies' cricket match. She was a pleasant, robust girl, fond of dancing, parties and amateur theatricals – which he was not – and of hockey and cricket – which he was – but with few intellectual interests to match his. However, she was kindly, cheerful and practical, and along with many other middle-class virtues possessed a strong loyalty to her husband and a determination to push him on. She made him a staunch and faithful companion, well suited to what then appeared to be his modest ambitions in life, and liked to call him by what seemed to many the inappropriate pet name of 'Tiger'.

Thus he proceeded prosaically on his way to middle age; not quite a businessman nor yet a countryman. (Astley Hall to which he moved four years after his marriage had a hundred acres of land but he let off all but twenty to a neighbouring farm and left the management of such few cows, pigs and chickens as he owned entirely to his wife, keeping in touch with them only for oratorical purposes.) He was an amateur 'man of letters' without the self-discipline to be a scholar, a faithful but undistinguished member of Worcestershire County Council and Worcestershire County Cricket Club, a Justice of the Peace, a kindly employer, a devoted husband and father of six children. That such a man should in due course stand for Parliament in the Conservative interest was only to be expected, and in the General Election of 1906 he duly presented himself to the electors of the Kidderminster Division, a safe Conservative seat neighbouring his father's constituency. 'If my son is returned to Parliament,' his father told the voters, 'he will be an honest representative.'

Baldwin found electioneering uncongenial, 'cleansing' his mind of it each evening, as he later told the Classical Association, by reading Homer and Horace. However, even though the tide was running against the Conservatives in the country as a whole there seemed no reason to doubt that the electors of Kidderminster would do their duty by a local man, especially since on the as yet unreformed register they numbered only 4,697, solid citizens all. In the event they proved no fonder of Baldwin than he of them. When the votes were counted it was found that he had succeeded for the first and only time in its history in turning what had hitherto been a safe Tory seat into a Liberal one, to the deep hurt of his father who walked away from the count, his Jehovah-like head with its great flowing beard bowed in sorrow, through a crowd that opened to let him pass, shocked into silence by the enormity of what it had done. There was even less enthusiasm when he subsequently offered to stand as the champion of the Conservatives of Worcester City in a by-election. Not even his father's local influence could get him past the selection committee. He was, as he wrote bitterly later, turned down 'in my own country town in favour of a stranger'.

It seems very doubtful whether those who knew him locally would ever have brought themselves to the pitch of choosing him to represent them had not his father's sudden death from heart failure in 1908 made the loyal people of Bewdley feel that the least they could do to honour his memory was to offer his seat to his son. He was returned unopposed and represented Bewdley for the rest of his political life, never again being called on to fight a hotly contested seat.

He was forty, a good age for entering Parliament, but there was nothing to suggest that he would make any particular mark on it or become at the best more than a reasonably good local member, a conscientious County Councillor and Justice of the Peace transferred to a larger stage. Such fires as may once have burned within him had, it seemed, long been damped down. He appeared a modest, ruminating man, square of face and build, provincial in manner and ideas, who had come to terms with what life offered and shelved ambition along with discontent as inconvenient appendages to a commonplace existence.

Yet within fifteen years of his father's death he was Prime Minister of Britain, to reach in that office a peak of public adulation scarcely paralleled in democratic politics, only to fall when he was old into the extremes of public dishonour and contempt. It was not a fate anyone could have envisaged for the middle-aged man from Worcestershire as he took the oath.

2. Struggle with the Devil

THERE is nothing in the history of modern British politics to parallel either the speed or the unexpectedness of Stanley Baldwin's rise. The rapidity of this advance, the fact that he came to the premiership less skilled and experienced in politics of the first rank than any man before or since, was important in determining his future role in the life of the country.

He spoke only five times in his first six years of parliamentary life and although he was to become one of the great masters of the House of Commons found himself at first singularly un-at-home in it. Even midway through the first world war, and a mere six years off becoming Prime Minister, he was still so despondent about his chances of making anything out of the political life that he had a mind to resign and 'go back to the County Council'. It was his wife who persuaded him to 'give it another two years'.

By the time these two years were up the scene had changed. Not very dramatically. Not yet with any great promise of the future. But sufficient to make the parliamentary life seem worth while. Ironically this was due, in part, to one whom he was later to distrust more than almost any man in public life and who was to become one of his bitterest political enemies – Max Aitken. Aitken was not yet Lord Beaverbrook. But already he was a power in the land because of his intimate relationship with his fellow Canadian, Bonar Law, and Bonar Law as it happened was looking for a Parliamentary Private Secretary. It occurred to Aitken that the unambitious ironmaster from Worcestershire might very suitably fill the bill. He was rich enough to entertain back-bench M.P.s on his master's behalf, unimportant enough to have no enemies, and sufficiently unassuming not to cause any rivalries. The Unionist Chief Whip, Lord Edmund Talbot, endorsed the opinion. Baldwin, he affirmed, according to Wickham Steed, later Editor of *The Times*, was 'discreet enough to be safe and stupid enough not to intrigue'. With these impeccable references Baldwin got the job. Two years later in consideration of his faithful service his Chief secured his promotion to the Junior Ministerial rank of Joint Financial Secretary to the Treasury. He had reached one of the foothills of power.

From this lowly vantage point he observed the life of Parliament for four years. He did not greatly like what he saw, particularly after the Khaki election of December 1918. 'The prevailing type is a rather successful-looking business kind which is not very attractive', he wrote to his mother. And to Maynard Keynes, who later quoted the remark as from 'a Conservative friend', he observed more succinctly that the new House seemed to be composed of 'hard-faced men who look as if they have done very well out of the war'.

He had done fairly well himself. But, unlike many of these whose leader he was so surprisingly to become, he did not enjoy it and very characteristically did what he could to reduce the burden of unsought guilt by an anonymous, but later famous, letter to *The Times* over the initials 'F.S.T.' (borrowed from his post as Financial Secretary to the Treasury). In this he announced that he had decided to give twenty per cent of his total wealth to the nation by offering £120,000 of war loan to the Exchequer for cancellation. Other rich men, he suggested, would be happy to do the same. In this he proved mistaken.

He was now over fifty. He had dreams of some day becoming Chancellor of the Exchequer: 'That is the limit of my ambitions', he said. Neither Bonar Law nor his new chief at the Treasury, Austen Chamberlain, found it easy to conceive of him as a successful Head of a Department, his merits seemed more appropriately recognized by an Australian Governorship or the offer of the High Commissionership of South Africa. Both of these he modestly rejected: 'Not my line but a compliment', he said when he wrote to tell his mother. There was even an idea that he might become Speaker. 'I don't know whether there is anything in it and if I were offered it I haven't an idea of what I should do', he wrote to a friend. But it came to nothing.

After four years as Financial Secretary to the Treasury some promotion was almost unavoidable, and when Bonar Law's illness and withdrawal from political life in May 1922 brought about a Cabinet reshuffle Lloyd George was persuaded to pay some of his Tory debts by giving Baldwin the Board of Trade. Here he proved patient, amiable and competent in an unassuming way, liked by businessmen because he was one of themselves, popular in the House for his good humour in answering questions: a moderate, trustworthy man who, although unlikely ever to be thought indispensable, was worth his place as part of the unpretentious furniture all administrations need to set off their better pieces. In Cabinet he seldom spoke.

This was a period of great men in politics. Lloyd George, Winston Churchill, Birkenhead, Austen Chamberlain, Curzon, Balfour, Robert Horne, Beaverbrook, were all active in affairs. Even if one denies the supreme adjective to any but two or three of them, the others were all men of stature and large reputation, infinitely more experienced in politics and the manipulation of power than Baldwin. Yet in the end Baldwin superseded, surpassed or out-manœuvred each one of them. How did he do it?

When he left London at the end of that parliamentary session on what was to become an annual ritual, a summer holiday in Aix-les-Bains where the waters were good for his wife's rheumatism and the surrounding hills provided him with suitable ground for the long walks and solitary contemplation he so much enjoyed, Baldwin was a member – a minor member – of an Administration of all the talents. When he returned from Aix on 29 September 1922, it was for the purpose of seeking to destroy it.

There is something at once touching and absurd in the picture of this eminently undistinguished member for Bewdley, who found it possible so rarely to summon the confidence to speak in Cabinet, tramping twenty miles a day over the hills above Aix-les-Bains, brooding on the means to drive permanently from office one of the greatest men in Europe, and returning to his hotel in the evening to play patience with his wife. It must have seemed even to him an extraordinary and formidable undertaking. But in those long solitary walks he was, as he told an old friend much later, gradually persuaded that he had been chosen by God, that long-time confidant of his father's, for this special purpose.

'Does little Baldwin think he can turn us out?' Lloyd George was to ask incredulously when he heard what his President of the Board of Trade was up to. Little Baldwin did, and strengthened by those solitary broodings on the hills above Aix, little Baldwin succeeded. Not unaided, of course, for Lloyd George had many enemies. But Baldwin's part was a large one. As large perhaps as Beaverbrook's although Beaverbrook was unwilling to admit it. For Baldwin the means flowed from the motive, and the motive provides a key to the character of this most unlikely Prime Minister.

Headed by, and composed mainly of, those who had led the country to victory in the First World War, this Ministry of all the talents had shown no more success than a less talented one might have done in meeting the economic problems of the post war period. On average seventeen per cent of the insured population had been out of work throughout the previous year, and the total number of unemployed had risen at one stage to more than 2,300,000. In the mining industry the first of the stoppages that were to bedevil so much of the 'twenties had only just ended with a capitulation by the miners which did nothing to solve the problems of the industry and left them sullen and resentful, determined to fight again. Engineers, shipyard workers, building workers, dockers, seamen, cotton operatives, agricultural workers, were all facing heavy cuts in pay.

But although humane and kindly and much concerned about the lot of the industrial workers in accordance with that tradition of benevolent paternalism he had inherited from his father, it was not economic failure that moved Baldwin to act against his colleagues.

He had no plans for industrial improvement he wished to set against theirs.

In foreign policy Lloyd George had upset his Tory supporters by his apparent eagerness to engage in military adventure – backed, it is true, by some moral arguments – in defence of the Greeks against the Turks. But although the fear of foreign involvement helped to create the atmosphere of crisis in which the destruction of the Lloyd George administration became possible, it was not because of this that Baldwin acted – indeed according to Lord Beaverbrook, who had means of learning a good deal that went on in Cabinet, he supported the pro-Lloyd George majority on this issue. In any event the Near Eastern crisis and the open quarrel with France, which supported the Turks, whereas Lloyd George, backed by Curzon, Chamberlain, Churchill, Balfour, Birkenhead and most of the Cabinet, supported the Greeks, had gone off the boil before he acted, though it was to remain a grave international issue for some time.

In its Irish policy the Government, by signing a Peace Treaty giving qualified independence to an Irish Free State, had brought about its head the anger of many reactionary Tory interests, even though Birkenhead (Galloper Smith) endorsed it and indeed had been most active and helpful in the final negotiations. But Baldwin was not a reactionary Tory and was wholly in favour of the Irish settlement.

National and international circumstances gave the opportunity. In Baldwin's case, as in Beaverbrook's with his passionate doomed loyalty to Empire Free Trade and his suspicion of foreign adventure, they provided the means. The motive came from a sense of moral and political discomfort that tells a good deal about Baldwin's character.

Baldwin's conservatism derived from ethical and social attitudes perhaps more common in country communities than cosmopolitan ones; more readily found among old-fashioned local magnates, County Councillors, Justices of the Peace and so on, than among rising young politicians in London – and less common even in such places than once they were. It was innate, slow-moving and, above all, constitutional; the framework for a way of life which, although rooted to a degree he never liked to admit in economic interest and inherited position, was, to his mind, essentially governed by public obligations and duties. He was an intense Party man – again and again his national decisions were based, to an extent exceptional even in a Conservative leader, on considerations of Party. But he was so because he had convinced himself that the Conservative Party – his Conservative Party, the true Conservative Party – was the best reflection of the nation. 'What is good for General Motors is good for America', said a famous American at a much later date. What was good for the Conservative Party, thought Baldwin, was good for the country.

Such a man could hardly be at ease in the Cabinet of Lloyd George. The personal life of the Prime Minister (in talking or writing of him to his wife Baldwin invariably referred to him as 'the Goat', whereas most of the rest of his colleagues called him 'the Big Beast' – meaning the monarch of the forest) shocked and disturbed him. Lloyd George's woman hunting, his cynical use of the honours system, the whiff of chicanery and corruption that came from so many of his political manœuvres, all these offended and appalled the Member for Bewdley. The restless energy of Lloyd George's imagination, his noble if intermittent vision of greatness in national and world affairs, being so contrary to Baldwin's own habit of mind, made no counterbalancing appeal. He distrusted Lloyd George's dynamism and habit of personal rule. Both were dangerous to the Conservative Party and hence to the nation, indeed to the constitution itself which surely depended on a system of parliamentary and cabinet government in which the Prime Minister should be no more than the first among equals.

Baldwin was not, of course, alone in his distrust. It was shared by many, indeed most, active Conservatives in the constituencies, by the Chief Conservative Agent, and by a goodly number of back-bench Tory M.P.s, who saw no reason to tolerate the little Welsh solicitor now he had served their purpose. But the belief that he could be dispensed with was contrary to the considered views of the Conservative leader, Austen Chamberlain, and most senior Ministers in the Cabinet, including Lord Balfour, Lord Birkenhead, Lord Curzon (although he was to change his mind when it suited him), Winston Churchill and Sir Robert Horne. So long as they, and more particularly so long as Austen Chamberlain, titular leader of the Conservative Party, remained of that opinion, it was difficult to see how he could be overthrown.

It was on this situation that Baldwin – that unimportant Minister without personal following in the country or even in the Conservative Parliamentary Party – brooded as he tramped the hills above Aix. So little was he concerned with current events that according to his son he did not bother to read any English newspapers during this time: like his father in his dialogues with God he was concerned with deeper matters than the day to day movement of affairs, even when they were taking so threatening a turn as in the Graeco-Turkish war. '... It was obvious', he wrote to a friend many years later, '... that the first thing to be done was to pull the country together: to make them realize the brotherhood of man. It seemed simple and obvious, but how to do it? The bitterness in the country was of the devil.... One thing was clear to me, that under the then Government, which was Lloyd George, F. E. Smith and Winston, buttressed by the respectability of Balfour and Austen Chamberlain, things would get rapidly worse....'

When, on 29 September, he was summoned back to London for Cabinet meetings concerning the Near Eastern crisis his mind was already made up. He must dare to be a David. Nor was his decision modified by an easement in the Near Eastern crisis itself. Goliath must be cast down.

In retrospect it seems plain enough that Lloyd George's run was nearly over – especially if one's retrospective view is obtained through the sharp, malicious yet at times extraordinarily magnanimous eyes of Lord Beaverbrook, whose superb personal records of the political intrigues of the time in which he played so considerable, yet ultimately so unrewarding, a part, have put all students of this strange period in his debt. Yet one must avoid being swept away by Lord Beaverbrook's skill in narrative and his eye for the damaging detail. It was by no means so clear at the time as it seems now that the power of Lloyd George really had departed and the Big Beast was no more than meat for the pack whenever they cared to turn on him. Churchill, Birkenhead, Bonar Law, Balfour, Derby – none of these masters of the various arts of politics thought him as vulnerable as he turned out to be. They thought him still indestructible. So did Austen Chamberlain, who almost alone in the inner political circle of the time always did his best to think and behave like a gentleman so that his views do not count for much. Most of the major figures in politics were still hypnotised by the Lloyd George reputation and the dexterity of the Lloyd George magic – and also in some cases, let it be said to their credit, by loyalty to the war leader.

In fact the magic had lost its public power and the reputation almost fallen away. As was to be shown when the issue was put to the test, the insiders, plotting and planning the various moves in an entrancing game, were knowledgeable about everything except what the electors actually thought of Lloyd George three years after the war's end. For the most part, until that moment came, they do not seem to have bothered very much about the wishes of the electors, or even the feelings of the ordinary members of their own party, except as pawns in a game whose rules were made exclusively by and for the best people. Even Parliament had lost its significance in the eyes of these leaders except in so far as its moods could or could not be harnessed to their own ambitions for place and power. What strikes one most as one looks back upon that period is the general disarray of political life, the absence of firm principle in most of the moves and counter moves hatched at the country house gatherings and private dinner parties round which political activity on its higher levels revolved. The war fought for democracy had produced at the centre an atmosphere more like an oriental court at which favourites struggled unceasingly for position than anything seen in Britain for a century or more. And, like a potentate in decay, Lloyd George, whose touch had once been so sure and who even now had moments, but decreasing ones, of magnanimity and intellectual vision, played off one against the other with the old ruthlessness but only a shadow of the old skill, twisting and turning first one way then that, prepared for almost any bargain that would postpone the moment when the power, that had long since ceased to be an instrument of principle and became no more than a prop for insatiable vanity, should be lost to him – and lost, it was to turn out, for ever.

Against all the odds this age in which principle had ceased to count was ended by two men of principle – Beaverbrook and Baldwin. To call Beaverbrook such may seem strange. Certainly it is contrary to the political label most usually pinned on him during a long and active life of political intrigue. Yet although the most adroit and cunning of intriguers, ready to use either friend or foe for his own purposes and to be found near the centre of every stratagem and plot of the time, Beaverbrook was guided in his activities by loyalty to a principle he never abandoned – the romantic and unrealistic policy of Empire Free Trade. If he made mischief it was – allowing for the licence one must grant a master in any art – for this end only.

Much as he delighted in intrigue for its own sake, greatly as he loved power and desired to be at the centre of things, Beaverbrook was not, as most of his intimates on the political scene were, concerned with personal place. His one permanent concern was the furtherance of the political dream he had brought with him as a louche young millionaire from Canada. For its sake he had attached himself to the hesitant and sombre figure of Bonar Law, of whom Asquith once said that he had 'the intellect of a Glasgow baillie' and Lloyd George that he was 'honest to the verge of simplicity'. To this alliance of opposites Beaverbrook contributed all the force, ambition and decisiveness that Bonar Law seemed incapable of generating on his own, while Beaverbrook in his turn derived from this unlikely source a centre of stability and authority that gave to his magpie operations a consistency they would otherwise have lacked and, above all, the possibility – never in fact achieved – that the Tory Party might be won over to his own dream of empire. It was this fidelity to principle in an unprincipled society that gave authority to Beaverbrook's stratagems, only for them to fall apart at the moment of victory when the friend on whom he had pinned so much refused to risk the policy in which they both believed because others warned him that it would be unpopular in the country. Never did a Warwick put so much faith in so infirm a Prince and stoop to so few recriminations when all he had planned for was wrecked.

The principles that actuated Baldwin were more diffuse than the single vision that inspired Beaverbrook, but they were no less compelling. Although in the circles in which Beaverbrook and his intimates moved he seemed a man of small account, they gave him a hold over the mass of ordinary Tory M.P.s such as Beaverbrook could never aspire to. Nor, though Beaverbrook scarcely gives him credit for it in *The Decline and Fall of Lloyd George*, was Baldwin's part in the defeat of the Prime Minister by any means inferior to Beaverbrook's own. And it was certainly more durable. His square figure and homely personality expressed in a special way the deep disquiet of the solid core of the Tory members at a position which seemed to them to make nonsense of the authority both of Parliament and the Tory Party. He led the ranks of mediocrity against the brilliant and sophisticated, and though the mediocre were to do much damage to the nation in the end they had a case. Their revolt had other less admirable features, but it was rooted in a genuine revulsion against the smell of corruption and scandal, the atmosphere of cynicism and conspiracy that invested the Lloyd George Government in its last years.

It is ironic that the chief obstacle in the way of restoring to public life the standards eroded by Lloyd George should have been Austen Chamberlain who, unlike most of the others in that *galère*, held to the old-fashioned belief that it was necessary to conduct oneself in politics like a man of honour. There was not much personal loyalty circulating in Westminster at the time but most of what there was was encompassed in Austen Chamberlain's monocled and, if the truth is to be told, somewhat pompous figure. He had committed himself to Lloyd George and this commitment he would not break.

He thus provided the main stumbling block to both Beaverbrook's and Baldwin's ambitions. So long as he retained control of the Conservative Party Lloyd George was safe, for not only was he determined to keep the Tory Members in the Government, he was no less determined that when a general election was fought – and with the Government in the disarray one could not be long delayed – the Tory Party must fight under Lloyd George's banner. To do otherwise, he was convinced, would, such was the Lloyd George magic, mean inevitable Conservative defeat and perhaps the birth of a new Centre Party. On 11 October, when the Cabinet finally agreed that an appeal to the country could no longer be delayed, it was found that almost all the Conservative Ministers shared his view. There were only two unimportant exceptions: Stanley Baldwin and one other, now almost forgotten, Sir Arthur Griffith-Boscawen. No one felt it necessary to pay much attention to them.

At the National Union of Conservative Associations due to hold its Annual Conference on 15 November it was a different matter. There was plenty of evidence that the anti-Lloyd George feeling in the Constituency Parties was strong and growing stronger and that perhaps a majority of the Constituency Party Chairmen and Tory agents who would then meet would like nothing better than to fight an election untrammelled by what they now regarded as the bondage of the Coalition Liberals. Conservative leaders are not bound by decisions of the political lower orders, but an adverse vote at the Conference and perhaps a resolution calling on Conservative Ministers to withdraw from the Coalition would nevertheless be awkward. It was in these circumstances that Chamberlain and his Conservative colleagues in the Cabinet called the famous meeting of Conservative M.P.s and Conservative peers in the Government at the Carlton Club on 19 October, for the purpose of carrying a vote of confidence in Austen Chamberlain's leadership and in the Coalition Government, and a resolution of support for an early general election on a Coalition ticket. If this were done Chamberlain and his colleagues – who suffered from a common political illusion as to their own indispensability – had no doubt that the National Union would see where its proper duty lay. Nor did they doubt that the Carlton Club meeting

– or a sufficient majority of those summoned to it – would act as required, for although many junior Ministers took the Baldwin line, and many more Tory M.P.s were deeply disgruntled, a sufficient number were thought to be persuaded that their own seats depended on the support of Lloyd George votes to come to heel when the leader of the Party required them to do so. Moreover, by restricting the Tory peers invited to actual office holders, mischief-makers such as Beaverbrook were cleverly excluded. Austen Chamberlain and his friends did not therefore doubt that they would end the day victorious.

Nor, though determined to fight, did Baldwin. He could, he told his wife when she returned from Aix, see no outcome but his own enforced resignation from the Cabinet. 'They will follow the G [the Goat: Lloyd George] and I can't,' he wrote to his Lucy, 'so it means I shall drop out of politics altogether.' Neither she nor he were dismayed at the prospect.

Yet there was one card in the pack capable of trumping the Chamberlain ace if only it could be played – Bonar Law. Bonar Law believed that although the Tories had little chance of winning an election on their own, to fight as part of a Coalition would destroy the Conservative Party. But he was ill – much worse than his friend Beaverbrook, who saw in him the indispensable hammer of the Free Trade enemy, would allow himself to believe. The vacillation that had always been part of his character was worse than ever. He could not make up his mind or hold to it from one day to the next. He cared deeply for the Tory Party – more deeply perhaps than for anything else now left to him in life. But he could not rouse himself to act. He had withdrawn from the political battle nineteen months before when, weary of the strain of working with Lloyd George, whose foreign adventures and ambitions he distrusted, and depressed by an attack of influenza, he had given up the leadership of his Party and made way for Austen Chamberlain. He retained his seat in Parliament. He enjoyed the political gossip his friend Beaverbrook laid before him so lavishly. But he disliked activity. In his long and cordial wartime partnership with Lloyd George – a partnership which had immensely benefited the nation and encouraged much that was best in both men – he had always shunned the supreme decisions, and he shunned them now. Asquith had once described him as 'meekly ambitious'. For a time Beaverbrook had cured him of the meekness and given his ambition fire. But in his retirement he had grown used to being out of things. It was not easy to put flame in dead embers.

To this task, that of bringing Bonar Law back to the leadership, Beaverbrook and Baldwin, united, though they scarcely acknowledged it, in their determination to end the Coalition, now bent their energies. Whose influence was the greater in bringing Bonar Law to the sticking point? The common view is that it was Beaverbrook's, but Beaverbrook has been his own historian. Baldwin's relations with this grey man of politics whose instinct it was to be fearful of doing the wrong thing were certainly not so intimate as Beaverbrook's. But he had served him as his Parliamentary Private Secretary and they liked and trusted each other, and he had a courier in J. C. C. Davidson, who had served even longer in that capacity, and before that as Private Secretary. Davidson was now Baldwin's P.P.S. and loyal friend, and an active intermediary between the two. Moreover Baldwin's and Bonar Law's interests in this matter were more nearly identical than were those of Beaverbrook and Bonar Law, for the latter was only partially an Empire Free Trade man but wholly a Tory. It was the saving of the Tory Party that most nearly touched him and it was for the rescue of the Tory Party – the real Tory Party, their Tory Party – that Baldwin could appeal to him in a way that Beaverbrook, the brilliant gad-fly of politics whose Party loyalty was, to say the least, intermittent, could not.

Baldwin's own assessment of their relative influence on the hesitant leader is characteristic. 'Beaverbrook and I fought for the soul of Bonar Law', he told G. M. Young. 'Beaverbrook wanted to make him a great man after his own fashion. I showed him there were better things to be.' One may smile at the typical note of tribute to his own moral integrity, yet it is possible that the arguments he and Davidson brought to bear were capable of moving Bonar Law most – even though the final word that he would go to the Carlton Club meeting was given to Beaverbrook.

How far any of these contestants for the soul of the reluctant and ailing leader looked beyond the immediate goal it is hard to judge. Bonar Law had been given by his doctors no more than two years of active life. He himself judged his likely term to be no more than a year. In fact it turned out to be six months. Would Beaverbrook have had second thoughts if he had known the time was to be so short? Would he have stopped to ask himself what was likely to happen after Bonar Law went? As it turned out the outcome was fatal to Beaverbrook's own political ambitions. He failed to win Bonar Law to Empire Free Trade while he still lived, and when he died found himself exiled as completely and as permanently from the courts of power as the man he had helped to overthrow on his behalf. He was betrayed by his most persistent weakness as a politician, the journalistic mind habituated to thinking in the short term, and by his readiness to adopt almost any method, however dubious, to achieve his ends. The methods were remembered, the core of principle forgotten, especially perhaps, by Baldwin.

How far Baldwin let his mind dwell on the fact that Bonar Law could not last long, or asked himself on whom the choice as Tory leader would fall when he was no longer there, it is impossible to say. Such weighing of political chances would have been out of keeping with his character as then known – though not perhaps with that of the astute politician he was later to be recognized as.

Bonar Law was the one indispensable man, but Baldwin did not concentrate his energies on him alone. In his task of saving the soul of the Tory Party he was tireless in canvassing support in every conceivable quarter.

In these manœuvres he disclosed for the first time that talent for manipulation which was later to make him, in Sir Winston Churchill's words, 'the greatest Party manager the Conservatives had ever had'. To some, later, this talent seemed at odds with his real character. It was not really so, for it derived much of its strength from what was a very characteristic rural curiosity about the minutiae of people and events. The House of Commons was his village. He had an ear like an old man sitting in the sun outside a village inn. To the gift for knowing what was afoot he added the ability, essential to a successful politician, to wait on events and let them work for him. What gave him his greatest strength, however, was that he never seemed to be a mere political intriguer but always, even at his most subtle, a man of principle. And this indeed he was – only it was principle grounded in the conviction that the preservation of the Tory Party was the main requirement of national life. Whenever occasion seemed to require it he was therefore always able to put Party before Country in the honest conviction that in so doing he was serving the permanent interests of the British people.

At the Carlton Club meeting he also disclosed another talent which was to have a great part in giving him a dominant place in public life for so long – it was also to prove his greatest weakness – a talent for what G. M. Young well describes as 'a new eloquence: direct, conversational, monosyllabic: rising and falling without strain or effort between the homeliest humour and the most moving appeal'.

His words to his fellow Conservatives at the Carlton Club immediately before Bonar Law spoke and made clear his readiness to resume the Tory Leadership were as plain as any of them could desire.

'I will not beat about the bush but will come right to the root of the whole difficulty which is the position of the Prime Minister. The Prime Minister was described this morning, in the words of a distinguished aristocrat, as a live wire. He was described to me, and to others, in more stately language, by the Lord Chancellor, as a dynamic force, and I accept these words. He is a dynamic force and it is from that very fact that our troubles, in our opinion, arise. A dynamic force is a very terrible thing; it may crush you, but it is not necessarily right.

'It is owing to that dynamic force, and that remarkable personality, that the Liberal Party to which he formerly belonged, has been smashed to pieces; and it is my firm conviction that in time, the same thing will happen to our party.'

It was enough. It was the end of Austen Chamberlain, the end of Lloyd George. Bonar Law moved into the leadership and from there, after a general election he did not expect to win, to Downing Street. Six months later he was dead and Baldwin, whom none could call dynamic, was Prime Minister.

3. *The Man Who Understood the English*

TO a degree exceptional in British politics a judgment of Baldwin as Prime Minister has to be made without the aid of evidence from previous political activities or appointments. MacDonald, it is true, had even less experience of office than Baldwin when he went to 10 Downing Street: none at all, indeed. But he had been for many years a leading and controversial figure in public life, fighting his way to the front the hard way, and subject to constant scrutiny under the glare of publicity; a Prime Minister with a political if not a ministerial ancestry. Not so Baldwin. For him life began at Downing Street. He was a Prime Minister almost without a political past.

The atmosphere of 10 Downing Street is inimical to the kind of discipline that Ministers commonly learn at the head of great Departments for it is aloof from the actual administrative organization of government, almost ostentatiously so. The fact that it is the Prime Minister's home as well as his office, staffed only by a small group of private secretaries, its furnishing and the view of the garden and St James's Park from the Cabinet Room, all combine to give the impression of a small country house in which the master is looking quietly through family papers in the library before going out for a stroll with a gun.

Moreover the office of Prime Minister is one of extreme flexibility. It is free of routine, responsive to the personality of the holder in a way that a great Department where executive decisions must daily be put in motion can never be. A Prime Minister may be an initiator of policy or an arbitrator between the policies of others. He may be the dictator of his Cabinet or its Chairman, or he may swing between the two according to the issues involved. He may be constantly on the heels of his Ministers urging them forward with demands for action, or he may sit quietly in the Cabinet Room with a clean sheet of paper in front of him waiting for them to turn to him for advice if they need it. He may read assiduously all the papers and telegrams that flow across his desk or he may leave them unread. He may do a great deal or very little. The choice is his: the office what he makes of it. He cannot, of course, hope to escape ultimate responsibility for the decisions his Government takes, but the extent of his direct share in making them may be large or small according to his temperament and habit of work. And it is often very difficult for anyone outside the Cabinet to know how large or small it in fact is.

The kind of Prime Minister a man is likely to be can normally be estimated with some accuracy as he steps into 10 Downing Street by reference to the qualities he has already shown in political life and the methods of work he has employed in earlier offices. When the time comes the historian, probing for deeper understanding, can similarly refer back for light on the character of the Prime Minister to the record of the Minister. This is scarcely possible with Baldwin. He was a Prime Minister almost without apprenticeship – one of the few in our history.

As President of the Board of Trade he was safe but undistinguished, possessed, according to his officials, of an attitude of humorous detachment toward detail interrupted by occasional bursts of resentment when he was pressed too hard. There is nothing much to go on there. His period as Chancellor of the Exchequer under Bonar Law, offered more as a reward for what he had done to bring down the Lloyd George Coalition than a recognition of intrinsic merit, though shorter, is somewhat more illuminating if only because it produced a settlement of the American war debt on terms that led Bonar Law to declare: 'I should be the most cursed Prime Minister that ever held office in England if I accepted them.' Nevertheless, accept them he did, only for them to turn out, as Maynard Keynes, Lord Beaverbrook and others had said at the time that they would, a hindrance to British and world recovery before they collapsed of their own contradictions within twelve years.

It is, however, the light thrown on Baldwin's political methods by the American Loan Agreement that is interesting. Recalled for consultation with the Cabinet, which had been shocked by his recommendations, he arrived at Southampton on board the *Olympic* on 29 January 1923, and without waiting to meet his colleagues at once gave a press interview. In this he declared the terms offered by the American negotiators to represent a tremendous advance in American opinion, and to be in his own view the best that could be got. This threw the Prime Minister into a fury and caused the King to write asking how it could possibly come about that a Minister could make such a statement before receiving Cabinet approval – a question to which Bonar Law could provide no answer. But Baldwin's object was achieved. Although Bonar Law threatened to resign rather than accept (he had already gone to the extraordinary length of writing an anonymous letter to *The Times* over the signature 'Colonial', attacking the proposals his Chancellor was bringing back), the rest of the Cabinet, while for the most part liking the agreement no better than he did, felt it impossible publicly to repudiate the Chancellor after what had been said in his press interview. The Agreement was accepted. Baldwin got his way.

It has since been argued by his friends that Baldwin's action in giving a press interview before meeting the Cabinet, which he knew disagreed with him, was due to innocence. If so, it was a very guileful innocence. What he did, in fact, was to try out a technique of which he was later to become a master, that of appealing over the heads of his colleagues to the country. Having committed himself to the American offer without much economic understanding, for economics was no more his subject than foreign affairs (indeed when Bonar Law summoned him to explain the proposals immediately after his Southampton interview he hardly spoke one word during the two-hour interview, leaving advocacy of the agreement entirely to Colonel Harvey, the American Ambassador), he could not bring himself to lose face by retracting. In his defence it can be said that he saw the

American Loan Agreement, as he saw so much else, not in financial but in moral terms. He was not guided by economic argument any more than the mass of ordinary people were, but by the sturdy British belief that however it may be with lesser breeds, honest Englishmen pay their debts and receive in due course their reward from God and society. Keynes's argument that America was at our mercy, just as we were at France's and France at Germany's, because 'it is the debtor who has the last word in these cases', would have struck him as dishonest if he had taken any notice of it.

'The public will applaud now, in five years they will bitterly censure those who have agreed to cripple Britain financially', said Bonar Law prophetically. But Baldwin was not looking five years ahead. He spoke to the heart of the public without fear, or intimation, of the future. It was his unique, his almost never failing gift.

It was this gift he took with him to the Premiership when less than four months after that disastrous debt settlement fatal illness compelled Bonar Law to resign before he could heal the divisions in the Conservative Party and bring back Austen Chamberlain as his natural successor.

Baldwin had held senior office for no more than two years. He was still almost unknown in the country: 'Not even a public figure, a man of no experience, of the utmost insignificance', said Curzon bitterly when the news was broken to him that his own long and distinguished service was to be passed over in favour of this pipe-smoking nonentity.

Aneurin Bevan once remarked to me apropos Hugh Dalton's resignation as Chancellor of the Exchequer in consequence of a silly indiscretion to a journalist that there is 'no immaculate conception of disaster'. But the same is equally true of success. If the Conservative Party had not been divided there would have been no possibility of Baldwin becoming its leader either then or later. Even as it was it is improbable that Curzon would have been passed over so summarily had it not been for two things. One was that Balfour, who was consulted by the King, was determined that Curzon should not benefit from breaking the pledge he had given to his colleagues in the Lloyd George administration not to take office under Bonar Law. The other was that the decay of the Liberal Party and the rise of the Labour Party had left a situation in which the official Opposition was unrepresented in the Lords. To have had a peer as Prime Minister would have been a deliberate affront to them. To this extent Baldwin was the beneficiary of circumstances. On the other hand it has also to be said that he had taken much trouble since the Carlton Club meeting to establish a commanding position of trust among the great body of Conservative M.P.s. His very deficiences were to them a recommendation. They were tired of greatness – as was indeed the country as a whole. They wanted tranquillity, not glamour. They wanted to be assured that they represented the solid middle part of the nation. This Baldwin understood better than anyone else, just as he understood better than most the inevitability of the rise of the Labour Party, and set himself not to fight it but to tame it.

As it happened the Labour Party required no taming. It was tame already. Too tame. The claim on which later Baldwin most prided himself, that he had taught the Labour Party to be constitutional, was ludicrous. No one was required to persuade Ramsay MacDonald to embrace the constitution or, for that matter, Arthur Henderson, J. R. Clynes, Jimmy Thomas or the millions of solid trade unionists who provided the backbone of their party. These were not hell-bent revolutionaries waiting to tear down the Establishment. All they wanted was to be accepted as a part of it. Yet behind his claim there is this at least: to a degree attained by no other public man, Baldwin did at this time reflect the mood, fumbling, vaguely progressive and conciliatory, of a large part of the nation and, because he did so, did less to exacerbate relations with political Labour than probably any other Conservative leader would have done. It is too much to say that he saved Labour from becoming revolutionary, but at least he did nothing to drive it into revolution.

Baldwin himself was in no dubiety about the matter. He believed it to be God's will that he should go to Downing Street. Like others who have felt the same he was not above jogging God's elbow. When the issue between himself and Curzon still seemed in doubt he made sure that a memorandum from his Parliamentary Private Secretary and intimate friend J. C. C. Davidson (later rewarded with the Chancellorship of the Duchy of Lancaster) should reach the King's Private Secretary, Lord Stamfordham, setting out the reasons why Baldwin should be preferred to Curzon: 'A representative of that section of privileged Conservatism which has its value but which in this democratic age cannot be too assiduously exploited.'

'Quite unfitted for it, with little experience, I had never contemplated it but I was never in doubt', he wrote of the Premiership to a friend towards the close of his life. 'I could see the hand of God in it and I recognized that my peculiar life had been a preparation for the very work that lay before me. The problem was to get at the soul of the working class.... The lines of my policy grew clear and *I knew* that I had been chosen as God's instrument for the work of healing the Nation.' There is a Victorian solidity about the assurance. It was never shaken.

With the certainty that the call was from the highest quarter he took on the leadership of a Government of the second eleven from which almost every person of public eminence in the Conservative Party, with the exception of the wounded but magnanimous Curzon, had voluntarily absented themselves. Within six months he had led it to electoral disaster.

His motive for deciding to go to the country without consultation with his senior colleagues, indeed to their complete mystification since he had previously assured them that he contemplated no such thing for at least twelve months, on an issue, Protection, which practically every electoral expert in the party regarded as foredoomed from the start, is obscure. To his credit he was deeply concerned about unemployment and believed that Protection could offer a chance, perhaps the only chance, of industrial recovery. But this does not seem to have been his main reason for embarking on an election when he did. Indeed if it had been he would surely have given himself more time to prepare the country and persuade it that it had now become essential to abandon the guarantee, previously given by Bonar Law, that there would be no change in the tariff system.

It seems likely that the true motive for this premature appeal to the country was more characteristic of him; to save the Tory Party from Lloyd George once again. Baldwin had received a report, quite mistaken as it turned out, that the ex-Coalition leader, then in America, was contemplating a programme of tariff reform, and feared that if he did so a new group would coalesce round the man he most hated in public life: 'I had information that he was going protectionist and I had to get in quick', he told Dr Thomas Jones. 'I got the Cabinet in line. But for this move Lloyd George would have got Austen Chamberlain with Birkenhead and there would have been an end to the Tory Party, as we know it.'

The Tory Party. It was always the Tory Party he thought of. But the Tory Party under himself. After his defeat at the polls Lord Stamfordham, the King's Private Secretary, passed on to him a suggestion that the King should send for Austen Chamberlain and ask him to try to form a Government. 'This did not seem to appeal to him.'

In the end he proved right. Having scourged his party with the whip of electoral defeat he did in fact succeed in uniting it – although only after coming near to losing it. The element of the gambler in Baldwin's character, the Celtic unpredictability and impetuosity that sometimes made him act so contrary to his public image, must not be overlooked, and on this occasion the gamble paid off.

Yet at first it was generally assumed that the electoral defeat meant the end of his political career.

'He [Sir Samuel Hoare] thinks it quite impossible for him to go on as our leader, in which I cordially agree', noted Lord Derby in his diary, quoted by Mr Randolph Churchill. It was the common view. What saved him, what saved him again and again, was his public image. It was too strong for his critics – just as it was, in the end, too strong for the Labour Party, over whose first steps in minority government he brooded with exemplary benevolence for the next ten months.

This image which was Baldwin's greatest contribution to the public life of his times, much more effective as a bulwark of political power than any of the things he actually did, was founded on perhaps the most profound, potent, and dangerous egotism ever to befall a Prime Minister – the belief that he alone knew the mind of the people. 'My worst enemy', he said to his official biographer, 'could never say that I do not understand the people of England.' It was by this conviction that he governed. He did not need to lead the English people. It was enough that he understood them.

Sitting passively in the Cabinet room or broodingly on the Front Bench, or gossiping in the smoking room with those older working-class members of the Labour Party for whom he had an especial affection ('He always seemed more at home with our people, particularly the older trade union people, than with his own lot', Attlee once remarked to me), he *knew* that he contained within himself the truest sense and deepest desires of the nation. Ultimately this profound egotism was to prove tragically corroding. Yet in some measure it was justified. He really did reflect and represent as no one else did a large part of the hopes and emotions of the mass of ordinary English people of all parties: their distrust of violence and extravagant opinion, their nostalgia for a past more simple, or so it seemed in retrospect, than the complicated and dangerous present, their tolerance and decency, their awareness of basic national unity, their trust in common sense.

This identification with what he conceived to be the virtues and aspirations of the great middling mass of ordinary English people was, however, not natural but contrived. It was not his true nature that he thus presented, but a synthetic composition. In the end it became almost second nature. But it bore hardly any relation to the Baldwin underneath. The real Baldwin was complex and passionate, a bundle of nerves, fears and anxieties that showed themselves not only in the involuntary nervous tics and gestures to which he was prey but in the collapse which so often followed moments of decision. What he presented to the world was an outer skin. This skin, one suspects, had begun to grow long before this – as a defence, perhaps, against the anxieties of his childhood and youth, against the seething emotions beneath the surface in his relationship with the father who imposed self control like a religion, and the mother towards whom he felt both affection and guilt. Against the frustration, also, of a career he hated but had brought upon himself by retreat into failure at his school and university. There were some who saw beneath the skin. A perceptive American observer wrote in the *Philadelphia Public Ledger* early in 1926: 'Within him storms a chaos. He has himself under admirable control, but everything he says or does is the issue of tense inner conflict.' To most, however, he seemed what he had set out to make himself: a commonsensical, equable, intuitive representation of idealized English qualities, the embodiment of that most difficult and most un-Celtic of virtues, moderation.

It was in its way a remarkable achievement. But it was too good to be true.

If this view of himself was synthetic so also was the picture he gave the English of themselves. It ignored, when it did not actually denigrate, the qualities the English most needed at this time; toughness, combativeness, anger and resolution. It was, moreover, in essence, literary rather than political, suitable for evoking words rather than action, static not activist. Being synthetic it was like a clever copy of a painting that lacks the power of the original to set its own forces of creative energy stirring in men's imaginations.

In Baldwin himself this idealized conception of the ordinary Englishman found its most satisfying expression in speechmaking. This man of silence in the Cabinet was an inveterate talker outside it. He was the prime advocate in innumerable speeches on innumerable occasions of a Utopian view of the virtues of the English and their society, and of the old and valuable English tradition of the decent man. Unfortunately he was also a victim of his own oratory, enslaved by the old harlot of the arts for whose power over others he was always on the watch, without recognizing it in his own case because she came to him dressed so modestly and so plainly – but no less seductive for that. Too often he seemed to feel that if a thing had been well said there was no need to do anything about it. He moved easiest among large generalities and found it pleasanter to enunciate moral ideas than to apply them in detail. And indeed he put so much energy into the making of his speeches and broadcasts – in which latter he excelled every political leader of his time – that it is not surprising that he often seemed to have none left over for anything else.

'Before an important speech', says his son, the present Lord Baldwin, in a biography which does credit to his filial devotion, 'the colour would leave his face, the sweat would sometimes roll off his brow and he has confessed time and time again he felt he might be sick.'

Each speech, each broadcast, was a work of art. The creative energy employed in producing it left him empty and inert when it was over.

Most successful politicians seem able to draw upon unlimited resources of energy. Their batteries are self-charging. The excitements and challenges of the political life provide all the fuel they need to drive onward in their extroverted lives. It was not so with Baldwin. Perhaps because so much of his emotional energy had been driven below the surface, there to be dissipated in hidden conflicts that were only rarely allowed to reveal themselves, he was subject to collapses of nervous energy that sometimes seemed to rob him of initiative and will at the moment when both were most needed. The engine stalled. The car came to a standstill and could not be restarted. Capable of bursts of intense energy and decision – indeed as has been remarked earlier of an impetuosity in action that bore no relation to his normal habit – he could not keep it up. Such plunges into activity were paid for in bouts of an almost pathological incapacity to maintain an interest even in matters of the greatest importance. He lacked the stamina of the long distance political runner.

This lack of stamina was never more clearly shown than during the General Strike. This unique and unnecessary interlude in British political life brought him, ironically enough, a nation-wide moral authority such as he had never reached before and never quite reached again. Looking back it is difficult to understand why.

His Administration's responsibility for the economic conditions in the coal industry to which the General Strike was a moving, if ill-judged and ill-considered, response of working-class loyalty, was clear and definite.

No single action played a larger part in creating these conditions than did the decision to return to the Gold Standard at the prewar parity of 4.86 dollars to the pound, a decision taken with the Prime Minister's full support by Winston Churchill as Chancellor of the Exchequer, the least appropriate of all the posts to which this great man's talents could have recommended him but offered, to his own amazement, as a means of bringing him back to the Conservative fold and reducing the danger of a rival political alignment.

By this return to gold at the old parity the exchange value of the pound, and consequently the price of British exports to foreign buyers, was at once raised by ten per cent without any attempt to adjust internal prices to a comparable degree or bring about the reduction in production and manufacturing costs which were required to meet export needs if the most serious consequences on domestic living standards were to be avoided. It thus imposed conditions of trade which the mining industry, badly organized, inefficiently run and highly dependent at that time on export markets, was more incapable than most of meeting. To Keynes, the greatest economist of his age, to Ernest Bevin, the greatest trade union leader of his time, who as a member of the Ministry of Reconstruction Committee at the end of the war had from the first opposed the Cunliffe Committee's recommendation of an early return to gold, to Beaverbrook, and to many others, the inevitable consequence to Britain's economy of this return to gold at the old parity was clear. So was the direct relationship between the return to gold and the attack on miners' wages. But not to Baldwin.

'On grounds of social justice,' wrote Keynes, 'no case can be made out for reducing the wages of the miners. They are the victims of the economic Juggernaut. They represent in the flesh the "fundamental adjustments" engineered by the Treasury and the Bank of England to satisfy the impatience of the City fathers to bridge the "moderate gap" between $4.40 and $4.86. They (and others to follow) are the "moderate sacrifice" still necessary to ensure the stability of the gold standard.'

The Government's responsibility, Baldwin's responsibility (whether of omission, as was so often the case with him, or commission) was plain enough. But all this was forgotten when the threat of a General Strike was heard. To a large part of the public Baldwin became the man standing between the nation and revolution. However one judges the cause of the strike or rates the practical sense of what was, in essence, one of the most unselfish acts in history on the part of millions of ordinary workers, who voluntarily demonstrated at heavy cost to themselves their feeling of solidarity with the miners, no challenge to constitutional government on such a scale could be allowed to succeed. Very properly, and for once with a good deal of energy, Baldwin took steps to ensure through the Organization for the Maintenance of Supplies that the life of the country should not be brought to a standstill if a general industrial stoppage did occur. All this was necessary. Yet to a man chosen by God, as he so confidently believed, to 'get at the soul of the working-class', the threat of a General Strike, muted and uneasy as at first it was, surely also offered a supreme opportunity for statesmanship and conciliation.

This opportunity Baldwin seemed at first determined to take. To many of his Cabinet colleagues, including such otherwise disparate Ministers as Neville Chamberlain and Winston Churchill, he appeared, indeed, more sympathetic to the cause of industrial labour than was proper in a Conservative. He understood the feelings of the miners and the emotions of their fellow trade unionists. Nor did he seem tempted to misread the mood, in so many ways so close to his own, of the leaders of the T.U.C., who showed themselves anxious above all else to avoid the sort of conflict into which they felt themselves being pushed by the intransigence of the mine owners, the revolutionary fervour of a very few of their own people, and the resentment and loyalty of the great mass of their followers.

Moreover, once the T.U.C. took over the negotiations the men he had to meet – Pugh, Thomas and Swales – were of his own kind: responsible, cautious men, anxious to extricate themselves from an impossible situation with such safeguards for the miners and dignity for themselves as should prove possible; men, moreover, themselves much practised in the generalities that were Baldwin's stock in trade. They were ready to do almost anything to reach a formula which would allow them to call off the strike in good order and on the night of Sunday, 2 May 1926, they seemed very near getting it.

With Lord Birkenhead, who to the surprise of many had proved throughout one of the wisest and most conciliatory of advisers, and Sir Arthur Steel-Maitland, the Minister of Labour, Baldwin agreed a formula with the T.U.C. leaders, and himself put it into draft form. This done the three trade unionists accompanied by the Acting

General Secretary of the T.U.C., Walter Citrine, rejoined their colleagues of the General Council in a room set aside for them in the Treasury, there to await the arrival of the miners' leaders who had been hurriedly called back from making speeches in the country. The formula penned by Baldwin, and accepted by them, pledged them to 'urge the Miners to authorise us to enter upon a discussion, with the understanding that they and we accept the Report [the Samuel Report which recommended large-scale reorganization of the mining industry, State ownership of coal royalties and the introduction of profit-sharing schemes with, however, a temporary reduction in wages, although of a smaller order than that demanded by the owners] as a basis of settlement, and we approach it with the knowledge that it may involve some reduction in wages.' It was a vague formula. But, in the circumstances this was felt by all concerned, including Birkenhead, normally the least indefinite of men, to be an advantage. Because of the reference to the possibility of some reduction in wages, it was hardly likely to be popular with the miners. But the T.U.C. was prepared for that. 'Never mind what the miners or anybody else say, we accept it', said Thomas. The victory for 'moderation' and the spirit of 'peace in industry' of which Baldwin had so often and so movingly spoken seemed within grasp.

This hope was shattered by a telephone call to 10 Downing Street from Thomas Marlowe, the Editor of the *Daily Mail*, who had chosen to mark this particularly delicate moment in the negotiations with a leading article under the provocative title 'For King and Country', denouncing the General Strike as 'a revolutionary movement intended to inflict suffering upon the great mass of innocent persons in the community' and aimed at 'destroying the Government and subverting the rights and liberties of the people'. It called upon 'all law-abiding men and women to hold themselves at the service of King and Country'. This leading article the machine-men of the *Daily Mail* refused to print.

Their action was unpremeditated and unofficial and was at once condemned by the leader of their own trade union, George Isaacs, when it was made known to him. It was entirely outside the knowledge of the members of the T.U.C. negotiating committee who, when the telephone call came, were already on their way back to the Treasury with the Prime Minister's formula, which they were fully determined to persuade the miners to accept.

But for the Cabinet – and for Baldwin – the telephone call from the

36

Daily Mail transformed the situation. Only Lord Birkenhead remained calm, remarking, when told of the printers' refusal to print Marlowe's inflammatory leading article, that it was 'a bloody good job'. Most of the rest, and especially Churchill, Chamberlain and Joynson-Hicks, were incensed, although Amery still felt it desirable to continue negotiations so long as the faintest hope of agreement remained.

In this situation all depended on Baldwin. His standing in the country was now such that no Minister could, on such an issue, have withstood him. Everything that had gone before, the mood of the T.U.C. negotiators, their acceptance of the formula he himself had drafted, the whole atmosphere of the talks which had only that moment been adjourned, might have been expected to incline him to put this trivial incident in its true perspective and refuse to be rattled by it.

But Baldwin was lying back exhausted in his chair. The emotional reaction had come. He had no more energy for argument. It was easier to let the angry members of the Cabinet have their way. The trade unions had failed him. Without even being given a chance to speak to the miners' leaders the T.U.C. negotiators were summoned back to 10 Downing Street. There they were met not by the Prime Minister or by any of the Ministers with whom they had so recently been in friendly communication, but by Baldwin's secretary, Col. Waterhouse. He handed them a note informing them that it had come to the knowledge of the Government that not only had specific instructions been sent under the authority of the T.U.C. directing their members to carry out a General Strike, but also that 'overt acts have already taken place including gross interference with the freedom of the press'. A withdrawal of the strike instructions and 'a repudiation of the actions referred to' was therefore demanded before the Government could agree to continue negotiations.

The T.U.C. leaders were baffled by this communication. The matter of General Strike instructions had already been fully discussed with Baldwin and other Ministers earlier that same day and assurance given that they could and would be withdrawn if the conversations led to a resumption of negotiations. It was in the light of these very assurances that Baldwin had drawn up the peace-saving formula to which they had agreed and of which they were now waiting to inform the miners' leaders. As for 'overt acts', of these they were completely ignorant, since they had not at this time heard of the *Daily Mail* incident.

37

They returned to their room at the Treasury and, as soon as they were able to discover from Isaacs what had happened, drafted a reply repeating their previous assurances regarding the strike notices and protesting that so far as the *Daily Mail* printers were concerned they could not be held responsible for an incident of which they had known nothing and which the printers' own leader had condemned as soon as he heard of it. They could not, they added, believe that the Government could contemplate breaking off negotiations now at so hopeful a stage over so trivial a matter. The note given them by Col. Waterhouse specifically called for a reply, and Pugh and Citrine hurried to 10 Downing Street with it. When they got there the house was in darkness. The Cabinet had dispersed and Baldwin had gone to bed. Anxious to do his best by his father in all circumstances the present Lord Baldwin has described this as 'A pardonable muddle that has been stretched into a scandal.' Other apologists have gone further. Robert Blake, for example, has managed to persuade himself (in *The Baldwin Age*) that Baldwin's responsibility for the breakdown is 'a complete myth', on the grounds that although Baldwin had, it is true, retired to bed there were four secretaries still awake – as the office-keeper who turned the T.U.C. delegates away could have told them had they asked him. No doubt there was a footman or two around as well.

But the T.U.C. was under the impression that it was concerned in negotiations at the highest level in an attempt to avoid a national disaster. When its representatives were informed that Mr Baldwin was unwilling to remain out of bed for half an hour to receive a reply to a document that seemed to make nonsense of all that they and he had been doing to reach a settlement they ought perhaps to have asked humbly for five minutes with a secretary, or even have pleaded for a word with the Prime Minister in his night cap. They did not do so. They assumed, and it is hard to blame them, that they had been given the brush-off, and that the Cabinet was now determined to use any pretext for a breakdown.

Even so they did not abandon their efforts. They met again the next morning and, after long and angry exchange with the miners, persuaded the General Council of the T.U.C. to approve a memorandum drafted by Ernest Bevin designed to offer a way out. These proposals Bevin himself took to the Ministry of Labour with the urgent request that they should be conveyed to the Prime Minister so that he might consider putting them before the House when he spoke that evening. If he did so, said Bevin, he had Arthur Henderson's assurance that they would be accepted on behalf of the Labour Party. But Baldwin was no longer interested. The T.U.C. proposals were not mentioned. The strike that nobody wanted began.

These events and the ones that followed are important in trying to penetrate the character of the strange man who was to hold the first place in British political life longer than any peace-time Prime Minister since Gladstone. They not only throw a sharp if fitful light into some of the darker recesses of his personality, but also set a pattern that was to recur on even more ominous occasions in the future.

Having failed to give battle in the Cabinet Baldwin did nothing – except, of course, make speeches – all through the General Strike and for some time after it. He was, says his official biographer, sunk in 'moods of exhaustion and collapse', enervated beyond power of recovery by 'the effort to maintain his nervous balance, to suppress his natural timidity'. A Cabinet colleague is quoted as saying: 'As soon as it [the General Strike] began he was a passenger.'

One need not accept Young as invariably correct in his assessment of Baldwin to believe him so on this occasion. There is ample confirmation from Baldwin's doctor, who, according to Baldwin's Principal Private Secretary, foreshadowed a complete collapse within six months unless the Prime Minister got away.

Yet although, on the evidence of several colleagues, he was unwilling or unable to participate in Cabinet decisions once the strike had begun, Baldwin used it for one of his most moving and effective broadcasts.

'I am a man of peace. I am longing and working and praying for peace', he told the listening millions. He promised that if the strike were called off there would be no victimization or exploitation and asked, 'Cannot you trust me to ensure a square deal for the parties – to secure even justice between man and man?' It was moving because it seemed to those who heard it to express the sincere emotions of the man above party concerned only to heal wounds that could cripple the nation; it was effective because, hearing it, millions of strikers and their leaders, caught up in a struggle they had never wanted and confronted by a potentially revolutionary situation they did not know how to handle, were persuaded that the strike should be ended quickly, and could be ended with honour. Yet hardly was it ended than Baldwin put his authority behind the punitive anti-trade union legislation of the Trades Disputes Act of 1927, a measure, said Lord Reading, that 'offered no single ray of light for British working men ... more vague, more indefinite, more lacking in precision in respect of the crimes which it indicates and the penalties which follow upon them than any Bill I have ever seen or any Act of Parliament I have had to construe either as a law officer or as a judge'.

On such evidence it is sometimes tempting to regard Baldwin as a man wholly without principle, careless of promises even beyond the bounds expected of politicians when they make public speeches.

To do so would surely be wrong. He was a more complicated character than such simple analysis allows. The picture of himself he presented to the nation in his broadcast was true: this was the man he was – or at least the man he wished to be. But faced with a crisis, with the need to assert himself and to fight, his instinct (unless the all important unity of the Conservative Party on which he so much relied was directly involved) was always to disengage, to retreat into a private world that the harsh demand for action could not contaminate. He had done so in the crisis of his boyhood at Harrow, and at Cambridge when he found Dr Butler there before him. It had been his response to his god-like father's insistence that he should adopt a business career that he hated. All his middle years had been lived on two planes. On the one the life of the businessman his father required him to be; on the other, the life of the man of letters, the philosophically inclined country gentleman he would have liked to be. Yet the surface equanimity to which he had schooled himself was never wholly complete. It was capable of degenerating quite suddenly, as it now did, into a mood of exhausted despair. At the heart of that apparently assured and benign nature there remained always a shrinking nerve.

In any consideration of his character one must also take into account the effect of the first world war. When it began he was forty-seven; well-off, comfortable, unambitious, too old for active service. His fate was to stay at home and grow richer out of others' sacrifices. He could not escape the sense of guilt. He hated physical pain: even to go to the dentist for a minor operation would turn him pale and sweating; to drive in a motor-car in fog was an agony, he would crouch in his seat, his fingernails biting into his palms, almost incapable of speech, and he was never able to bring himself to travel by plane. Yet out of the physical agony and danger of others he now found himself growing richer than he had ever expected. He could not bear it.

The war profits on his business investments, about £200,000 in all, he gave away, most of it – including the £120,000 to the Treasury – anonymously. But that was not sufficient to bring him peace: 'I felt,' he said later, 'no use to God or man.'

He belonged to a generation more used than the present to thinking itself in direct personal touch with the Deity. But from his letters and some of his speeches there seems no doubt that to a degree unusual even for his generation, and certainly so for most of those of the thrusting, ruthless, opportunist political life of the war and postwar years whose leader he became, he began in his middle years to feel himself a God-selected, God-directed man. He believed himself personally chosen, to quote his own assessment of his destiny, 'to pull the country together: to make them realize the brotherhood of the human family', and thus to expiate in some measure the guilt of non-participation in the bloody sacrifice that had engulfed so many of his countrymen.

He must have been immensely reinforced in this by the ease with which the power of Lloyd George, whom he had come to regard as the most destructive and corrupting influence in the national life, collapsed before him; and confirmed in his conviction that 'the hand of God was in it' when he found himself Prime Minister after so short an apprenticeship. There is also his enormous private egotism, the defence against youthful failure, to take into account; the belief that he alone understood the English people, that what he liked to call his 'peculiar life' had been no more than a novitiate for what lay ahead.

It is no wonder he often found it difficult to argue about concrete matters in his Cabinet. In such exchanges he had really nothing to offer. He was a man from outside, a political prophet the real nature of whose witness was disguised by his short, stocky, undistinguished provincial appearance, his square face with its broad nose and humorous mouth, his sandy hair and his half-crown cherrywood pipe.

This innocence, which was genuine enough, was not incompatible with a wily skill in political tactics and a certain ruthlessness in human relations. It seldom is – Gandhi provides another example. It was, however, incompatible with a good deal of the daily work of politics whose concern is the translation of ideas into practice, whereas his was with 'the soul of the nation': a task calling for exhortation and speech-making rather than legislation. Deeply persuaded, as he wrote to a friend in old age, 'that in my public life I have been increasingly led and I mean to be led to the end', he often seemed to feel that it was enough to speak in the correct emotive words for difficulties to dissolve; sufficient to declare as he did in a famous speech in the House of Commons quite early in his public career: 'Four words of one syllable each ... contain salvation for this country and the whole world, and they are Faith, Hope, Love and Work', for salvation at once to be manifest.

In his official biography G. M. Young concludes that the key to Baldwin's character was a longing for the 'sympathy, fondness and understanding' that had been denied him in youth. 'Public affection – not popularity, but sympathy and understanding – became', he suggests, 'a good, almost a drug, which he could not bring himself to forgo. He came to listen for the echo – so long friendly; and he shrank from the angry noise of a people in discord with its rulers and itself.'

The matter goes deeper. Baldwin had come to active politics late in life with certain rather simple general principles which he innocently believed provided a universal solvent of all political problems. When these failed him, or when his belief in his unique understanding of the English people, that understanding which 'not even my worst enemy can deny', let him down, the virtue went out of him. It did so when the *Daily Mail* printers threw him off balance on the eve of the General Strike. It was to do so again and again with even more tragic consequences in his conduct of foreign affairs.

4. Rise and Fall of an Idol of the People

'BALDWIN, Rt. Hon. Stanley ... confesses putting party before country.' So says a famous index reference in Churchill's *The Gathering Storm*, subsequently much debated and criticized. In the context in which it is used it is perhaps not wholly fair – although less unfair than many of Baldwin's friends would have us believe – but it expresses an important general truth. To Churchill a political party was an instrument to be used for purposes greater than itself according to its fitness at the time – or rejected if unfit. But to Baldwin the unity of the Tory Party was a thing of absolute value in itself because he could not conceive that without a united Tory Party England could survive.

He was not a man able to change the habits of a lifetime even when employed on a divine commission. By birth and upbringing he was a moderate Tory who had never been anything else: even as a young man at Cambridge he had never felt the temptation to lust after strange gods. To him Toryism was part of the stuff of that traditional England in whose image he found such sustenance: the solid Labour men in whose company he found himself so much at ease were to him (and he may have had a point) no more than strayed Tories whose heresies arose more from a failure of Toryism to make itself understood than to any original sin on their part. His allegiance was the stronger because it did not arise from any intellectual conversion but from an old habit long worn: to break with, or break up, the Tory Party would have been as unthinkable as to break up his marriage. Naturally he was not so modest as to be unaware that the public image of himself was his party's greatest electoral asset, nor so innocent as not to know that many of his colleagues grumbled after some of his speeches that if he wanted to lead the Liberal Party he should become a Liberal, if he wanted to be a Socialist, join the Labour Party. He wished to build the Tory Party in his own image but he was always very careful not to push his differences with his right wing to the point of a split.

There were some who thought he would do so on India. And indeed he came very near to it over the Government of India Bill of 1935. But here his instinct was right. In his bones he knew the country was with him, and that because it was the Tory Party would in the end see reason, though Churchill might not – but then he did not mind losing Churchill, another of those dangerous dynamic fellows like Lloyd George. He could smell the change in the climate of opinion among the ordinary people of Britain weary of the responsibilities and dubieties of imperial power, and though he did not bother himself with the details of an Indian settlement, he was at home with the moral principles involved for the ordinary run of English people – just as he was at the Abdication. Broad moral principles were always his strongest line, these and rules of conduct and propriety on which he felt instinctively as the great mass of ordinary respectable English people of all classes did.

If the sole duty of a Prime Minister were to reflect the broad middle movement of opinion in the nation and act as a secular pastor to his people, he would have been a wholly admirable one. But there are even greater demands, and these he could not meet. Moving habitually in a world of good intentions in which words not actions were king, he seems, for example, to have been almost completely without understanding of the real nature of the economic issues that faced the country and the world in the 'twenties and 'thirties. He could deplore unemployment, he could do little or nothing to cure it. The kind of creative energy that Roosevelt brought to bear on economic issues in the United States was wholly beyond his scope. And to an even more tragic degree, though he could reflect accurately enough the longing of ordinary people for a peaceful world, he could do nothing to secure it for them.

To read Baldwin's speeches during the 'twenties and 'thirties is to catch again and again the authentic voice of millions of ordinary men and women confronted by problems of war and peace that seemed too immense for them to deal with. The phrases echo across the years. They are eloquent. They come from the heart. They express the profound horror of all civilized men and women for the idea of war. One cannot but feel warmth and sympathy for the man who spoke them.

'I tell the House that I have been made almost physically sick to think that I and my friends and the statesmen in every country in Europe, two thousand years after our Lord was crucified, should be spending our time thinking how we can get the mangled bodies of children to the hospitals and how we can keep the poison gas from going down the throats of the people....'

'I think it well also for the man in the street to realize that there is no power on earth than can protect him from being bombed. Whatever people may tell him the bomber will always get through....'

'The only defence is in offence, which means that you have to kill more women and children more quickly than the enemy if you want to save yourselves....'

'Since the day of the air, the old frontiers are gone. When you talk of the defence of England you no longer think of the chalk cliffs of Dover; you think of the Rhine....'

'Most of us, when we consider the subject, do not see great movements, deep moral or legal issues, grouping of Powers or any of those "huge cloudy symbols"; we catch our breath and think of something far more intimate, much more dear, the lives of our children and grandchildren, of the familiar sights and institutions of our own land, all the boundary stones of our spiritual estate. We live under the shadow of the last war and its memories still sicken us. We remember that war has no glory in it but the heroism of man....'

'We think perhaps of the level evening sun over an English meadow with the rooks trundling noisily home into the elms; of the ploughman "with his team on the world's rim creeping like the hands of a clock", one of those garnered memories of the long peace of the countryside that a wise man takes about with him as a viaticum. To what risks do we expose our treasures, irreplaceable treasures, for you cannot build up beauty like that in a few years of mass production. Make no mistake: all the life that we and our fathers have made in this land, everything we have and hold and cherish, is in jeopardy in this great issue....'

'If the world – Europe and the world – can find no other way of settling their disputes than the way of war even now, when we are still finding and burying the bodies of those who fell twenty years ago – if they can find no other way, then the world deserves to perish....'

'War is a very terrible thing and, when once let loose in Europe, no man can tell how far it will spread, and no man can tell when or how it will stop. I am quite content in these circumstances to be called a coward if I have done what I could, in accordance with the views of every country in Europe, to keep my own people out of war....'

'To my mind war is the greatest folly that can afflict mankind. Whoever starts it knows that he is condemning to mutilation and famine as many civilians as may be killed in the fighting services. Of the great works of man, works which distinguish him from the beasts, more may be destroyed in a few years of bombing than Goths and Huns and Vandals could accomplish in a century....'

'Now that question [peace] will in the end be answered not only by Governments but by peoples. There may be Governments deliberately planning the future, leading reluctant or unsuspecting people, into the shambles. It sometimes looks as if it were so. I confess that in my own political experience I have not encountered Governments possessed of all these malevolent qualities. Most Governments seem not better or worse than the people they govern. Nor am I on the whole disposed to conclude that the people are such a helpless ineffective flock of sheep as those who claim to speak in their name often imply. They have a way of making their opinions known and heard when they feel deeply....'

'I certainly do not know how the youth of the world may feel but it it not a cheerful thought to the older men that, having got the mastery of the air we are going to defile the earth from the air, as we have defiled the soil during all the years that mankind has been on it.... When the next war comes and European civilization is wiped out, as it will be, and by no force other than that force, then do not let them lay the blame on the old men. Let them remember that they, they principally or they alone, are responsible for the terrors that have fallen upon the earth....'

That war was horrible and unthinkable. That if it came European civilization would be wiped out. That if this were to happen the blame would not be only with the 'old men' (although the old men were for the most part in control of the world's affairs) but with the young. That when it came to the issue 'the people' would not let it happen, they not Governments would give the answer. These are recurring themes in his thoughts throughout the 'thirties. They conditioned his actions – or what was more frequently his inaction. He had never moved easily among foreign affairs, nor wanted to know much of foreign nations. 'What should they know of England who only England know?' his cousin Kipling had asked. But he knew Worcestershire – and Aix-les-Bains. It was enough. His only quality of genius was, as he knew with an immense, a touching egotism, to understand his own people.

Firm in his conviction that 'The Englishman is all right as long as he is content to be what God made him, an Englishman, but gets into trouble when he tries to be something else' and (to quote from another speech delivered more than twenty years later), 'our people are alive and flourishing and have avoided many of the troubles that have fallen to less happy nations because we have never been guided by logic in anything we have done', he could not help but feel that if one refused to worry too much things would turn out all right. He had, as he said to the Combined Empire Societies in May 1937, always been a 'home-keeping man, much occupied in this little island'. In his own life he had moved not very far in space, not very far even in time. When he thought of England, as he constantly did, it was of an England that was already passing, and which, even when it existed, had not had much meaning to most of those who lived in it, to the crowded workers in the industrial north, the technically-minded dwellers in the Midlands, the black-coated workers in the great new suburbs.

It was the sounds and sights and scents of his youth half a century before that were most real to him and to which he most constantly turned for inspiration – for inspiration and the assurance to do nothing: 'The sounds of England, the tinkle of the hammer on the anvil in the country smithy, the corn-crake on a dewy morning, the sound of the scythe against the whetstone, and the sight of a plough team coming over the brow of a hill, the sight that has been seen in England since England was a land and may be seen in England long after the Empire has perished and every works in England has ceased to function, for centuries the one eternal sight of England.' The plough horses were going from the land and the tractors beginning to take their place even as he spoke, but what was that to him? There were better things to think of: 'The wild anemones in the woods in April, the last load at night of hay being drawn down a lane as the twilight comes on, when you can scarcely distinguish the figures of the horses as they take it home to the farm, and, above all, most subtle, most penetrating and most moving, the smell of wood smoke coming up in an autumn

Mister Baldwin

New Statesman, 4 November 1933

evening or the smell of the scutch fires: that wood smoke that our ancestors, tens of thousands of years ago, must have caught on the air when they were coming home with the result of the day's forage, when they were still nomads, and when they were still roaming the forests and the plains of the continent of Europe. These things strike down into the very depths of our nature and touch chords that go back to the beginning of time and the human race, but they are chords that with every year of our life sound a deeper note in our innermost being.'

His public personality reflected all that is romantic and nostalgic in the English character: surely it is one of the great impertinences of history that it should fall to him, who could never even bring himself to enter an aircraft, to confront the mechanized violence of the twentieth century.

Among the qualities of the English that most evoked his affection and admiration (for he had no false modesty in this matter and never sought to deny that the English were superior to all other nations) he once listed that 'they do not look ahead, may not heed warnings, may not prepare, that they grumble but do not worry' (unlike some foreign nations 'who worry but do not grumble'), and thus kept their nervous systems sound and safe. He talked much about the horror of war from the air. But he could not bring himself to believe in it. He had no aptitude for martial speech and although, contrary to some of the myths that have grown around him, he did on a number of occasions bring himself to warn Parliament and the public of the speed of German rearmament, there was always something half-hearted about it.

Antipathetic to detail by nature, his dislike of the very thought of war made him even more reluctant than usual to examine the documentary evidence, and he permitted himself to be so falsely optimistic about the size of the German Air Force that he had to apologize to the House of Commons for misleading it.

His reputation would stand higher if he had had the courage to be more explicit, instead of being content for the most part to paint the horrors of war in phrases of a generalized despair that, as Churchill said, seemed often more designed to create anxiety and perplexity than anything else. But a nation has a right to more than warnings from its leaders. It expects them to act, and it was only after long hesitation that Baldwin could stiffen himself to do so. He was temperamentally incapable of subjecting the Air Ministry to the probing and spurring it needed, or of readily involving himself in decisions that might seem to accept as inevitable that rain of destruction from the clouds of which he spoke so movingly.

He was not, of course, alone in this attitude. The majority of the Labour Party was of like mind: more resistant, indeed, even than he to the idea of large-scale rearmament. But it could at least claim to be faithful to the idea of collective security, and although the League, it is true, was not much of a prop to lean on, it need not have been quite so weak a one as Baldwin and his colleagues made it.

Morally, Baldwin was on the League's side, as he was on that of all expressions of human goodwill. But he could never bring himself to be interested in it in practice. It is surely a staggering fact that in all his years of office he visited Geneva only once, though all his summer holidays were spent no more than a few miles away. Like all else that lay beyond the physical frontiers of his beloved England it seemed to him unreal. It was both his own and his country's tragedy that in an age that called imperatively for a world view he was neither internationalist, nor imperialist, but obstinately Little Englander. Lacking firm convictions of any kind on foreign policy he could never make up his mind whether to go for the League or for power politics and so became a sort of bigamist of diplomacy, committed to both but faithful to neither, his heart in Worcestershire all the time.

His Policy towards the League was in consequence like nothing so much as the indecisions of a colourblind motorist at a traffic crossing. When President Hoover, the year before Hitler came to power, proposed a plan for qualitative disarmament that might, if adopted, have brought the United States into permanent cooperation with the League of Nations and have abolished the very weapons of offence that Japan, Italy and Germany were later to employ with such aggressive success, he first agreed privately, only to allow the plan to be publicly rejected by Simon in Geneva a month later in terms so contemptuous that one British delegate wrote: 'I saw the U.S. delegation go white with rage in the face of the insult.' He fought a general election on the undertaking that 'The League of Nations will remain ... the keystone of British Foreign policy', and that there would be no wavering on sanctions against Italy, only to abandon this policy four weeks later in favour of the Hoare-Laval pact partitioning Abyssinia, and then to repudiate Hoare in his turn when public opinion erupted. Such hot and cold meanderings were duplicated many times.

Nor was his progress any the less erratic when he used the other leg of the dual policy on which Britain hobbled into the dangerous world.

If his Government lacked confidence in the League of Nations and a genuine attempt at collective security then the alternative was to build up British defences unilaterally and develop the Anglo-French Alliance to keep German aggression on the leash. Yet when Hitler marched into the Rhineland and France wished to act Britain refused. 'Either now or in 1939', said the French Ministers, and 1939 it was. If the two had acted together in 1936 and compelled the withdrawal of German troops 1939 would have been a very different year. And when in that same month of 1936 the British Government at last produced a Defence White Paper promising formidable and coordinated expansion of forces on land, sea and in the air in order to retrieve the broken promise of two years earlier, that Britain would 'in no conditions' accept a position of inferiority to Germany, Baldwin appointed as the Minister of Defence to do the job a nondescript wheel-horse of the Tory Party – Sir Thomas Inskip.

Two years later in the House of Commons Winston Churchill gave his judgment on Baldwin's record in these matters in these words: 'When I think of the fair hopes of a long peace which still lay before Europe at the beginning of 1933 when Herr Hitler first obtained power, and of all the opportunities of arresting the growth of Nazi power which have been thrown away ... I cannot believe that a parallel exists in the whole course of history. So far as this country is concerned the responsibility must rest with those who have had the undisputed control of our political affairs.... They exploited and discredited the vast institution of the League of Nations and they neglected to make alliances and combinations which might have repaired previous errors, and thus they left us in the hour of trial without adequate national defence or effective international security.'

It is a harsh verdict. Yet who, looking back on the evidence, can regard it as an unjust one or deny the validity of the bitter Churchillian comment that this was a Government 'decided only to be undecided, resolved to be irresolute, adamant for drift, solid for fluidity, all-powerful to be impotent'?

The truth is history played a dirty trick on Baldwin. He who had been cast by nature and the conflicts and stresses of his youth and middle age for the contemplative life, for words not deeds, preaching not practice, and whose truest role was that of an essayist of the English countryside, found himself called on to play the leading part in a tragic drama that demanded a man of heroic action. He did his best. But he was the wrong actor, in the wrong part, in the wrong play.

At first he was able to rely on the voices: the voice of God who had touched him on the shoulder in 1921 and called him from mediocrity to 'some special work'; the voice of the people whom he 'understood' as no other could. But when the voices failed, what then? For now the time was coming when he had to lead instead of being 'led', and could find nothing to guide him but a discordant babble of sounds like a man whose hearing aid has gone wrong.

Communication had, of course, faltered before. He had twice been rejected by the electorate. But these rejections, although annoying, were no more than were to be expected in the normal run of business, part of the inexorable law of the pendulum. Had they not, after all, given him the opportunity to make one of his greatest contributions to the spirit of the age, to stand by and give Labour a chance to learn how to govern? Nor had these defeats seriously affected his personal popularity. Some of small faith in the Conservative Party had revolted. Malevolent characters like Rothermere and Beaverbrook, who could not understand the deep heart throb of the English people and that there were times when it was wisest to do nothing, had been given a chance to make mischief. The chief agent of the Conservative Party had so far lost his senses as to pen a disillusioned memoranda saying that the Tory Party could never hope to win an election so long as Baldwin was its leader. But none of this had mattered. Such attempts to subvert the course of nature had been easily routed whenever his wife persuaded him it was time to hit back. She was always the one to persuade. 'Tiger Baldwin, Tiger Baldwin', she would cry triumphantly when she succeeded in rousing him from the lethargy that so easily overcame him in time of crisis. And even when they had voted for someone else the people had continued to love him, seeing in him as always a reflection of themselves: the true Englishman, 'the most generally trusted and acceptable personality in public life'.

As the 'thirties advanced, however, things began to happen to the public mood that Baldwin could no longer understand. Or it would be truer to say, perhaps could not bring himself to understand because they struck to the heart of the conflicts in his own nature. They robbed him of confidence – that apparently unassuming but rock-like faith in his own instinct for the middle road – by challenging him to define, if only to himself, what he was really about. He had always been against definitions. 'I would say one more thing – don't let us be too keen on definition … it was the attempt to define that split the Christian Church into fragments soon after it came into existence, and it has never recovered from that', he said once. But now the need to define was upon him. He was faced with a moral dilemma that generalizations could not bridge. And he could not bring himself to take it out and look at it.

If he had dared to be honest with himself he would, one suspects, have admitted in the privacy of his personal stocktaking that he could not bear the idea of war in any circumstances. Temperamentally he was a passive resister. His nervous horror of violence, his fear of strong emotion, his acceptance, 'as a sensible man', of what life put before him even while he 'cordially hated it', all these inclined him to a pacific role. So did his imagination, that powerful instrument that could bring back to him so evocatively the scent and sounds of the vanishing rural world that had solaced him in his youth, but which now summoned no less vividly before his eyes, until he was almost physically sick with the horror of it, the 'mangled bodies of women and children' and the 'poison gas going down the throats of the people'.

Temperament and imagination both ranged him on the side of those who wished to close their minds to thought of war. Yet his responsibilities as a national leader, his loyalty to his Party, the criticism of his opponents, his whole instinct to conform to the broad sweep of national interest required that he should not do so. Well might he have cried with Hamlet – and beneath that so carefully phlegmatic exterior there lurked a good deal of Hamlet – 'The time is out of joint! Oh cursed spite, That ever I was born to set it right.'

Feeling as he did, torn as he was, he was not only peculiarly susceptible to the strong emotions of pacifism that were actually to be found among the British people, but also to the temptation to magnify them and sometimes, indeed, to see them where they did not exist. Thus a by-election in East Fulham in the Autumn of 1933, when a 'safe' Tory seat was lost by 7,000 votes to Labour, threw him off balance completely. He at once became convinced, as he told the House of Commons in a speech of 'appalling frankness' three years later, that it had been won and lost on 'no issue but the pacifist'. Contemporary campaign reports, confirmed by the experience of those who, like the present writer, actually participated in the contest, show however that in any accurate meaning of the word pacifism was at no time a major issue at the election.

The Labour victor, John Wilmot (later Lord Wilmot), had served in the Royal Naval Air Service during the war. At no time in his life had he been a pacifist or unilateral disarmer. He was not one then and did not become one later. His closest affiliations in the Labour Party were with those, like Hugh Dalton, who were the most intransigent opponents of pacifist attitudes and the most consistent critics of the Parliamentary Party for voting against the Defence Estimates. The biggest single issue in the election was that of local housing conditions, which were very bad and brought Wilmot many votes from people who did not normally vote Labour. Wilmot was by profession a banker and Secretary of the Shareholders Protection Association, which he had helped to found, and his campaign for middle-class votes rested a good deal on a well-documented exposé of the threat to small savings resulting from operations of City speculators whom the Government refused to control. In foreign affairs he was an advocate of defence through collective security, taking a position very close to that subsequently reflected in the League of Nations Ballot of 1934 when out of the huge total of more than 11,500,000 votes seventy-four per cent were cast in favour of military sanctions against aggression.

It is, of course, true that there were a good many people in the country, including, no doubt, some who backed Wilmot at Fulham or subsequently voted in the League of Nations Union referendum which came to be misleadingly known as the 'Peace Ballot', who put more emphasis on disarmament than on collective security – even when they voted for it. No doubt there were many more who did not trouble to ask themselves what was to be done if effective collective security proved impossible. More still, no doubt, who were in no mood to consider how large the bill for collective security might be. These were all matters on which they could have been instructed by a determined Government.

It must be remembered that when the Fulham by-election was fought in 1933 the 'vast institution of the League of Nations' had not yet, in Churchill's words, been 'exploited and discredited'. Abyssinia lay ahead though Japan had, it is true, been allowed to get away with aggression in Manchuria. It was still perfectly sensible to believe that the League could be made stronger, not weaker, if one or two great powers were ready to show that they meant what they said when they talked, as they did continuously, about Collective Security. Germany was rearming. But she had not yet marched into the Rhineland and was still relatively weak militarily – indeed a year later Baldwin was still assuring the House of Commons that her real strength was 'not fifty per cent of our strength in Europe today'. Although it might later come to seem a little naïve – as sensible ideas that are allowed to fail often do – a vote for Collective Security, in so far as the Fulham vote could be counted such, was in these circumstances very far from being one for pacifism. What was most notable about the Fulham poll, in fact, as about the 'Peace Ballot' later, was the extent it indicated that the pacifist view that had been popular a few years earlier had become a lost cause. Many voters distrusted Conservative policy because they thought it insufficiently internationalist. But far from being pacifist, public opinion in so far as it showed itself in the Fulham by-election and the League of Nations ballot, had shifted decisively to acceptance of the unpleasant fact that it might be necessary to use force to check Nazi and Fascist aggression.

Yet for no adequate reason Baldwin chose to see in this by-election a decisive vote for pacifism, reflecting, as he went on to declare without one iota of evidence, a feeling 'common throughout the country'.

It is hard not to believe that he did so because this explanation best reflected the colour of his own mood. In the moral dilemma in which he found himself he chose, not wholly consciously perhaps, to read into the Fulham result his own anguished resistance to the distressful but implacable logic of international events and made it a cloak for his own failure in resolution.

Looking back on it three years later in that speech of 'appalling frankness' to which reference has already been made and which did so much damage to his reputation he had this to say:

'Supposing I had gone to the country and said that Germany was rearming and we must rearm, does anybody think that this pacific democracy would have rallied to that cry at that moment? I cannot think of anything that would have made the loss of the election from my point of view more certain.'

It is, of course, on this last sentence that the celebrated reference in the index of the *Gathering Storm* is based. Heavy counterattacks on Sir Winston Churchill's interpretation have since been made and it can perhaps be argued that it was overharsh. Baldwin was musing on probabilities rather than confessing to actual misdemeanour. Yet who can doubt the insight the words offer into his mood and the effect on him of the Fulham result? According to Young, he referred to this election result again and again: 'It was a nightmare', he said.

Yet what he made of it was quite untrue. On the evidence of Fulham, and even of the 'Peace Ballot' later, if he had gone to the country and said, 'In the light of current Nazi policy and Nazi military expenditure more arms are essential to make the League of Nations effective against aggression, and will become even more essential for our own defence if the League fails', he would have got them. In fact when he did finally screw himself up to saying something like this two years later he was sent back to power with a great majority.

It was untrue. Yet it was a wonderful excuse for failing to do what public duty demanded but his nature resisted. Only the Tory Party could save the country: that had been the central creed of his faith from the beginning. He was more sure of it now than ever as the clouds gathered. But the people were not ready. They would not vote for a Tory Government that wanted more arms. They, not he, were pacifist. He was absolved from blame.

Yet still the nagging doubts must have persisted.

'Tell the truth,' said Churchill, 'tell the truth to the British people. They are a tough people and a robust people.' But he had not told them the truth. Or only a little of it, and that little late. Whether this was because he could not trust them to face it or could not face it himself – who shall say? But even his long habit of self-justification can scarcely have saved him from all knowledge that he had failed.

One cannot help but feel some sympathy for him. He was an honest and honourable man. He had believed himself called to public life 'to pull the country together', to make it 'realize the brotherhood of man', and had done his best to reflect in his character those qualities the British most esteem, even when they do not seek to emulate them. But now the age he had wished so earnestly to shape had turned sour on him. Even his virtues had become liabilities. His wish to believe that all men (except Lloyd George) were good, and Governments no 'better or worse than the people they govern' had become a shameful evasion of the facts. There is nothing odder in all this odd time than the extent to which Baldwin avoided acknowledging, even to himself, what was happening in Germany. Where in all those speeches, on so many occasions, to every imaginable gathering from the Federation of British Industries to the Bible Society, from the Leys School, Cambridge, to the Brotherhood Movement and the City of London Conservative and Unionist Association, is to be found the note of horror and indignation that a man so committed as he to human kindness and dignity must surely have felt when he learned what had been done to the civilized values in Hitler's Germany? By 1936 all the world knew the meaning of Nazi anti-semitism. And all the world knew also that murder and torture were the customary instruments of Nazi racial and political policy. Yet Baldwin could still tell a great audience that although he had often been told of 'malevolent' governments he had never come across one.

There is something both pitiful and profoundly tragic in the extent to which the moral dilemma of good will, war and peace, became too much for him. To some extent, perhaps, it always had been so. Perhaps that was why he always found it so much easier to pretend that conflicts of class and interest did not exist than to examine their causes, to speak in broad general terms about human values than to govern. He was growing old – and watching him in the House of Commons he often now seemed older than he was. Even his mastery of Parliament – the skill in lowering the temperature of debate that had so rarely failed him in the past – began to fail him. One became uncomfortably aware that the lethargy that had so often taken over in difficult times was now becoming deeper and more obstinate. His touch was going and with it his assurance of his own skill. It was, as he himself felt, time – past time – for him to go.

Fortune, which had favoured him so often, had one last favour to offer before he went. She gave him the Abdication. It was the perfect curtain. Here he was on his own ground. On such an issue all his old powers could be brought into play, and he made no mistakes. To the plaudits of all of the nation he cared for he ushered off – a little unctuously – one King and welcomed another in his place. On the drive from the Coronation of the new King the cheers for him were scarcely less loud than for the monarch. 'I feel tired, happy and at peace and mighty humble', he wrote when it was all over. '... I still have that sense of wonder that the Blessed Damozel showed in her face when she leaned over the gold bar of heaven.'

The Garter and an earldom came to him, as was his due. At a party at the Athenaeum the Archbishop of Canterbury said that 'in him was to be found the spirit of England behind all parties: the Happy Warrior that every statesman would seek to be'.

If only it could have been the final end. But of course it was not. The wheel had yet to turn full circle.

He went back to Worcestershire. He was tired and empty of nervous energy. For a year he could find no rest even in his books. It took him a long time, he said, to 'recover his poise'. When he did he settled into the comfortable routine of honourable retirement. He was elected, it was very fitting, President of the M.C.C., and Chancellor of the University of Cambridge. There were meetings to attend, friends to

visit, speeches to make. He went to Canada to give three lectures at the
University of Toronto as an old and honoured statesman of the Commonwealth, and to the United States, to Columbia University, to
lecture on Citizenship. And all the time the war against which he had
tried so hard to close his eyes, and on whose horrors his mind had so
often dwelt, was drawing nearer. It broke as the ship bringing him
back from America reached English waters.

He was seventy-two and in the tumult of those days there was no
place for him. He went back to Worcestershire, to Astley. It seemed as
though the English people had forgotten him. But in the spring, as the
German tanks roared across France and the ill-equipped British forces
fought their way back to Dunkirk and the little ships, they remembered. And now they remembered with hate. He symbolized for them
England in the wasted, complacent years and as they looked at the
consequences of those years they turned on him – and on themselves.

He was advised for his own safety not to come to London. When the
gates in his garden, many of them old and beautiful or of historic
significance, were taken for scrap months before others a Tory M.P.
won himself a cheer and much press and public approval by asking,
'Is the Hon. Member aware that it is very necessary to leave Lord
Baldwin his gates in order to protect him from the just indignation of
the mob?' Day after day at Astley the letters arrived, savage, accusing,
contemptuous. They were piled on the library table. He had no
secretary now. He opened them and read them himself. Only Churchill was magnanimous, inviting him to Downing Street and finding
time amidst all the pressures of war to treat him with kindness and
courtesy and even to flatter him a little with talk of what was being
done and how the situation looked.

From the English as a whole there was no magnanimity. He had
been the tribal god of the 'twenties and 'thirties and the magic had
turned sour: all that they could remember was the half truth that he
had confessed to misleading his country in order to save his party.
There were demands in some newspapers that his pension as an ex-
Prime Minister should be taken from him. A. L. Rowse, forgetting
that historians should let the dust of time settle before they make their
judgments, wrote scathingly that he was allowed to sit in his comfortable home while the world crashed, 'in possession of his honours, if
not his honour, and presumably of a pension for his services'. A
journalist went down to Astley and planted a poison tree in the
grounds. 'I planted it well', he told his admiring readers. 'Grow up,

little tree! Blossom and flower and bring forth many fruit. For you are on famous ground.' And all the time the letters came.

It is not a pleasant time to remember. The English people, whom Baldwin believed himself to understand so much better than any other man could, had much to forgive him – him and themselves. But they do not come out of the final transaction well. 'They hate me so', he said. When he was persuaded to make an excursion to Dorchester to unveil a memorial to Thomas Hardy, those who saw him were shocked by his appearance. 'He seemed', one of them said, 'to have death in his face.' In his diary Baldwin wrote that one night as he lay in bed he seemed 'for what must have been a couple of minutes to see with extraordinary and vivid clarity, and to hear someone speaking to me. The words at the time were clear but the recollection of them had passed when I seemed to come to, as it were; but the sense remained, and the sense was this: "You cannot see the plan." Then, "Have you thought that there is a purpose in stripping you one by one of all the human props on which you depend, that you are being left alone in the world? You have now Me upon whom to lean and I have chosen you as My instrument to work My will. Why then are you afraid?" ' In defeat as in success he had to feel himself a 'chosen man'.

Gradually the letters stopped. The English people had other things to think about, better things to do than curse him. They forgot him again, and he was left alone. He suffered from arthritis and he was growing deaf. His wife who in the past had been his chief prop, now needed his support. She had always been gregarious. The isolation, the sense of hatred surrounding them, broke her spirit. When they went for their small strolls in the garden, carefully avoiding those places where they would be reminded of the rape of their gates, it was she who had to lean on his arm.

They had few visitors now. When the sun shone they would walk a little on the terrace and in the evenings they would sit silent at their separate card tables 'working out perpetual games of patience or crossword puzzles which they would interrupt', their son tells us, 'to stand "at rheumatic attention" when the anthems of the allied nations were played before the evening wireless bulletins' – those allied nations in which he had found it so very hard to interest himself in the days of his power and glory.

In June 1945 as the war was drawing to its conclusion his wife died. He lived on for two and a half years with his widowed daughter to look after him. There were occasional visits from friends, occasional family gatherings, but most of his days he spent alone in his library, looking into the fire, thinking, but about what he never said, or doing crosswords, or going through old family papers: but the locked volumes of his father's diaries he could not bring himself to open. He died in his sleep on 13 December 1947 and his ashes were laid with those of his wife's beneath the nave of Worcester Cathedral. Afterwards a few of his Worcestershire neighbours had the idea of putting up a small red sandstone memorial to him on the roadside beside his home. A subscription list was opened, no more than a hundred pounds or two were required. But there was small response and a letter in the county newspapers brought little more. Only the intervention of Winston Churchill, who heard of the pathetic outcome of the appeal and sent a large subscription, enabled the simple monument that had been planned to be erected and maintained. Astley Hall itself became a home for backward children.

'I have had my hour. I pass soon into the shade....' Baldwin had said to the Rally of Empire Youth at the Albert Hall in the last speech he made as Prime Minister, and to his Canadian audience on his journey to Toronto just before the outbreak of war, he said, 'There are statesmen who have never made a mistake. I am not one of them. I leave judgment to those who come after. None of us is free from blame.'

Even in his worst moments he cannot have imagined that the shade would be so complete, the judgment so rejecting. The English people had got him out of their system at last.

Ramsay MacDonald

Born 1866; illegitimate son of John MacDonald, ploughman; educated at Drainie board school, Morayshire; Secretary of the Labour Party 1900-12; Labour M.P. for Leicester 1906-18; Chairman of Independent Labour Party 1906-9; Leader of Labour Party 1911-14; Treasurer of the Labour Party 1912-24; Labour M.P. for Aberavon, Glamorgan, 1922-29; Chairman of Parliamentary Labour Party and Leader of H.M. Opposition 1922; Prime Minister 1924; Prime Minister 1929-35; Labour M.P. for Seaham, Co. Durham, 1929-31; National Labour M.P. for Seaham 1931-35; Lord President of the Council 1935-37; National Labour M.P. for the Scottish Universities 1936-37; died 1937.

1. *Young Man on the Outside*

JUST about the time that the young Worcestershire ironmaster Alfred Baldwin and his bride Louisa were setting off on their honeymoon, a Scottish servant girl on a farm near Elgin found herself with child by the head ploughman, a Highlander named John MacDonald from the Black Isle of Ross. There was no question of marriage between them and when her condition could no longer be concealed Anne Ramsay packed her bags and went back home to her mother in a two-roomed stone cottage in the fishing village of Lossiemouth on the Moray Firth. There on 19 October 1866 she gave birth to an illegitimate baby boy who was to become the first Labour Prime Minister in British history and share the government of Britain with the only son of Alfred and Louisa Baldwin for nearly a decade and a half. He was christened James Ramsay MacDonald.

Anne Ramsay's mother does not seem to have been disturbed by the absence of a legal father for the baby. Hers was a matriarchal household. Her own husband had turned his back on her several years previously leaving her with four small children – of whom Anne was the youngest – to fend for. She had managed to feed, clothe and educate all of them by her own efforts and saw no reason why the rearing of a grandson should daunt her.

It was otherwise with MacDonald himself. He shared the 'taint' of illegitimacy with two other great leaders of Labour, Keir Hardie and Ernest Bevin, but it appears to have left a greater mark on his personality than it did on theirs. As a boy he was in trouble for seriously wounding a school-fellow who called him a bastard and in later life he did his best to conceal the circumstances of his birth from his own children. Its disclosure by Horatio Bottomley in *John Bull* during a particularly nasty campaign in the first world war left him utterly distraught. 'Thank God my mother is dead', he said over and over again, 'for this would have killed her.'

In the close possessive care of these two women, his mother and grandmother, and under the stern but kindly eye of the Dominie of Drainie village school, MacDonald spent the first eighteen years of his life. In assessing the resources of personality he later brought to politics, these years are important on both the credit and debit sides. In Lossiemouth he was a triton among the minnows but, because of his birth, a vulnerable triton moved by romantic longings and imaginative passion, at the same time suspicious, secretive and almost wholly lacking in humour. That he was not to be put to the plough like his missing father or to fishing like his contemporaries, neither his mother nor his grandmother ever doubted. Nor did the Dominie. Nor did MacDonald himself. He accepted it as natural that they should pinch and scrape to keep him at school long after most of his fellows were at work.

He was an apt pupil and earnest in self-education, able to read Latin and Greek and well versed in the works of Scott, Carlyle, Ruskin and Hazlitt. Cassell's *Popular Education* and *Science for All* provided him, as he later said, with his university, textbooks on biology and the natural sciences picked up in a secondhand bookshop gave him an ambition to be a scientist. Despite these achievements no path to a career offered itself to the prize pupil of Drainie school. Solitary, proud, on the look out for insults, he studied the situations vacant pages of *The Scotsman* and sent off innumerable letters without success. No one had any use for his talents.

He was by this time a dark, handsome young man with something of the noble bearing and magnificent voice that thirty-nine years later were to set political hostesses (anxious for a reassurance that they would not be murdered in their beds by Bolsheviks) agog with the gossip – so contrary to the facts but so grateful to MacDonald's ears – that he was really the by-blow of a Scottish Duke: 'One of us', as Milly,

Duchess of Sutherland, said to her sister Lady Warwick, 'the illegiti-mate son of the old Duke of Argyll.' 'Of the Duke of Richmond', corrected a rival hostess.

Neither his looks nor his talents were at first able to open doors for him to that wider life which he and his mother and grandmother and the Dominie felt – correctly as it turned out – to be his destiny. Even when on the Dominie's recommendation he managed to get a job as a Christian young man to help in the organisation of a Church Club in Bristol it did not last long. In less than two months he was back in Lossiemouth, living on his mother and grandmother again, well aware, no doubt, of what the Lossiemouth neighbours had to say about it. Later he would sometimes rhapsodize about 'the fine lot of the ploughmen who lived about us … you could hear them across field after field singing as they laboured'. He showed no wish to share their idyll. Neither to him nor his mother and grandmother does it ever seem to have occurred that he might earn his living by his hands, even temporarily. All three were conscious that he was of superior clay.

It was at this time that he became a socialist. But although he had been introduced to the political creed of socialism by a branch of the Social Democratic Federation in Bristol the socialism he evolved for himself as he mooned away the long hours in Lossiemouth waiting for a job was very different from the Marxism of the S.D.F. Nor had it anything in common with the left wing fervour of the new trade unionism which had begun to show itself among the ill-organized, unskilled general workers in Bristol, as elsewhere, and was to make its first big public demonstration in the great London dock strike four years later – at about the time that the loyal employees of Baldwin's celebrated the coming of age of the young master with the presentation of an illuminated address. MacDonald's socialism was nurtured by the radicalism then current in the air of Lossiemouth, as in most of rural Scotland, where hatred of landlordism was strong, and by a sense – very necessary to MacDonald's own esteem of himself – of what he liked to call 'the aristocratic virtues of the poor'. But its main ingredient was a belief he had acquired during his amateur reading of the natural sciences. He called himself a socialist because he believed himself to be a scientist.

Such confidence in the evolutionary and liberalizing role of science was natural enough at the time. To MacDonald, as to H. G. Wells and other eager young men like them, scientific advance seemed the one certain way of lifting from the backs of the young and the poor the inert weight of the elderly and plutocratic, with their baggage of privilege and superstition, religion and social snobbery. It was exciting, disreputable and romantic, the powerful *régisseur* that could bring the temples of privilege and orthodoxy tumbling down about the ears of the smug and open wide the gates of progress to what Wells called the 'adventurous outsiders'. Although Wells later listed MacDonald as one such along with Bottomley, Shaw, Basil Zaharoff, Maundy Gregory, Birkenhead and himself (an odd mixture), he was in fact far from being so. He was an outsider who longed to be inside. Unlike the militant trade unionists and the Social Democrats he did not want to wage social war, he wanted to be accepted. He was not concerned to tear the class system apart. All he wanted was an assurance that it would change of its own accord and take him in.

Meanwhile he was compelled to live on his mother and grandmother in Lossiemouth, writing interminable letters and suffering from the most desperate of all the diseases of youth, the fear that no one would give him a chance to show his quality. It is to his credit that he did not despair. Even when, on the strength of a letter from a Bristol acquaintance who had moved, there he arrived in London with a few shillings given him by his mother and grandmother to find that the job he hoped to get had been filled the day before, he remained resolute. To have returned defeated to Lossiemouth a second time would have been to deny his destiny. He took cheap lodgings in Kentish Town and set out on a sombre search for work, tramping the streets from factory to factory, office to office, haunting the public libraries for an early glimpse of the situations vacant columns in the morning newspapers, living on oatmeal and hot water while he grimly hoarded his shillings. He was talented, ambitious and, by English standards, educated far above his station. He was ready to take on anything – and no one wanted him. It might have made him bitter. It did not. There was at no time any element of revenge in MacDonald's socialism. He wanted too much to belong.

He seemed, rather oddly, to have found his first taste of what he was looking for in the Fabian Society when, after at last managing to find a job as an invoice clerk in a warehouse at fifteen shillings a week, later increased to a pound, he continued his political education by circulating from one political society to another. Fabianism as such did not, it is true, appeal to him greatly; he had a natural antipathy to its insistence on practical detail. Nor was the Fabian oligarchy much attracted to him; Mrs Webb was later to describe his socialism as 'Conservative collectivism tempered by muddle-headed Utopian socialism', and to add waspishly, 'It hurts my pride to see the Fabian policy of permeation guyed by him.' But in the comfortable drawing-rooms of the Fabian Society's better-off members he found a society – middle-class, intellectual and consciously élite – in which he felt at home as he had in no other. This product of a brief affair between a ploughman and a servant girl was an instinctive member of the professional classes. Several of the Fabians, Shaw among them, took him at first to be an army officer. None, so far as is known, made the mistake of thinking him a member of the proletariat.

What the Fabian drawing-rooms began, his subsequent employment (at a salary of £75 a year) as secretary to Thomas Lough, a wealthy Liberal with political ambitions, continued. This appointment was, indeed, almost as decisive in the creation of MacDonald the politician as his marriage to Margaret Gladstone, great niece of Lord Kelvin and daughter of Dr John Hall Gladstone, F.R.S., eight years later. It made him free of that ample middle-class world of the intellectual and cultured, the prosperous and politically-minded, to which the Fabian Society had introduced him and which he felt to be his natural habitat. It brought him in touch also with men concerned not merely with political ideas but with their practical application and administration. It might even have made him a Liberal if the Liberal caucus had been more willing to open its doors to the talented but impecunious young. But though when the Liberals snubbed him he turned to the I.L.P. he did so with, odd though it may superficially seem in one of his antecedents, an aura of the middle class: 'He was', said one of its trade union members, 'a Godsend to us. He came to us from another world.'

Marriage set the seal on his social transformation. It was a love match. To Margaret Gladstone, MacDonald was the ideal knight of whom, as Lord Elton tells us in his uncompleted biography of MacDonald, she had written in her diary three years before: 'I wonder whether I shall meet him in this world. I mean *My* him, my sir, my knight. I believe that each of us will meet her him or his her in some world.... Oh God, Thou hast not given me Thy best gift. Oh let me make no mistake about it, and if I should use it for myself and him instead of for Thee and Thy other children, keep it from me until I am ready to have it, however far away that time may be.' To him she was one who 'saw spirit in everything'. Until her tragic death fifteen years later they were ideally happy.

As well as being a love match this marriage was also the corroboration of MacDonald's social hopes. As Thomas Lough's secretary he had found a place in the world first glimpsed in Fabian drawing rooms, but a tenuous and ambiguous one only. Now he was there of right. By the standards of the very wealthy his wife was not rich. But she had an assured private income sufficient to make both of them economically independent, and a social background that lifted MacDonald far above the anxieties and dubieties of his own beginnings. It was a setting that suited him admirably. They could afford to travel, and this they did abundantly, so that he became by far the most internationally knowledgeable of the members of the young Labour Movement. They could afford to entertain and this they did, not luxuriously but after a free and easy Bohemian style that made their flat in Lincoln's Inn Fields and their cottage in Buckinghamshire natural centres for left wing intellectuals, and the host an obvious leader among them. MacDonald had never felt himself a member of the working classes. He now, as his biographer Lord Elton approvingly remarks, assumed, as one who had found his way home, 'the manners although not the prejudices of what is called the ruling class'.

The independence given by his wife's means was of great importance in 1900, when the newly formed Labour Representation Committee came to elect him as its first Secretary. (Six years later the Committee became the Labour Party, with MacDonald, duly elected M.P. for Leicester, as its leader.) The fact that he was in no way dependent upon the trade unions for a living and could provide the infant committee not only with much voluntary work but also with a home in his flat in Lincoln's Inn made him an ideal choice enjoying an independent status the Secretary would not otherwise have had. All the advantages were now his. He was indubitably of humble origins. But he was no less indubitably a member of the superior classes from which the English working classes have almost always liked to draw their political leaders. Moreover Margaret MacDonald was warm and generous of heart, with an outgoing nature which admirably compensated what was aloof and egocentric in her husband's personality. She made a bridge between him and simple people and she gave him a sense of belonging.

'To turn to her in stress and strain', he wrote in the *Memoir* of her he published privately after her death, 'was like going into a sheltered haven where waters were at rest and smiling up into the face of heaven. Weary and worn, buffeted and discouraged, thinking of giving up the thankless strife and returning to my own house and children and household shrines, I would flee with her to my Buckinghamshire home and my lady would heal and soothe me with her cheery faith and steady conviction and send me whole to smite and be smitten.' The phrasing has that touch of the mawkish that disfigures so much of MacDonald's writing – and some of Baldwin's – but the emotion was genuine. She made him a larger man than he was without her.

But in September 1911 she died. The loss was all the greater in that it came seven months after the death of his mother, two years after the death of his grandmother. He had depended all his life upon women's support. He was now bereft of it. He had no men friends. Although in the nature of the political life there were many acquaintances on the public periphery of his activities there was no room in his nature for men who offered friendship on equal terms. From men he required an acknowledgement of his uniqueness to be satisfied only in a leader-follower relationship. He disliked most of his principal colleagues even more than they disliked him.

Something of what had happened to him he recognized: 'I feel the mind of the solitary stag growing upon me', he wrote early in 1914 to Mrs Bruce Glazier (it was natural that the confession should be to a woman and one who like his wife came from the upper middle classes). 'My fireside is desolate. I have no close friend in the world to share either the satisfaction of success or the disturbance of defeat. So I get driven in upon myself more and more, and I certainly do not improve.'

Yet in a curious way his solitariness, the fact that he was so unrepresentative, contributed to his eminence in his Party. In a movement that was still largely an uneasy federation of the politically homeless it was a source of strength rather than weakness to be entirely trusted by none of the major conflicting groups. It kept him from the danger of being thought wholly committed to any. In his mastery of Parliamentary tactics, his 'consummate art as a political performer', to quote the reluctant tribute of Beatrice Webb, and his power over mass audiences on whom his romantic presence, magnificent voice and rich if confused phraseology acted like Highland music uplifting the heart and enervating the mind, he was without rival.

His socialism remained biological. 'The biological view', he wrote in a passage characteristic both of his literary style and of his mode of thought, 'emphasizes the possibilities of existing society as the mother of future societies, and regards idea and circumstance as the pair from which the new societies are to spring. It gives not only an explanation of the existing state of things. It also views every form of existence on its actual process of movement and therefore on its perishing – very different from perishable – side. It lays the very slightest emphasis on its "critical and revolutionary" side because it is mainly constructive and the idea of "clearing before building" is alien to its nature.'

Yet by an odd irony this misty, moderate, talented, egotistical and hollow man, whose one wish was to be thought a benevolent traffic policeman directing society along its biological road to 'community consciousness', became in the public mind in the course of his career the symbol of the most extreme socialism.

All public men, of course, tend to become archetypal figures, taking to themselves the characteristics their supporters and enemies most need to see in them, their images constantly enlarged by the accretion of misconceptions essential to the political life. Because MacDonald's personality, while superficially so distinguished, was in its real texture so amorphous, he was more susceptible than most to the advantages and disadvantages of being misunderstood. He was a peg built to hang myths on.

Thus although he was never a pacifist, and indeed until nearly the end of the 1914-18 war was not even an advocate of a negotiated peace but of a fight to a finish, he came to represent in the minds of many millions of ordinary people the extreme pacifist view, arousing in the majority the virulent hatred proper to 'a pro-German', while to a minority who opposed the war he was a hero and martyr. Neither side, it would appear, read what he actually said.

'Victory must be ours. England is not played out. Her mission is to be accomplished.... We cannot go back now. Nor can we turn to the right. We must go straight through. History will in due time apportion the praise and the blame, but the young men of the country must, for the moment, settle the immediate issue of victory ... I want the serious men of the Trade Unions, the Brotherhood and similar movements to face their duty. To such men it is enough to say "England has need of you"; to say it in the right way. They will gather to her aid....'

Such were his words in a letter – the occasion is significant – to a mass recruiting rally at the De Montford Hall in Leicester in September 1914. Yet when a few weeks later he came to the decision that, although too old for combatant service, he ought to find some means of actively participating in the war and volunteered for service with an ambulance unit on the Belgian front under a friend, Dr Hector Munro, he was arrested as a dangerous person by the local British military authorities

as soon as he arrived and sent back to England – only to return a fortnight later with an omnibus pass from Lord Kitchener himself.

The public cannot be blamed for finding his position obscure. As
one goes through his speeches and writings at that time it is extraordinarily difficult to discover what his attitude to the war was. That
he was never a pacifist is clear enough. But his suspicion of Sir Edward
Grey led him on occasion into utterances as difficult to reconcile with
the sentiments he expressed in his recruiting appeal as those sentiments
were with his reputation as a pacifist. Within a few days of the outbreak of war, for example, and a week or two before the recruiting
rally at Leicester, he was writing an article in the *Leicester Pioneer*
which, not content with drawing attention to the deficiencies of
British diplomacy, seemed to put the whole responsibility for war
with Germany on Britain.

'When Sir Edward Grey failed to secure peace between Germany
and Russia he worked deliberately to involve us in the war using
Belgium as his chief excuse', he declared. From this he moved to a
conclusion subsequently widely quoted by German propaganda.
'There is no doubt whatever but that, when all this is over and we turn
back to it in cold blood and read it carefully so as to ascertain why
England has practically declared war on Germany, we shall find that
the only reason from beginning to end in it is that the Foreign Office
is anti-German and that the Admiralty was anxious to seize any opportunity of using the Navy in battle practice.'

There were others who held views not very different from his.
Many of those in the Labour Party who did so, like Hardie, Snowden,
Ponsonby and Russell, became absolute pacifists in regard to this war.
MacDonald, on the other hand, could declare that 'the only reason
from beginning to end' why Britain had become involved in war was
that the Foreign Office was anti-German and the Admiralty wanted
battle practice for its ships, and yet subsequently take the stand that
'The war has broken out, we are in it. We must see it through. Every
step to that necessary end must be taken. Let there be no mistake about
that.'

In logic these two positions were of course not incompatible. They
were occupied by many others, including several members of the
Asquith Cabinet, who believed that war had been brought on the
British people by the negligence, folly, and worse, of Asquith and
Grey, but that in the circumstances Britain's moral commitment,
given additional force by the invasion of Belgium, was so strong that

war could not be avoided – and that once war had begun the patriotic view, 'my country right or wrong', was the only proper one. For MacDonald to have taken a positive stand of this sort would have been to alienate those upon whose support in the I.L.P. he had now come to depend. This he could not bring himself to do. Accordingly he continued throughout the war to make speeches which were capable of almost totally different interpretations according to the mood of the audience that heard them. Reading them one sometimes has the curious feeling that one is listening to a man haunted by an image of himself in the witness box required to prove by exact textual reference that he did not say what the other side accused him of.

One can feel some sympathy for him. He hated militarism. He could not pretend that he thought this a holy war. But neither could he bring himself wholly to oppose it once it had begun. His intelligence, by habit subtle and dialectical, was not at home among the blacks and whites that war makes popular. Rejection of commitment, admirable in a philosopher, is a disability in a political leader whose trade requires that in moments of decision he shall decide, and fatal to those who make public speeches to large audiences, since the end result is likely to be that they are either misinterpreted or mistrusted or both. It is significant that in the end MacDonald attracted to himself much more public hatred than those who, like Snowden or Lansbury, opposed the war utterly but were recognized, however reluctantly, as men of principle, whereas MacDonald often seemed to be speaking in two voices at the same time and so got none of the credit that his confused and sometimes anguished attempt to be honest with himself deserved. Not that even this attempt always succeeded. Expediency would keep breaking in. Reading his speeches it is often hard to determine where the man of principle ends and the man anxious to keep a foot in both camps at the same time takes over. Perhaps he did not always know himself for he found it impossible to resist the appeal of a large crowd or the temptation to say what it most wanted to hear, and as the war proceeded he took more and more of his colour from the temper of those I.L.P. audiences who were always so ready to cheer his 'pacifism' and hold out to him the cloak of their uncritical adulation for protection against the icy blasts of public hatred.

Yet at the beginning his attitude was very similar to that of many Liberal leaders, including Sir John Simon, Charles Masterman, Lord Morley and even Lloyd George, with all of whom he was in constant communication right up to 4 August. They, like him, distrusted Grey and Asquith and opposed their French commitments. Like him they thought Grey had failed to clarify the issue of Belgian neutrality or give Germany sufficient warning of the consequences of invasion. And like him they had little stomach for an alliance with Imperial Russia, the most tyrannical and reactionary regime in Europe.

In this they were right. By successive stages from 1905 onwards when Colonel Repington first made contact with the French General Staff and cleared the way for official talks promoted with vigour by General Sir Henry Wilson, Director of Military Operations at the War Office, right up to the time of the meetings of the Committee of Imperial Defence after Agadir when the plan for a British Expeditionary Force as the centre piece of British strategy in the event of a European war was accepted, Britain was manœuvred into a position where the moral commitment to fight alongside the French became virtually inescapable. Yet this was done without any formal commitment and with the knowledge of only three members of the Cabinet, Asquith, Grey and Haldane. By August 1914 the French fleet had already withdrawn to the Mediterranean, leaving her northern coasts to be protected by the British Navy, and the French Army had been assured that it could count absolutely on a British Army Corps on its left wing. Irrespective of the invasion of Belgium, Britain was thus wholly committed without public knowledge, and without prior warning to Germany to fight on the side of France if war came.

MacDonald was right in his criticism of Grey and he showed courage in making it. He was right in thinking the public substantially misled. He was right in suspecting that Asquith was more concerned to cover up the follies of his Administration and the deficiencies of the military high command than to tell the people the truth. (There was a startling example of this a few weeks later on 31 August when with ineffable arrogance Asquith reprimanded *The Times* for reporting the initial allied defeat on the Belgian frontier, which forced British troops to fall back well over a hundred miles in ten days. 'It is impossible', he told the House of Commons, 'to commend too highly the patriotic reticence of the press as a whole from the beginning of the war up to this moment. The publication to which my Hon. friend refers would appear to be a very regrettable exception. I trust and believe that it will not recur.' The business of ordinary people was to fight, not to ask for the truth from their betters.)

All this MacDonald felt, and had the courage not to be silent. But he could not make up his mind about his subsequent position. His speech in the House following Grey's announcement of the British ultimatum to Germany was a parliamentary disaster, not because it was critical but because at the end of it no one could be sure whether he was for the war or against it. Where a plain statement was required he gave a metaphysical discourse. It was a habit that was to grow on him. It was, indeed, endemic to his personality. He could not bear to slam any door.

Although over-subtle for the times his opinions were intrinsically not of a nature to cast him for the role either of a hero of the pacifists or an enemy of the people. Yet because of them, or rather because of the myths that accrued around them and him, he, who in this matter as in so many others was desperately trying to find a middle way between the extremes his nature abhorred, became a symbol of extremism, rejected by the mass of his own Party from whose leadership he was forced to resign, reviled by the great majority of his fellow country-men, idolized by and forced into ever closer association with the very people with whom he was temperamentally least in sympathy, the left wing 'phraseologists' of the I.L.P. It is perhaps characteristic of him also that in this confused situation the blow that hurt him most according to his friend and biographer Lord Elton was his expulsion by seventy-five votes to twenty-four from the Moray Golf Club in Lossiemouth. However, he found comfort in perusading himself that 'the place is infested by snobs and "penny gentry" during the summer', and that 'the true quality' were on his side: 'Some of my swell Tory friends are rallying round me splendidly', he reported to Mrs Glasier. 'The old dowager Countess and her daughter are coming up next week just to show me countenance....'

As the war ended, the symbolic quality in his personality that had earlier served him so well – and was similarly to serve him again – seemed to have contributed most to bringing his political career to ruin. He was crushingly beaten at Leicester in the General Election. 'The haunting memory', he wrote, 'is of the women – bloodthirsty, cursing their hate, issuing from the courts and alleys crowded with children, reeking with humanity' – an odd phrase surely for a socialist – 'the sad flotsam and jetsam of wild emotion.' And although he could still count on the almost hysterical responses of the mass audiences of the Left with whom he had least natural affinity he was disliked and distrusted not only by a large part of the great middle section of his party, including most of the trade union members, but by most of his fellow *leaders* of the I.L.P. He was very much better known to the public at this time (though mainly to his disadvantage) than his almost exact contemporary Baldwin, and had, as has been seen, packed a great deal more political activity into his fifty-two years. But he seemed no more likely to reach 10 Downing Street than did the amiable iron-master from Worcestershire, with whom in a spirit of mutual amity unusual in political rivals he was to govern Britain turn and turn about for thirteen of the most momentous and unlucky years in British history.

2. The Doors Swing Open

IT took MacDonald four years to get back into Parliament. It had been plain that in a general election immediately on the heels of victory candidates with the Lloyd George coupon would sweep the country, but the level of personal vituperation to which the campaign sank was a surprise and MacDonald was overwhelmed by the Leicester result. He found it hard to believe that a constituency that had known him personally for twelve years could turn upon him so bitterly.

He went abroad to recover his balance. 'The moment the peoples of Europe question things', he had said in one of his wartime speeches, 'the moment they ask why, how and wherefore – that moment the spell of war will be broken. They will come together in their sorrow and demand peace and lay the foundations of peace.... It is the old order that is crumbling and breaking to fragments, filling the air with its dust and noise and confusion of its downfall.... We go back into the world to do our duty, to reconstruct society, to rebuild the fabric that has fallen, to make good the walls that have been crushed; to put a new idea, a new beauty, a new holiness into the lives of the peoples of Europe.'

In the shattered societies of Europe many were already questioning. Among Continental socialists and liberals MacDonald found himself made much of for his wartime attitudes. In such company the sincerity of his hatred for militarism and the force and energy with which he had campaigned against what he believed to be the criminal prolonga-tion of the war by the refusal of the Allied Governments to consider a negotiated peace were recognized and admired. His evasions were not known.

He came back restored in confidence to take up again the round of I.L.P. meetings whose audience rose to him as to a Messiah, and in

1921 made another effort to get back into the House at a by-election in Woolwich, a safe Labour seat long held by Will Crooks. He lost it against a Coalition candidate with a distinguished war record, Captain Gee, V.C. But despite a venomous campaign against him by Tories, Liberals and Coalition Labourites, and the intervention of Horatio Bottomley, whose travelling circus, not content with attacking his war record, devoted itself to blackening his private life in the most slanderous terms (thus greatly restoring his prestige in the Labour movement for whom he became a socialist martyr), the result was sufficiently narrow to show that public opinion was, as Baldwin inside the Coalition Government was also becoming aware, on the move. He was beaten by only 683 votes in a total poll of over 26,760. He did not have to wait long for another chance. In the general election of 1922 he was returned for Aberavon.

He was the most skilled parliamentarian on the Labour benches. He had played as large a part as any man living – if not the largest – in the birth and development of the Party. With Arthur Henderson and Sidney Webb he had had a major hand in drafting the two statements of policy, 'Memorandum on War Aims' and 'Labour and the New Social Order', which, together with a new Party constitution providing for individual membership of Constituency Labour Parties, gave Labour a much greater appeal to the middle classes than it had had before. But he had been out of Parliament for four years and out of the Leadership of the Parliamentary Party for eight.

Although his claims on the leadership were high they were, therefore, by no means assured. It was only by the narrow margin of five votes out of a total of 117 cast at the meeting of the Parliamentary Labour Party on 14 November, with twenty-two members absent, that he was elected. These five votes were to make him Prime Minister within fourteen months.

The narrowness of his majority was not due to his war record. That had now become an advantage. What held back many, including some like Philip Snowden who had had long experience of him in the I.L.P., and others, like several of the trade union members who had worked with or under him in the past, was suspicion as to what there actually was behind the moving and eloquent words that poured out with such torrential ease before enthusiastic audiences of the left. These men found him hard to pin down. They thought him able but were not sure they could trust him. If Arthur Henderson had been standing against him for the leadership he would have had little or no

chance. But Henderson had contrived to lose his seat at the general
election and had, in any event, decided that his best service for the
Party lay in organization rather than parliamentary leadership. It was
therefore a much weaker candidate MacDonald had to beat, J. R. Clynes.

Clynes had been Minister of Food in the closing years of the war.
He was a middle of the road trade union leader, shrewd, honest,
practical, but physically unimpressive, possessed neither of Mac-
Donald's talents as a parliamentary personality nor Henderson's massive
administrative authority. Sincere but mediocre, his reputation for
excessive moderation was out of key with the mood of the postwar
Party. That even so MacDonald was only able to beat him by so
narrow a margin indicates in pointed manner the extent of the ill will
the idol of mass audiences had managed to attract from those with a
closer view. In fact, on any sensible assessment of parliamentary
qualifications, MacDonald was the only possible choice at this time.
Not only was he the best known figure in the Party, nationally and
internationally, and its ablest speaker, but apart from Snowden, who
had other defects, there was no one of any popular standing in the
party to compare with him intellectually. The tragedy of the choice,
if, as many later came to believe, it was a tragedy, was not that the
Parliamentary Party chose wrongly but that there was no one else to
choose. The Conservative Party could afford to reject glamour and
turn to what appeared to be the safe mediocrity of Bonar Law and
Baldwin. The Labour Party, because it was still above all a party of
propagandists, could not. It had to have someone who could attract
attention and who would be accepted in the country as of a parliamentary stature comparable to that of the leaders of the older Parties.
MacDonald was the only one who filled that bill. He may not have
been a real leader but as Beatrice Webb observed he was 'a magnificent
substitute for one'. For the Parliamentary Party to have elected
Clynes instead of him would have been to carry loyalty to the point of
political idiocy: not that this would necessarily have ruled it out for
the Labour Party.

Some of those who voted for MacDonald were no doubt fully
conscious that whether they liked him or not, there was really no
alternative. However, the main reason for his success, moderate
though it was, was the mistaken belief of many new M.P.s, particularly
those from Clydeside, that MacDonald was a revolutionary left-wing
socialist who would give the Labour Party bite. They expected him
to lead them in a socialist crusade.

This mistake was not unnatural. Many of MacDonald's speeches during the war, particularly those to I.L.P. audiences, might have been specifically designed to give exactly this impression. Certainly they conveyed it to those actually present, subject to that golden voice and romantic presence, although when analysed in cold print they rarely conveyed quite the same meaning. At any rate it was in this conviction that Emanuel Shinwell speaking for the whole Clydeside group nominated MacDonald for the leadership. It was in the same conviction that they voted for him.

MacDonald thus found himself elected leader of the Parliamentary Labour Party by the votes of those in his Party to whom he was temperamentally and intellectually most antipathetic, while the moderates who were closest to him in political attitude mostly voted against him. Elected in such manner his natural inclination to stand alone was intensified. Aloof, impatient of criticism and very conscious of his intellectual superiority to most of his colleagues, he found himself leading a Party with most of whose members he had little or nothing personally in common.

Philip Snowden, the only other long-standing member of the Party with gifts which, though narrower, were comparable, but with a mordant tongue that made enemies, and a snobbish and unpopular wife, detested MacDonald, finding his high-flown generalities and personal vanities totally uncongenial. Arthur Henderson was willing to support him – it was indeed largely Henderson's doing that the war-time breach between MacDonald and the trade unions had been kept within bounds that made reconciliation possible. But he did so only because he thought MacDonald's parliamentary talents essential to the Labour Party: there was no warmth between them. Nor was there anyone else of comparable stature with whom MacDonald felt able or ready to discuss politics on that informal and confidential level between equals which is essential to a balanced judgment of affairs.

Yet in many ways the image the Labour Party could now present to the nation was much closer to MacDonald's heart than it had ever been before. The adoption of the new constitution in February 1918 had transformed the original loose federation of trade unions and socialist societies into a nationally organized party with strong local branches. Although still federal in principle – for that was the only way the organizational and financial support of the trade unions could be preserved – its doors were now wide open to individual members of all classes. Through these newly opened doors thousands came in, including many who had formerly been adherents of the Liberal Party before its division and decline. Moreover the Labour Party was now for the first time formally a socialist party and as such able to appeal to the idealism of a much wider cross-section of national society than previously. It was still founded on the trade unions. They provided the firm base that gave it a solidity none of the continental socialist parties could match. But it was much less a trade union party and much less a class party than before.

This fact was reflected in the new Parliamentary Party of which MacDonald now became leader. In the 1918 election the Party's new constitution and its statements of broad socialist purpose at home and abroad had not had time to make any impact on the electoral results. Nor even with more time could it have withstood the flood of postwar emotion behind the Lloyd George appeal. By 1922 its new look had its effect. Helped by the break up of the Coalition and the new forces at work in public opinion, this election returned a Parliamentary Labour Party not only greatly increased in size but significantly changed in composition. In 1918 no more than 57 M.P.s had been elected of whom 48 were trade union nominees, 25 from the Miners Federation. The Parliamentary Party MacDonald was elected to lead in 1922 was 142 strong, and though the trade union group had increased in size to 85 (42 of them miners) the rest were from the local Labour Parties or socialist societies, mainly I.L.P. or the Divisional Labour Parties. They included for the first time a sprinkling of middle-class members like Clement Attlee, the first Oxford graduate to be returned for a Labour seat, Arthur Greenwood, who had been a university lecturer, Sidney Webb, moving for the first time from the Fabian wings to the parliamentary stage, and two former Liberal M.P.s, Charles Trevelyan and H. B. Lees-Smith. And there were several others like A. V. Alexander, David Kirkwood, James Maxton, Thomas Johnston, John Wheatley and Emanuel Shinwell, who soon showed themselves capable of making their mark in the House in one direction or another.

Although inexperienced it was thus by no means either a negligible or a narrowly based parliamentary team of which MacDonald now found himself in command. The question was what would he do with it. The Clydesiders were not alone in believing that they had been sent to Parliament to challenge the old order of things at every turn and to replace it by a new society that would, in MacDonald's words, 'put a new idea, a new beauty, a new holiness into the lives of the peoples of Europe'. They wanted to use their parliamentary position to extend the range and force of socialist propaganda for this new kind of society and to demonstrate that the Labour Party was as different as possible from any other.

MacDonald's ambitions, however, were quite other than this. He did not want Labour to stand outside the political establishment. With an ardour no less intense than Baldwin's he wanted it to become a part of the establishment. To the dismay of the Clydesiders he at once made use of the opportunity provided by his speech on the Address to declare that Labour would have not less but more regard for the constitutional proprieties than the Conservatives, who during the Irish dispute, 'seemed to me to be snipping, snipping away with the shears, at those tender cords of consent, restraint and good sense that alone keep the complicated fabric of civilized and international relationships together. I shall never be a party to such conduct.... We shall do our best to state our case in home affairs, in all their great perplexity, and in foreign affairs in their still greater perplexity; and I ask from you – and I know that I will get it – and I ask from the Right Hon. gentleman and his followers on the other side of the House that fair play, that generosity of treatment, which no man doing his best has ever been denied by this House.'

What MacDonald was most concerned to do, as he made clear in an article he wrote in the *Socialist Review*, was to convince the electorate of Labour's political respectability: its capacity to be an alternative Government. 'The weakness of the Labour Party', he wrote, 'is the fact that it is a "Red Terror" to the minds of large masses of people who know little about it but who read a profusion of absurd criticism of its immediate projects.' He rebuked in tones magisterial those members of the Parliamentary Party who failed to realize that 'while demonstrative enthusiasm may be understood by those who know all the circumstances it tends to antagonize people who read of it in the papers next morning'. The task of the Labour Party was to convince the nation that 'it thinks of the whole community and subordinates interests and functions to the common well-being, it regards society as a unity ... its influence upon institutions is to transform them into instruments of the distinctive ideas and aspirations of these times'. (It might have been Baldwin talking about the Conservative Party.)

Nor did he retreat from this high level when in November 1923 Baldwin so unexpectedly flung the country into the general election that was to have the totally unexpected result of making MacDonald

Prime Minister. Coining several phrases that were to become part of the permanent stock of his oratory he told a mass meeting at Bristol that the Labour Party was 'the expression of a great uprising of the human spirit, never old, never satisfied, never finding a permanent habitation in any of the stable habitations that men build, but always like the Bedouin sleeping in tents that he folds up in the morning in order to go on his pilgrimage. But, my friends, I see no end of the journey. We have come, we shall journey, and we shall go, and our children coming after us will go on with their journey, and their children will go on with theirs. And, my friends, you and I have to take care is that the journey is both onward and upward.'

It is hard to be fair to MacDonald when one reads his speeches. Robbed of that handsome presence and the rise and fall of that magnificent Scots voice they seem fabricated of such secondhand fustian that even when one reminds oneself of the ineffable tedium of the generality of political speeches one wonders how they could ever have been listened to with patience. But of course there was more to MacDonald than this. He was an excellent chairman of committees, and in practical affairs was sometimes capable of a realism that bore no relation to the misty rhetoric of his speeches. His vision of the world, although romantic and imprecise, was noble. He had much courage, great energy and a zeal for the general good. Although self-consuming his ambitions were neither small not mean in their essentials. As a parliamentary performer he towered not only above his colleagues in the Labour Party but above most of those on the other side as well: he was certainly, as Sidney Webb used to tell his colleagues in moments of depression, 'the best leader available'.

Yet one cannot help but feel him unfortunate in both his casting and his timing. He would have been more at home in a Liberal Cabinet in the first decade of the century than, as he was so soon to become, head of the first Labour Government in British history – there was, indeed, an oddly Edwardian air about many of his political and social ambitions, including his avid passion for great houses. He was once described as 'the nearest to a Gladstone Labour ever had'. It would have been closer to the truth perhaps to have said that he was the closest Labour ever came to an Asquith. Or, possibly, despite his personal dislike of that Liberal Foreign Secretary, a Grey. For, as was soon to become plain, it was foreign affairs that most engaged his interest. As Foreign Secretary, which he combined with the Premiership, for he could not bear that anyone else should have it, he could function, as he liked to do; a statesman on a world stage, moving with charm, patience and the most punctilious courtesy, informal yet never forgetful of protocol, in a world of great affairs in which the appearance as well as the realities of the life were still important and Foreign Offices were still staffed by gentlemen. 'The Foreign Office is far too pleased with MacDonald', complained George Young, an ex-diplomat recruit to the Labour Party, and it was said in the Foreign Office itself that in losing Curzon and getting MacDonald they 'had got rid of a cad and found a gentleman'. 'He is', said Mrs Webb with a minatory snap, 'a born aristocrat.' It was as the legatee of the liberal aristocratic tradition in politics that this socialist leader, born so very much out of character as the illegitimate son of a ploughman, most often seemed to see himself.

His conviction that Labour must move from its purely propagandist past and show itself fit and able to govern in constitutional terms was, of course, valid, the commonsense of practical statesmanship. The real misfortune lay in the fact that, called so unexpectedly to form a Government in 1923, Labour had not yet thrown up any specifically socialist leader capable of demonstrating its constitutional principles in terms that had real relevance to the genuine roots and true social purposes of the Labour movement. Henderson might conceivably have done so – although he was more of an organizer than a Parliamentarian. So, a little later, might Wheatley the Clydesider who was one of the few positive successes of the first Labour Administration. MacDonald could not. If he had been required to work under a leader hewn out of a tougher more genuinely Labour timber, MacDonald might well have fitted in admirably as a distinguished Foreign Secretary. As Prime Minister he was obsessed by the need to evolve an Administration indistinguishable from any other. The great doors of the establishment had swung open. He marched in, proud and happy to be home at last.

3. Survival of a Myth

WHEN the first Labour Government in British political history came to an end after less than nine months in office MacDondal wrote in his letter of resignation to the King that Labour had 'shown the country that they have the capacity to govern in an equal degree with other parties in the House'. A less friendly critic, Beatrice Webb, took a markedly more pessimistic view. MacDonald's Premiership, she thought, provided 'a melancholy example of demoralization when a man becomes pre-eminent in his own sphere, uncontrolled in the exercise of power – especially a man who is wholly unaccustomed to and untrained for these giddy heights of personal decisions on great issues'.

It is part of the enigma that MacDonald constantly presents to the inquirer that there is almost as much to say for either judgment. It is hard to think of any political figure of comparable eminence less consistent in performance or character than MacDonald. One never knows where one has him. One moment the face is that of a statesman of world stature, intelligent, far-seeing, and resolute, the next of a politician of the pettiest kind, vain, amateurish, indecisive and infirm of judgment. He is like one of his own Highland landscapes: the great peaks jut into the sky with majestic and noble clarity but even as one admires them, the mist falls and all becomes indistinct, confused, and damp, and one is left standing ankle deep in a bog.

To find himself Prime Minister so soon and so unexpectedly delighted MacDonald, even though Prime Minister of a minority Government without real power, holding office at the whim of Conservatives and Liberals able at any moment to turn him out by combining against him. Later he described this first Administration of his as an 'insane miracle'. It fell a good deal short of the miraculous both in achievement and intention. It can more fairly be called a gamble – one that did not quite come off.

During the course of this Administration MacDonald displayed in bewildering sequence what was both frivolous and serious in his character. He embraced with naïve vanity all that was repugnant in Court ceremonial, to the intense discomfort of the most dedicated of his followers, especially to those in the I.L.P. to whom he most owed his eminence. Such men and women were prepared, reluctantly, to accept the fact that a minority Labour Government existing by grace of Conservative and Liberal votes could not hope to carry through any large constitutional or economic changes. Many, including several of the party leaders, thought it should accept office only for the purpose of presenting an uncompromisingly socialist King's Speech on which it would be bound to be defeated, thus demonstrating in a dramatic way its difference from other parties and its dedication to sweeping change. With the aid of Snowden, Webb and others, Mac-Donald, by no means averse for his own part to governing with his hands tied against the kind of measures he least believed in, had no great difficulty in persuading such staunch souls that deliberately to invoke defeat on the King's Speech would merely convince the country that Labour was unfit to rule.

Yet being idealists of a simple and uncompromising kind they assumed that although their Government might have its hands tied on major issues at least it would show its dislike for what they felt to be the meaningless flummery of much public life with all its snobberies and glorification of class and caste. They discovered their mistake when they opened their morning papers and found in them a photograph of MacDonald looking handsome and proud in full Court dress complete with sword. It was perhaps a small matter. Better socialists than MacDonald were later to acquiesce without much controversy in the ceremonial trappings of office, considering them of no great importance either way. But in the atmosphere of 1924, when Lord Birkenhead, who often managed to combine one of the best minds in politics with the wit of a third form schoolboy at an inferior prep school, jibed that Labour Members slept three in a bed and the boring convolutions of London society provided rich imbeciles with the happy assurance that they were members of a superior race, it was a different matter.

What was significant about MacDonald's readiness to get himself and his colleagues into aristocratic livery was not that he thought it not worth making a fuss about but that he did. So far from wishing to strike a new note in political life, as his I.L.P. supporters assumed, he was anxious only to show himself a Prime Minister exactly like any other. More particularly he was concerned to show the King and the Court that far from wanting to upset the niceties of social precedence and ceremonial order by which King George V set so much store he would – and could – fit into the charade as to the manner born. To him, indeed, it was much more than a charade. It was the visible sign of belonging. Now he was truly inside. To stay at great houses, to mix as an equal in the highest society, to be smiled on by duchesses and approved of by their husbands, this was to conquer his anxiety at last. He did not so much succumb to the aristocractic embrace as fling himself into its arms. Like Lloyd George, he arrived at 10 Downing Street a stranger to the class and the tradition that has given Britain nearly all her Prime Ministers. To Lloyd George this did not matter. He had the assurance of genius. He made his own laws. But to Mac-Donald it was a constant mortification. If only he had really been 'one of us', as Milly, Duchess of Sutherland, whispered behind her hand, or even the scion of a military family with a social conscience that the Fabians had taken him for when he first appeared among them, how different it would all have been. Then he could have employed his political talents without having to bother about belonging.

But this was impossible to him. He had to be accepted. In the process he transformed into bewildered or cynical disillusion the naïve expectations of thousands of those who had believed that his presence in 10 Downing Street would bring a new wind blowing through society. It was his greatest disservice to his age. There was no possibility that a Labour Government taking office in the conditions this one did could bring a major alteration in the social and economic structure. But it might have sounded a note that would have made men conscious of new attitude in politics. Instead it succeeded in taking the heart out of much genuine social protest and in diverting a good deal of idealism into arid channels of doctrinaire controversy. No doubt this idealism was romantic. Perhaps, as is so often the fate of romantic idealism, it was doomed anyway. But it represented a genuine postwar emotion which might have had a pervasive influence on British society in the 'twenties if MacDonald's anxiety to convince the eminent, the established and the rich that there was nothing in Labour's social protest to disturb them had not denied it effective political outlet and driven, among others, many writers, poets, artists and scientists away from the main stream of British political life to dissipate their energies in flirtations with Communism in Bloomsbury drawing-rooms.

MacDonald did all he could to turn the twentieth-century Labour Party into a great eunuch of politics – incapable either of rape or creation. He did not quite succeed. But in the course of trying he did as much as any man – and did it earlier than most – to change the climate of hope and optimism that came with the end of the first world war into one of cynicism and disillusion.

He did not, of course, mean to do so. His socialism was genuine enough – only he did not mean what most people did by the word. He had listened so often to his own speeches that he had not only come to believe them but to believe that they were enough. One spoke of a new world and lo and behold! it was there. All that was needed for its painless birth was a whiff of twilight sleep and himself at the bedside.

Foreign affairs were different. Here his ideas were not only more explicit but of a kind not to run him into trouble with the Conservative,

Liberal and Court circles whose goodwill he valued: he regularly sent all important Foreign Office papers to Baldwin, whom he found much more congenial than most of his own Cabinet colleagues. Although his interest in foreign affairs was much livelier than Baldwin's the general approach of the two men was not unlike. Both were basically liberal imperialists with a strong suspicion of French ambitions.

'The people in this country', he wrote sternly to Poincaré, 'regard with anxiety what appears to them to be the determination of France to ruin Germany and to dominate the Continent without consideration of our reasonable interests and the future consequences to European settlement. They feel themselves apprehensive of the large military and aerial establishment maintained not only in Eastern but also in Western France. They are perturbed by the interest shown by your Government in the military establishments of the near states of Central Europe.'

And to make it quite clear that a Labour Prime Minister had just as much regard for British interests as any other he concluded in minatory tone: 'Finally they question why all these activities should be financed by the French Government in disregard of the fact that the British taxpayer has to find upwards of £30,000,000 a year in interest on loans raised in America and that our taxpayers have also to find large sums to pay interest on the debt of France to us to meet which France has herself as yet neither made, nor propounded, so far as they can see, any sacrifice equivalent to their own.'

Such barbs meant little to Poincaré. He knew what he wanted and was not to be turned from it by the complaint that what he wanted would ruin Germany. But Poincaré was soon replaced by Herriot whose views more nearly matched MacDonald's. In a glittering series of diplomatic triumphs MacDonald, reaching a level of practical achievement he was never again to match, persuaded the French to evacuate the Ruhr, stage-managed what seemed a workable, and was certainly a more rational, settlement of the Reparations problem by means of the Dawes Plan, and promoted a considerable advance toward the general acceptance of international arbitration as a first step towards disarmament, thus temporarily transforming the whole face of international affairs.

It was a remarkable record for so brief a span of office, due in no small part to his own talent for negotiation and conciliation. If his sensibility as a Foreign Secretary had been paralleled by similar qualities as a Prime Minister the first Labour Government might well have lived longer – or, at any rate, not have died so ingloriously as it did. But he needed the glamour of big occasions to stretch him. He had the star quality that responds to a great audience and the glare of limelight. He played best by ear. When his ear failed him, then even on large occasions his touch could go disastrously wrong.

The habit of solitariness that had grown on him steadily since his wife's death inclined him most to those occasions where he could play a lone hand. Like Neville Chamberlain later he rarely consulted or even informed his Cabinet on matters of foreign policy and, although he had sometimes to do so in domestic affairs, disclosed his real thoughts to them as little as possible. At times superb as a solo-performer, he was thus disastrous as the leader of a team. Autocratic both by tempera-ment and by the nature of the Prime Minister's office – which presents those thus inclined with all the circumstances most likely to feed their inclination – he manifested his contempt for most of his colleagues by neither taking them into his confidence nor asking for theirs. There was remarkably little friction in his Cabinet. But this was not due to agreement but to the absence of discussion. Each member concentrated on his own affairs while the Prime Minister sunned himself in the smiles of Lady Londonderry.

The only colleagues whose company he enjoyed were Lord Thom-son the Air Minister, a pleasant unassuming army officer who never troubled him with political ideas because he had none, Sir Patrick Hastings his Attorney-General who had none either, and J. H. Thomas, the Cabinet's self-elected man of the world (the poor man's Birken-head), whose eye to the main chance, contempt for high-faluting idealism, and talent for anecdotage gave MacDonald a comfortable sense of keeping in touch with trade union opinion without any of the usual ennui.

With most of the rest of his senior Ministers, Henderson, Snowden, Clynes, Wheatley and even the three most acceptable to him socially, Haldane, Trevelyan and Ponsonby, MacDonald was either on bad terms or kept personal contact to a minimum. There has probably never been a Cabinet with less intimacy or even ordinary friendship between the Prime Minister and its principal members.

In a Cabinet so uncohesive achievement depended on the capacity of individual ministers like Wheatley, whose Housing Act was one of the Government's few substantial domestic achievements, and Trevelyan who did well at the Board of Education. No broad measure of socialization was attempted and although Snowden's Budget of

1929 brought him much personal prestige (for this reason giving little pleasure to MacDonald) it did so mainly because of its extreme orthodoxy – Gladstone might have drafted it.

MacDonald's dislike of talking to members of his own party except in large halls had other unfortunate consequences. It had been assumed that the advent of a Labour Government would bring a period of industrial peace. The contrary proved to be the case. MacDonald's relationship with the trade union leaders was not of a kind to incline them to discuss industrial issues with him or stay their hands in the belief that political action would bring the reforms they wanted. As a result the brief history of the first Labour Government was marked by a series of strikes by dockers, transport workers and London Underground railwaymen, culminating in a threat by MacDonald to evoke the Emergency Powers Act put on the statute book by Lloyd George. This not unnaturally brought bitter protests from both the National Executive of the Labour Party and the General Council of the T.U.C. and created lasting bad blood between MacDonald and the most powerful of the new trade union leaders, Ernest Bevin.

Yet if apart from the Rent Act and MacDonald's own triumphs at the Foreign Office there was little in the Labour Government's record to inspire popular enthusiasm, there was nothing to suggest that its end would prove as squalid and inglorious as it turned out to be. Even now MacDonald's part in the events that led up to his Government's resignation and defeat in the general election seem well nigh incredible. How was it possible, one asks oneself, for a man so politically talented as MacDonald to lose his touch so completely – and however did he survive it?

It may be that with such triumphs as were immediately possible in foreign affairs already behind him, and trouble ahead over the Anglo-Russian trade treaty, he was, half-consciously at any rate, anxious for defeat. Certainly he sometimes acted as if he were. When the Cabinet had one of its rare general discussions on political prospects in September he remarked, according to Sidney Webb, that although he did not expect there to be an election on the question of trade with Russia, since only Lloyd George and Churchill wanted a fight on that issue, he was getting 'sick of it' – meaning by 'it' everything. The Parliamentary Executive, he said angrily, seemed to regard itself as a court martial and Labour's only paper, the *Daily Herald*, spent its time queering his pitch. For Labour to be returned with a majority at an election would, he added, be a misfortune: 'The Party [although not apparently the Cabinet] had shown itself unfit to govern.'

The possibility of such a majority was, in fact, so remote that there seems no reason for MacDonald to have worried. What seemed more likely as he himself earlier envisaged was 'a Labour Government in, off and on, for many years, neither the Conservatives nor the Labour Party having a clear majority in future Parliaments, and the decreasing body of Liberals throwing their force first on one side and then on the other'.

With this in mind he may well have thought it no bad thing to risk defeat while Labour's record in foreign affairs, which was what he most cared about, was fairly impressive. But if so surely common sense should have dictated that he pick an issue that would present himself and his party to the country in a good light. Instead he managed to give the worst possible impression by getting turned out over the prosecution, started and then hastily dropped, of J. R. Campbell, Acting Editor of the Communist *Workers Weekly* for publishing an open letter to the Forces urging them not to allow themselves to be used in industrial disputes.

It is useful to consider the various stages of this odd affair. When the article first appeared two Conservative M.P.s raised it in the House. The Director of Public Prosecutions thereupon investigated and advised Sir Patrick Hastings, the Attorney-General, that an action would fall under the Incitement to Mutiny Act of 1795. A week later the offices of the *Weekly Worker* were raided and Campbell arrested. There is no direct evidence that MacDonald knew of this in advance but it is almost inconceivable that he was not told. Patrick Hastings, a successful advocate with minimal political sense, was one of the few Ministers with whom he was on easy terms and it is hard to believe they did not talk.

The news of the arrest created a sensation. It was too close for the comfort of Labour members to the measures taken by reactionary administrations in the past against the founders and leaders of the Labour Party itself. Not only the left wing of the party but much of the solid middle erupted. Was it, one M.P. caustically asked the Attorney-General, intended to prosecute Members of the House expressing similar sentiments in their Constituencies at the weekend, 'because if so', he added with a wave towards the Treasury Bench, 'they will probably lose half their party'. Meanwhile the Communist Party announced that it was briefing Sir John Simon for the defence and would put the Prime Minister in the witness-box, since in the House of

Commons on 4 June 1912 he had defended Tom Mann against a charge almost exactly similar to the one now brought against Campbell.

What followed could scarcely have been more politically maladroit. The Attorney-General promised to look further into the case and after asking Maxton to come and see him announced that it would be dropped. Subsequently he insisted that there had been no political pressure and that he had acted purely as the result of further information. He had learned, for example, that Campbell was not the actual editor of the *Weekly Worker* but had merely been acting for him while he was away ill, a circumstance that scarcely affected Campbell's legal responsibility although it might be regarded as some mitigation of his offence. What weighed more with Hastings was that Campbell had not only served in the war but had been decorated for exceptional gallantry and badly wounded. 'I thought to myself,' he said, 'how would I look as the Attorney-General of England putting in the dock at the Old Bailey, as the only dangerous Communist I could find, such a person as that?' To the Conservatives, already in revolt against the proposal for a Soviet trade agreement and a trade loan ('No Money for Murderers', shrieked the *Daily Mail*), it was an opportunity not to be missed. They put down a vote of censure. However, a way was opened by which MacDonald could extricate himself. The Liberals put down an amendment proposing the appointment of a select committee instead. This was a reasonable enough demand in the circumstances. Had MacDonald accepted it he could have ridden the storm.

By this time, however, he was in a highly emotional state. He had been under attack in several newspapers for accepting a Daimler car and a gift of 30,000 shares in the Scottish biscuit firm of McVitie and Price from Alexander Grant, a self-made business man whom he had known as a boy. When the transfer of these shares had first been noted by a keen-eyed City reporter of the *Daily Mail* it merely provided the occasion for cynical stories about the socialist Prime Minister who had become a capitalist. But the matter took a different turn when the biscuit manufacturer was made a baronet. Cries of trafficking in honours were raised and questions asked in the House. They were not disposed of by the explanation that Grant, like many other self-made men, a Conservative, was a munificent benefactor to many good causes and had first been put forward while the previous Government was in office. Nor did the further explanation that the 30,000 shares were not an outright gift to MacDonald but were merely intended to provide him with an income to cover the cost of running his car, much reduce the criticism. The fact remained that, however deserving on general grounds, Grant had been given his baronetcy by a Labour Government directly after presenting its leader with a car. Even those who, as most did, discounted the suggestion of corruption could not help feeling that MacDonald had shown himself extraordinarily insensitive to the proprieties of political life.

Nor could his followers, whether in the House or in the country, understand why he needed so sumptuous a motor car, or so considerable an income to keep it up, or had been willing to accept such gifts from a political opponent. The whole business of hereditary honours to rich men who gave to charity seemed to them distasteful. They had not expected a Labour Government to perpetuate it. Looked at in even the best of lights, this affair, like the Court dress and the receptions at Londonderry House, seemed to provide one more example of how different MacDonald's socialism was from the socialism preached by ordinary members of his Party in hundreds of little halls all over the country.

MacDonald was genuinely astonished by this reaction. 'Why are they so incensed against me?' he asked when his peroration at a great public meeting was interrupted by a heckler's shrill cry, 'Biscuits'.

All this had combined by the time of the Campbell affair to bring him to a state of mind in which even the very reasonable Liberal demand for a select committee seemed like an attack on his honour. The debate on the Tory vote of censure opened with a contemptuous attack on MacDonald by Sir Robert Horne, but Sir Patrick Hasting's speech did much to transform the atmosphere. Indeed at the end of it most members were not only convinced of the Attorney-General's personal good faith but a good deal impressed by the abundant evidence he cited, including a letter from Sir Gordon Hewart, the Lord Chief Justice when the Attorney-General, and an exchange of memoranda between Lloyd George and Lord Birkenhead, which went to show that in so far as he had taken into account political considerations and the probable public reaction to a prosecution, he had done no more than previous Attorney-Generals in like circumstances. Two Conservative lawyers in the House, Sir Reginald Mitchell Banks, K.C. and J. J. O'Neill, went so far as to announce that if the vote of censure were pressed they would feel compelled to vote against their own party. Moreover in moving the Liberal amendment in what was to prove his last speech in the House of Commons Asquith was both detached and conciliatory. A Select Committee was, he pointed out the normal procedure when the House and the country had been disturbed by allegations which called for cool examination, and had been accepted by other Governments in similar circumstances without complaint. To remove any fear the Government might have that it would find itself in the dock before a packed jury he gave an assurance that the Liberal Party would not itself ask for any places on the Select Committee. The atmosphere seemed favourable to compromise.

But MacDonald was not to be placated. Wrapped in the dark cloud of his affronted honour he announced that if the House passed either of the resolutions on the paper 'then we go'. It may be that in so doing he calculated that the Liberal amendment and the Tory vote of censure could be beaten separately, neither party voting with the other and thus enabling him to survive. If so he was mistaken. Having heard his challenge the Conservatives switched their votes and supported the Liberal amendment. The first Labour Government was over.

It was a tawdry ending. Worse was to follow: the Zinoviev letter. In retrospect the letter iself seems a small matter to have created so large a stir: 'Why this particular rag should have been considered such a singularly tasty morsel I have never been able to explain to myself', J. D. Gregory, Head of the Northern Department of the Foreign Office, the Department particularly concerned, remarked later, adding with complete truth, 'People could at any time have had a whole meal off Zinoviev letters if they had wished.'

Whether this particular one was authentic or a forgery, or, as seems most probable, a combination of the two, is even yet not quite certain. Subsequent investigations have failed to produce credible evidence either way. Nor is it easy to judge how large a part it had in Labour's defeat at the general election. Although Labour mythology gives it a major role it is more likely that all it did was to turn certain defeat into a rout. But the light thrown on MacDonald's personality by the affair is revealing. So is the curious and unexpected effect it had on his reputation.

The matter of the Zinoviev letter has to be seen against the background of the election campaign. MacDonald had gone to much trouble to avoid the Anglo-Russian Treaty becoming the main issue of the election. Indeed this anxiety provides the only credible explanation of his singular ineptitude in the Campbell affair, since he may have calculated that it was better to be turned out on an issue that was likely to be no more than a nine days wonder than to go to the country on the Anglo-Russian Treaty, a cause for which he had little stomach. And in fact whatever the merits of the treaty as a whole the Labour Government was in a position of some vulnerability regarding the loan guarantee which accompanied it. On 18 June MacDonald had given an assurance to the House that in no circumstances would the Government guarantee a loan to Russia, only for such a loan to be included when the terms of the proposed new treaty were presented to Parliament a week or two later.

MacDonald himself had taken little part in the Russian negotiations. He left them to Ponsonby, keeping as aloof as he could from an affair he disliked and would have been glad to be rid of if opinion in his party would have let him. Although it was impolitic for a Labour leader to appear too strongly anti-Russian at a time when something of the first romantic fervour that had greeted the overthrow of the greatest tyranny in Europe still dazzled socialist eyes, he was no less anxious not to give Conservative and Liberal opinion any reason to think him pro-Soviet.

Probably all the political parties overestimated the importance given to the Anglo-Russian Treaty by electors. They were much more influenced by a desire for stability and by the feeling that with the Liberals out of the race they were more likely to get it from a Conservative Government led by Baldwin, than from Labour. Certainly Labour had shown little sign of possessing a key to the millennium when in office, or even of wanting to find one; it was still an uneasy consortium of warring elements of left and right which neither deserved, nor expected, a popular majority. It was safer to trust the Tories.

It seems likely that MacDonald himself would not have disagreed with this view privately. He had long since come to the opinion that his party was unworthy of him and his general demeanour and the lack of clarity and vigour in his election speeches all suggest that he was reconciled to defeat and perhaps even welcomed it. He was chiefly concerned not to do or say anything that might undermine his reputation as an international statesman of moderate views; the acceptable man. And like many Labour people he tended to assume that Conservatives behave like gentlemen, and was genuinely astounded by the venom of the personal attacks on him.

It was, no doubt, a combination of all these things, the fear of being thought pro-Soviet, the inertia of a man already resigned to defeat, and a genuine inability to appreciate how far the Tories would go to make sure of winning, that made him act the way he did when the Zinoviev letter appeared on the horizon.

A copy of this letter first arrived in London in the latter part of September, shortly after the publication of the proposed terms of the Anglo-Soviet Treaty and a few days after the Campbell case had first become a *cause célèbre*. It purported to be from the Executive Committee of the Communist International in Moscow to the Central Committee of the British Communist Party, and to be signed by G. Zinoviev, President of the Comintern, Kuusinen, the Secretary, and Arthur Macmanus, a British member of the Presidium. It was dated 15 September and the copy that arrived in London was sent to a British businessman by a friend said to be 'in touch with Communist circles'. The letter while instructing the British Communist Party to take every step to ensure that the Anglo-Soviet Treaty was ratified also ordered it in typically minatory terms to plan military insurrection in working-class areas, and subvert the allegiances of the Army and Navy so as to 'paralyse the military plans of the bourgeois' of whom the Labour Government was no more than an instrument.

So far as the sentiments were concerned there was nothing inherently improbable about the letter. Most of them were common form in Communist propaganda. But there were several things about the document itself to suggest that it might be a forgery. Arthur Macmanus, the British member of the Presidium had, for instance, apparently signed his surname only, a habit unusual even among Communists – unless they also happen to be peers. Still odder was the fact that although Macmanus was supposed to have signed in Moscow he was in London on the date given – an oddity recognized by subsequent versions from which his signature was dropped. Moreover the instructions contained in the letter indicated an ignorance of the British scene even beyond that customary in Communist circles and by any standards the style of the document was remarkably bizarre, suggesting that several disparate hands had been at work on its concoction. No original was ever produced and although there may well have been an authentic document of some sort it seems likely that to make it more saleable it had been a good deal embellished by one or other of the anti-Communist agencies that made a business of dealing in such things at that time.

The recipients of the first copy to arrive in London did nothing with it for some time. They may well have concluded that even if authentic it did nothing more than show that the Communists' hatred of the Labour Party exceeded their hatred of Conservatives. Not until the election had well begun were its possibilities as a last minute vote swinger perceived by the Conservative Central Office and the *Daily Mail*, to whom copies had been passed.

On 10 October another copy of the document, which had by now become a popular offering by right wing underground groups on the Continent, reached the Foreign Office. It was not at first taken very seriously. The military and naval intelligence services to whom it was shown considered it a fake. So did the Special Branch of Scotland Yard which was used to anti-Communist forgeries. MacDonald was briefly in London on 13 October and called in at the Foreign Office, but no mention was made of it to him then. Nor was it referred to Ponsonby, the Under-Secretary of State for Foreign Affairs, who was at the Office regularly and who was in charge of the Russian negotiations, or to Haldane, who was acting as Deputy Prime Minister during Mac-Donald's absence from London. However, it finally reached Sir Eyre Crowe, Permanent Secretary of the Foreign Office. His congenital inclination to think ill of the Russians disposed him to accept it as authentic and on his instructions it was included in a batch of Foreign Office papers despatched to MacDonald in Manchester with a minute suggesting that a protest should be sent to the Soviet Chargé d'Affaires and communicated to the press.

MacDonald received this on 19 October. He dealt with it that night. He agreed that if the letter were genuine a protest ought to be made and asked for a draft to be prepared. He added, however, that before taking action the greatest care was necessary in investigating the document's authenticity. A draft for an official protest was sent to him on 21 October. Owing to the fact that he was on the move this did not reach him until the 23rd. No evidence as to the authenticity or otherwise of the letter accompanied the draft which MacDonald rewrote and returned the following day. He did not initial it for he assumed that a fair copy would be made and sent to him when the investigation into the authenticity of the letter itself was complete – so far he had nothing to go on but Sir Eyre Crowe's unsupported opinion. The following day, Saturday 25 October, five days before polling day – he opened his morning papers to find the Zinoviev letter, together with his amended draft of the Foreign Office protest, splashed across their main pages. They had been given to the newspapers by the Foreign Office without any attempt to consult him – or even to reach him by telephone. Nor had there been any word from the Foreign Office to Haldane, Ponsonby or anyone else.

Subsequently the Foreign Office sought to excuse itself by stating that it had only learned late on the Friday that the *Daily Mail*, which had been holding on to its copy for the best moment to do the Labour Party down, already had the letter in type and was proposing to publish the next day. In these circumstances, said the Foreign Office, it was considered essential to publish the British protest at the same time in order to show that the Government had the matter in hand. Mac-Donald's handwritten corrections to the original Foreign Office draft were considered to give adequate authority for its publication, even though it had not been initialled by him and nothing had been done to provide him with the report he had asked for as to the letter's authenticity. The effect of the publication on the Labour Party's electoral fortunes was not, the Foreign Office explained, a matter to which they could properly pay attention. Not everyone found it easy to accept the Foreign Office story. However, MacDonald, who stood in considerable awe of Sir Eyre Crowe, apparently did so.

How far he himself had ever considered the electoral implications of the Zinoviev letter it is difficult to say. He did not discuss it with any of his colleagues nor did he mention it to the two Ministers, Lord Arnold and Lord Thomson, neither, it is true, very sharp politically, who were with him on his tour. He seems to have been principally concerned to show himself capable of dealing with the matter with detachment. Unlike Baldwin, who always put his party first and as a member of the 'gentlemanly party' felt under no obligation to behave like one in political matters, he was anxious to act like a Foreign Secretary and a gentleman.

The publication of the letter and Foreign Office protest without prior warning of any kind filled the rest of the Cabinet with alarm and dismay. 'We're buggered', said J. H. Thomas – ever practical. Most Labour candidates felt the same. It was not the Zinoviev letter itself that dismayed them most. This they would have been quite ready to dismiss either as a forgery or, if authentic, as merely one more among the many inept and violent epistles the Communist International was always sending about the world. Indeed they could have quoted its venom against Labour to strengthen their case that, so far from the Anglo-Russian Treaty being, as the Conservatives declared, evidence of Labour subservience to Communism, it was simply an effort to put Anglo-Russian relations on a sensible commercial basis which would help both countries.

The terms of the Foreign Office protest as apparently approved by their own leader, MacDonald, cut the ground from under their feet. Not only did this apparently take the authenticity of the letter for granted, it also assumed it to have been sent with the full approval of the Soviet Government in flagrant breach of undertakings made during the Treaty negotiations. And it threatened that the Treaty would be torn up unless the Soviet stopped the activities of agencies 'whose aim is to spread discontent or to ferment rebellion in any part of the British Empire'.

All over the country Ministers and Labour candidates waited for MacDonald's guidance. None came. Although he had a number of weekend meetings he made no reference at any of them to the one subject on which the country was waiting to hear from him.

On Monday the Soviet Government reply was published. As was to be expected it denounced the letter as a fabrication and demanded 'the punishment of officials concerned in the forgery'. MacDonald could no longer avoid some comment. But when it came it was so obscure and ambiguous that both the Labour Party and the country were left in complete doubt as to whether or not he regarded the letter as genuine and had or had not approved the Foreign Office note.

Manifestly the situation was delicate. Prime Ministers and Foreign Secretaries cannot readily repudiate their officials or shelter behind other people's mistakes. But if silence on some points was understandable, MacDonald could at least have given his followers some guidance on what ought now to be their attitude to the Anglo-Soviet Treaty and whether the situation regarding it was changed or not. He gave none.

Whatever may be thought of the Foreign Office's behaviour it can be argued that up to the moment of publication MacDonald himself acted in this bizarre affair with propriety and dispatch, if with a political innocence uncommon among Prime Ministers. He can hardly be blamed for not imagining the Foreign Office would act as it did without telling him, and in dealing with the letter itself he had been both expeditious and correct. It is, however, difficult to make political sense of his subsequent behaviour. Presumably his original intention had been to keep the matter in play until after the election. If he won he would then deal with it at leisure. If he lost, the record would show his successor how correct he had been. But as soon as the letter became an election issue it was obviously necessary for him to do something about it. He might have taken a strongly patriotic line and declared that although Britain had done everything possible to establish proper relations with the Soviet in the interests of world stability, it was not prepared to tolerate interference of this kind in its domestic affairs. Or he might have announced that he had set up an inquiry into the authenticity of the letter and the Soviet Government's responsibility in relation to it and urged the country not to prejudge the Anglo-Soviet Treaty meanwhile. He did neither.

'It makes my blood boil to read of the way in which Mr Zinoviev is speaking of the Prime Minister of Great Britain today', said Baldwin cheerfully at Southend – ever awake to the public mood. If Mac-Donald's blood boiled it boiled in private. He would say nothing definite either way. Never had Asquith's quip that he was like Johnson's Poll Carmichael, 'She was wiggle-waggle, I could never persuade her to be categorical', seemed more true. In the few days of the election that remained the Conservatives had it all their own way.

Yet oddly enough when the election was over with a net loss of forty Labour seats it was the Zinoviev letter that saved MacDonald. Those at the centre might rage about his habit of secrecy and his perpetual shilly-shallying or note like Beatrice Webb: 'The ex-Prime Minister is badly shaken in courage and self-confidence and I doubt whether he will recover his status in the Party.' The *Labour Monthly* might publish a venomous attack on him and talk about his moral and intellectual failure, and thirty M.P.s, including the whole of the Clydeside group, pledge themselves to be rid of him. But to the party as a whole he was again a hero. The Zinoviev letter had given it what the Labour Party always looks for first in defeat, an excuse. Because of it there was no need to admit, even to oneself, that Labour's own failures had contributed to rejection by the electorate. Almost certainly Labour would have lost anyway. But because of the Zinoviev letter the party had no need to look into its own faults. Victory had been snatched from it by an unscrupulous lie. Capitalism had shown once again that there was nothing it would not do to keep socialism away. On such terms defeat was almost sweeter than victory. It justified the propaganda of years.

On this wave of moral self-satisfaction the myth of MacDonald, dedicated leader of the left martyred by means of an unscrupulous forgery because he would not bow the knee to Tories and Liberals, sailed proudly back into the hearts of his followers. They did not, most of them, understand much about practical politics. They would, most of them, always feel happier in opposition than in office. But they knew capitalists were wicked and this election confirmed it. They sang the

'Red Flag' with renewed pleasure at their Annual Conference in September and gave their socialist leader a heart-felt tribute. He had a brilliant personal success.

MacDonald was not the first, nor was he to be the last, political leader disliked and distrusted by his intimates and rescued by a myth. But he was perhaps the only one to be sustained so completely in his position by a mass loyalty based on an almost total misunderstanding of what he really stood for.

4. The Appearance of Leadership

BEATRICE WEBB, on whom MacDonald's character, composed of talents she had to admit but could not admire, exercised a horrid fascination, once noted in her diary that he had the appearance but not the reality of leadership. One is tempted to think the same about the human being. Was he, one sometimes asks oneself, still there when there was no one to see him? Like the cow in the philosophic argument, what was left when the audience was gone? It is extraordinarily hard to know. One holds out a hand to touch him and lo! there is nothing there. The public person is clear enough, everyone can see that. But what of the private man behind the public figure, the human being inside the shell of the statesman? That is a very different matter altogether.

One does not have this difficulty with Baldwin. The public figure and the private man were not, of course, the same. But underneath that cunningly contrived appearance one is aware of a recognizable human being, a solid, even a likeable man. No one can doubt that Neville Chamberlain existed. One may not always like what one sees but it is real, there was never any question of him not being there when one ceased to look.

But the more one knows of MacDonald the less one knows him, he becomes not more but less tangible with acquaintance. When Churchill called him the boneless wonder he uncovered, one suspects, a truth more profound than the political jibe. For as one studies MacDonald the curious impression grows that the customary bony structure of a man is missing. There is no solid skeleton, only a voice and a presence – an ageing male Mary Rose invented perhaps by Barrie.

Possibly it would all have been very different if Margaret Mac-Donald had lived. She gave a solid centre to his life. Without her, despite his affection for his children, he seems a man disassociated. One is conscious of an absence of contact, a lack of human involvement such as one sometimes finds in affectionless children brought up in institutions – although he in his youth had been surfeited with the possessive, perhaps the altogether too possessive, love of two women. He seems, at times, not so much aloof from as incapable of entering into the lives of others, and this not so much by reason of a positive rejection of people as because there was nothing in himself to respond to what was in them.

He was of course an artist: 'The only artist, the only aristocrat by temperament and personality in a party of plebeians and plain men', said Beatrice Webb, and, still breathlessly pursuing the elusive will-o'-the-wisp of his personality: 'J. R. M. is, I think, the greatest political *Artist* (as distinguished from orator and statesman) in British political history.' She records (anyone who saw him on such occasions will recognize the aptness of the description) how at a Mansion House luncheon in his honour 'his handsome features literally glowed with the emotional acceptance of this just recognition of his great public service by the citizens of London: a glow which enhanced his beauty – just as a young girl's beauty glows under the ardent eyes of her lover'.

The scene changes. He is at Upper Frognal Lodge, Hampstead. There is a Richard Wilson on the wall of the entrance hall, another in the library, two Ibbotsons, a Samuel Scott. The *objets d'art* and stray pieces he has around him are tactful and distinguished; the books in his library display a catholic taste. Over lunch he talks of the Royal Family and pictures and books and again of the Royal Family. He is, as ever, the artist, but this time the part is that of the connoisseur of life and letters, the connoisseur and courtier, and he plays it well. And indeed it fits him best, for he is in his own way a superb if slightly anachronistic example of that peculiarly English brand of liberal culture that grew up in the latter part of the nineteenth century, born of intellectual freedom out of material security: all the more faithful to it because it was for him an ideal of life achieved, not an inheritance accepted a little guiltily. A portrait of Keir Hardie, as the shrewd, political diarist's eyes of Tom Jones observed, is hung out of the way behind a door.

Or he is at a reception at Londonderry House, handsome, distinguished, a model of old world diplomacy and the most exquisite courtesy; he has been staying at Dunrobin Castle with the Duke and Duchess of Sutherland after a few days at Balmoral and is hoping to find time for a day or two's relaxation after the rigours of London life with his dear friends and present hosts, the Londonderrys at Lock Choir – what would his constituents, the miners of Seaham, whose labours produced the Londonderry millions, say if they could see him now? Surely even they would have to admit that revolution is not the way.

Or one is at the back of the City Hall in Glasgow and there far away on the platform he stands, remote and calm yet with an inner intensity that sends its compelling vibrations across the great hall, the burden of the whole world upon those delicate shoulders. 'My friends', he begins, and as that golden voice rises and falls all criticism is stilled – it is sufficient to accept the benison of his presence.

One cannot doubt the art with which he lived each separate part, nor deny the virtuosity. But what, one finds oneself asking yet again, was there besides the art? What kind of man remained when the lights dimmed and the reception was over or the crowds dispersed and it was time to go home? To that question the answer is not so easy. One cannot find it in his friends, for he had none, at least of any degree of intimacy. Nor yet in his speeches, for in truth they wear badly in print and it is often hard to find any solid core of meaning in them, still less of character. His occasional writings and travel pieces have a certain dated charm but it is not a very revealing one, and although his more serious political works, particularly the earlier ones, often have a certain grace and lucidity of style the clarity of the language more often than not merely serves to illuminate the confusion of the thought. To claim, as does R. Bassett in his pietistic volume on the 1931 crisis, that in his writings MacDonald was an influential socialist philosopher, is to allow an agreeable desire to speak up for the man to addle the critical sense. Not, of course, that the smallness of MacDonald's contribution to political thinking should be held against him: practising politicians rarely contribute much to political philosophy, action not erudition is their trade.

That there was, or had been, a character of some staunchness behind the impressive presence is plain enough. No man could have overcome the handicaps of his beginnings and surmounted without bitterness the struggles and frustrations of his early search for work without a core of granite somewhere. Nor, although later it became almost obligatory in Labour circles to forget it, can the large extent and shrewd nature of his practical contribution to the formation of the Labour Party be forgotten. Nor the courage with which, despite some dubiety of purpose, he sustained his position during the war. There must have been something there once that was hard and real, even although it seeped away as the years passed.

Aside from a comforting faith in the gradual evolution of society to higher things, MacDonald was entirely empirical in his approach to affairs. He reacted to events, he did not try to shape them. Ignorant of economics and industry and possessed of no settled principle, or even attitude of mind, such as might have provided him with a chart to steer by in such matters, he tended to shy away from all problems of domestic policy, finding them both troublesome and uninteresting. The British were thus doubly unfortunate in the timing of their Prime Ministers in the 'twenties, alternating between one interested only in foreign affairs when what was required was a clear head for domestic issues, and another concerned only with the domestic scene when what really mattered was international policy.

Yet although MacDonald strikes one as a curiously empty character it would be absurd to put all the blame on him for the melodramatic twist given to his career in its later stages. The melancholy fact is that office came to him twice by an accident – the disintegration of the Liberal Party – which had nothing to do with the ability of either himself or his party to rule. Neither in 1924 nor in 1929 was the Labour Party ready for government. Its Parliamentary position reflected neither its true position in the country nor its intrinsic merits but merely the electoral urge to fill a vacuum.

As a mass movement Labour had behind it the pervasive power of much honest idealism plus the solid industrial strength of the trade unions. As a political party it was woefully immature, lacking either a cohesive doctrine of its own or the necessary public support to clothe with legislative and administrative flesh the vague socialism that animated it. It was the beneficiary and victim of the British liking for a two-party system.

In such circumstances MacDonald's Parliamentary superiority over his Labour colleagues was an added misfortune. Not only was he himself temperamentally averse to fundamental decision making but he represented none of the forces in his party from which decisions capable of giving it an independent identity might have come. He was not a manual worker and lacked the economic solidarity of the trade unionist while possessing neither the self-assurance of those of the professional and old governing classes who joined the Labour Party after the war nor the crusading moral zeal that inspired many members of the I.L.P. In so far as he represented anything but himself it was the most rootless of all British groups, the ambitious lower middle-class brain workers who had climbed out of their original setting without finding an assured home anywhere else, distrusted by those they had broken away from, not yet accepted by those they wished to join.

In the years between 1910 and 1914 MacDonald had wanted to merge the Labour Party in the Liberal Party and a progressive role in a traditional party would probably have suited his character better than the leadership of a new one, required by its nature to show itself capable of developing policies and programmes directed to fundamental social change. His strength was as a virtuoso of politics. The technical excitements of the trade, the professional small talk of the political and social life delighted him, but he skated only on the surface of ideas.

What strikes one most, in fact, about the 1929 election is the basic similarity between the Conservative and Labour programmes, despite the rival slogans, even more meaningless than such slogans usually are, of 'Safety First' and 'Socialism in our Time' (certainly nothing was further from MacDonald's mind than the latter). It was an election of Buggin's Turn. The Labour Buggin got office on the understanding, indeed the firm assurance, that he would do nothing new. There was, in MacDonald's own words, to be 'no monkeying'.

In the international field this presented no difficulty. Easily succumbing to inertia when asked to turn his eyes beyond the white cliffs of Dover, Baldwin had been happy to take over MacDonald's 1924 policy of friendship towards Germany and suspicion towards France. All MacDonald had to do in 1929 was to resume custody of the child. Germany's brief honeymoon with democracy was already nearly over, but for the time being everything seemed to be going swimmingly. The Young Plan for Reparations had been accepted and in Geneva the Preparatory Commission for the Disarmament Conference resumed its work. The last foreign soldiers marched out of the Rhineland, Russia signed the Kellogg Pact outlawing war, and MacDonald had an impressive personal triumph in the United States (he was much admired by Mayor Walker), where he went to prepare the way for a Five Power Naval Conference. Even his staunch critic, Beatrice Webb, found herself compelled to praise him for 'a feat of endurance and a triumph in political activity', and wrote in her diary of 'the P.M.'s magnificent rendering of a friendly neighbour and uplifting statesman' – rich praise indeed from such a pen. Some foreign triumphs Mac-Donald was regretfully compelled to share with Arthur Henderson who had insisted on having the Foreign Office – MacDonald's first bizarre idea had been to give it to J. H. Thomas, his second, rather than leave the world stage to a strong rival, to take it himself, and let Henderson be Prime Minister – a proposition unfortunately none of his colleagues were prepared to entertain. However, there turned out to be enough international glory for both, especially as Henderson's immersion in the day-to-day business of the Foreign Office and his increasing involvement in the Disarmament Conference left Mac-Donald free to move about the world with distinguished aplomb: 'Prime Minister Visits Britain' sardonically announced his old enemy, the *Daily Mail*, on his return from one of his trips.

His success was genuine. On this stage he came to life and his touch seldom failed. He may not have seen very far into the future or guessed how quickly the interaction between economic and political events would make nonsense of all his diplomatic triumphs, but then few others did either. On the civilized surface of world affairs he conducted himself like a grand master, delighting excessively in the plaudits of the audience but informed none the less by a genuine passion for international cooperation. He had turned his back on much of his past but his international aspirations – some would say his illusions – remained firm.

It is inevitable that some of MacDonald's diplomatic triumphs should seem hollow in retrospect – some worse than that. But they were real enough at the time and he deserves credit for them. If instead of being Prime Minister had he as he briefly wished, been Foreign Secretary his reputation today might stand higher than it does.

But he was also Prime Minister. As such he found himself in an unenviable position: his speeches were beginning to catch up with him. Along with every other prominent leader and theoretician of his party he had for years been saying on public platforms that industrial capitalism as then practised was both immoral and inefficient. Now the speeches turned out to be true. Life imitated art, economics copied oratory. It was most unfair.

True, there had been some advance warning. The 1929 election had been fought largely on the issue of unemployment, though Lloyd George rather than the Labour Party had made most of the running. By June, when MacDonald moved into 10 Downing Street for the

TRAMSAY.

second time, the numbers out of work had already risen to 1,122,700, 9·6 per cent of the insured population. He put J. H. Thomas, that incomparable raconteur, in charge, with Sir Oswald Mosley, not yet Hitler's mimic, and George Lansbury, to help. Within a year the total had risen to 1,912,000, 15·4 per cent of the insured population. Another six months and it was 2,500,000, one in five of the insured population. It was most annoying for MacDonald, who wanted to think about larger things.

It was also very annoying for the Labour Government as a whole. Here they were with one eye on the Tories and the other on the Liberals, neither of whom could defeat them singly but who could turn them out whenever they wished by combining, all set for a safe, moderate domestic programme – a new Factory Bill, ratification of the Washington Forty-Eight Hours Convention on hours of work, a Royal Commission on the Drink Traffic, an amendment to the Widows and Old Age Pensions Act, plans for urban and rural housing – only to find themselves interrupted by the capitalist crisis they had been prophesying for years. They were neither revolutionaries nor economists but practical politicians – children as MacDonald himself was, of the reformist aspirations of the nineteenth century and also of the nineteenth century's basic assumption of British economic stability. In so far as any of them had given thought to such things on any plane other than that of platform oratory, they were as much captives of the orthodox conventions about the international credit system and the sanctity of the Gold Standard as any banker: faithful servants of the Fabian policy of the inevitability of gradualness. And suddenly nothing was gradual any longer. All was sharp, swiftly changing and heading for disaster. It was as though a nonconformist minister comfortably preaching on the wrath of God should see his congregation struck down before him by fire from above.

Even if MacDonald had any idea what socialist measures were he was in no position to enforce them with a Conservative–Liberal majority against him. Nor did he wish to interrupt his diplomatic progress by risking a parliamentary defeat.

The I.L.P. shouted for nationalization. But that was socialism. The Tories urged tariffs. But that shocked Snowden, the free trade Chancellor. The Liberals urged expenditure on public works schemes. But that was Lloyd George. And then there was Ernest Bevin, who having served on the Macmillan Committee on Finance and Industry, wanted to abandon the gold standard. But Bevin was simply an ignorant trade

unionist – and hardly on speaking terms with MacDonald anyway.
There seemed nothing MacDonald, who had never pretended to
understand such things anyway, could do but appoint a Committee on
Government Finance under an insurance company Chairman, Sir
George May, to show how broadminded he was, and leave the rest to
Jimmy Thomas. But Thomas had trouble with Sir Oswald Mosley.
And instead of going away the crisis got worse.

A Franklin Roosevelt in such circumstances could show himself
capable of revising and revitalizing a whole national economy. There
was nothing in MacDonald's character to make him capable of doing
anything like that. He could only talk – hopefully but almost entirely
irrelevantly – as the dole queues lengthened. In Wall Street stock-
brokers leapt from twentieth-storey office windows, in Germany
Hitler's stormtroopers drilled against the day when financial crisis
would open wide the gates to power, and in Austria the collapse of a
bank, the Kreditanstalt, of which the vast majority of British people
had never heard, started a chain reaction which among its other consequences was to bring the Labour Government tumbling and transport MacDonald himself to a peak of popular adulation such as even
he can never have anticipated.

The Kreditanstalt had borrowed heavily abroad to finance Austrian
industry in which it was the largest partner. The disclosure that it was
in financial difficulty precipitated a run by domestic and foreign
lenders, and the Austrian Government was forced to step in and declare
a moratorium. Thereafter the centre of crisis moved to Germany whose
major banks were up to their necks in Kreditanstalt finance. In four
weeks the Reichsbank lost more than £50,000,000 in gold and foreign
exchange. As a result it was compelled to curtail banking credits so
sharply that the biggest of the German commercial banks, the Darmstädter and Nationalbank, closed its doors. Now bankers in London,
New York, Paris and Amsterdam took fright, calling in short term
loans to German banks and industries to the tune of nearly three
billion Reichsmark in a matter of weeks. Under the Young Plan, so
recently acclaimed as a solvent of international difficulties, Germany
was required to pay Reparations of £100,000,000 a year. With a major
financial crisis on her hands she could not do so. And without reparation payments from Germany how could the French pay the British
the interest on their war debts or the British pay the Americans? In an
effort to stabilize matters and provide a breathing space for recovery
President Hoover proposed a moratorium on all reparation payments.

But it came too late – too late for democracy in Germany, too late, as it turned out, for the British Labour Government which scarcely seemed to comprehend what was happening to it.

For this it can perhaps be forgiven. The merchant banks in the City, whose business international credit was, showed little comprehension either. For years they had lent abroad extravagantly, maintaining the City's reputation as the financial centre of the world by means which in retrospect seem touched with a fantasy so wild as to be engaging if the consequences had not been so harsh: £30,000,000 to the South American State of Colombia, for example, to build a railway to connect two valleys separated by a range of mountains 9,000 feet high for which there was no need since each valley had its own outlet to the sea. But above all they had lent to Germany which between the two years 1927 and 1928 alone had borrowed abroad, mainly from America and Britain, close on £800,000,000. As a result the City of London now found itself in the position of having vast credits abroad, a high proportion in the shape of long term loans which it could not recover, while at the same time it was the repository of an immense amount of international banking funds which could be withdrawn at a few hours' notice.

On 13 July 1931, the full extent of the City's own short term indebtedness was disclosed for the first time in the report of the Macmillan Committee on Finance and Industry. Two days later the Governor of the Bank of England received a cable from the Governor of the Federal Reserve Bank in New York. 'We are', it said, 'concerned and surprised at the sudden drop in sterling exchange today. Can you throw any light on this?' The Bank, odd though it may now seem, confessed itself unable to do so. 'I cannot', Norman cabled, 'explain the drop in sterling in relation to dollars and most European currencies. It was sudden and unexpected and resulted in the engagement of over £7,000,000 gold for these days including £4,000,000 for Bachmann' (President of the National Bank of Switzerland). Within a week the £7,000,000 had risen to £23,000,000 and the Bank Rate was put up to 3½ per cent to try to hold the position. But anxiety in New York, Paris, Amsterdam, Zürich – especially Zürich – had long since passed the stage at which it could be as assuaged by the offer of another one per cent interest. The drain continued. Another rise in the bank rate to 4½ per cent failed to halt it. So did credits of £50,000,000 hurriedly negotiated with the Federal Reserve Bank of New York and the Bank of France in the last two days of July.

The dates are significant. So is the sequence of events. Subsequently it came to be believed – perhaps even by the Labour Cabinet itself – that the financial crisis which brought the Labour Cabinet down and transformed MacDonald into Prime Minister of a National Government was entirely due to the weakness of the national finances disclosed in the Report of the May Committee. But although this report, published on the last day of July, added to the nervousness of the international money market, the run on the pound had begun more than two weeks before and was initially due, like the earlier stock market crash in New York and the banking failures in Vienna and Berlin, to causes outside Government jurisdiction. Still less was it due to the improvidence of the unemployed who were shortly to be called on to bear the main burden of the sacrifices required to repair the damage done by the excessive optimism of the financial houses of the City of London, many of whom had not, as was later disclosed, taken the elementary precaution of exchanging information with other banks to discover the total indebtedness of the foreign clients on whom they pressed loans.

Meanwhile MacDonald had more important matters on his mind. While the Bank of England grappled with the run on the pound he was considering what to do about the House of Lords. 'As you know,' he wrote to Sidney Webb on 14 July, the day the withdrawal of short term funds from London by foreign bankers began, 'I am in a most awful difficulty about the House of Lords. You may think I have been doing nothing but as a matter of fact I have been working at it weekend after weekend and am in a complete dead end. We have not the material in our Party that we ought to have. . . .'

One cannot help but feel sorry for him, so concerned over the inadequacy of his Party for those conventionalities of the political life that touched him so nearly, so impotent in face of real danger, so apparently unaware, indeed, that it was gathering around him.

'It is the old order that is crumbling and breaking to fragments, filling the air with its dust and with the noise and confusion of its downfall, nothing else than that', he had told a great audience in Glasgow in the years of his socialist oratory, enthralling them with the promise to reconstruct society and bring 'a new idea, a new beauty, a new holiness into the lives of the people'. But the day of the shaggy demagogue was over. The Prime Minister had taken his place. The old order was crumbling indeed but all the Prime Minister wanted was to shore it up in whatever way seemed most suitable to those in command of its institutions whose approbation he so much enjoyed. His words had often been revolutionary. His thoughts had never been so; certainly the radical reconstruction of a world in financial chaos had never been part of them.

There is something peculiarly ironic in the fact that MacDonald should have been Prime Minister of a Labour Government at such a time and in such a situation. Although the most telling propaganda for socialism was based on a view of economics very different from that which governed twentieth-century industrial capitalism he himself was the least economically minded of men. His socialism had nothing to do with how the economic business of the world should be conducted.

This lack of economic interest on his part might not have mattered if anyone else of stature in his administration had read, if not Marx, that was perhaps too much to expect, then Keynes at least, or been even as aware as Roosevelt that the old economic order really was crumbling and that Humpty-Dumpty could never be put back on his wall again in quite the same shape as before. But there was no one. Snowden, like MacDonald, was a socialist by ethical persuasion. In economics his principles were the purest Gladstonian orthodoxy, his twin gods Free Trade and the Gold Standard – deities less suited than almost any to answer the complexities and hazards of the time. Arthur Henderson was heavily engaged in problems of disarmament. To such economic issues as forced themselves upon him he brought no more than the strictly practical judgment of a trade union negotiator of the middle kind. Sidney Webb might have been expected to deploy a larger intellectual expertize, but he was primarily interested in running his old Department, the Colonial Office, and, as a good Fabian, too much committed to a belief in gradualist policies of social reform to recognize a world-wide economic depression when he saw one. In any event MacDonald never consulted him.

In fact what strikes one looking back is how little the members of the Cabinet as a whole concerned themselves with the economic and financial situation until the very last. They stuck to their Departments – writing minutes while the world crumbled. The first news of the run on the pound passed them by almost unnoticed. Even the May Report on 31 July, with its estimate of a £120,000,000 budgetary deficit and its recommendation that public expenditure should be cut by £96,000,000, including £66,500,000 off unemployment benefits, failed to excite them. They had, Sidney Webb reported to his wife who noted it in her diary for 4 August, 'a very jolly and cordial Cabinet meeting', at which MacDonald and Henderson told their colleagues how popular they had been in Berlin.

Britain's financial stability was in jeopardy. The number of unemployed was 2,600,000. In the world as a whole those unable to find work of any kind had, according to the estimates of the International Labour Office, reached the staggering total of at least 30,000,000. More than twenty countries were in default on their external loans and in almost every country great industries were running into bankruptcy.

The machinery of international exchange and trade had broken down as so many socialist propagandists had often said it would. But the British Labour Cabinet only talked socialist propaganda, it did not believe it, and MacDonald departed happily to Lossiemouth for his holiday.

5. Palladium of the People

MANY sinister interpretations have been put on MacDonald's movements after 10 August, on which date he returned to London by the night train to confer first with Sir Clive Wigram, the King's Private Secretary, and then with Sir Ernest Harvey, Deputy Governor of the Bank of England (characteristically Montagu Norman, the Governor, had had a nervous breakdown), and Edward Peacock, senior member of the Bank Court, a partner in Baring Brothers and a royal adviser on financial affairs in his capacity as Receiver-General of the Duchy of Cornwall. It is, however, more likely that the course MacDonald followed flowed naturally from his character. He reached the point where to stick a knife in the ribs of his party seemed the obvious course, not out of planned intent but because the right people expected it. It was not in his nature to oppose a King's Private Secretary and two bankers if he could any way avoid it.

Certainly the situation was serious enough. The £50,000,000 credit jointly advanced to the Bank of England by the Bank of France and the Federal Reserve Bank of New York was practically used up. The run on the pound was such that unless it could be stopped the Bank saw no chance of maintaining the freedom of exchange required by the gold standard. Nor had the two bankers, both honest men dedicated to the proposition that the City of London was the guardian of civilization, any doubts. They were confident that the cause of the monetary crisis lay, to quote their subsequent message to Neville Chamberlain (for they felt it their duty to communicate with the Opposition as well as the Government, and MacDonald acquiesced), 'in the complete want of confidence in H.M.G. existing among foreigners'. The remedy lay with the Government and could be summed up in one word: economy. This view MacDonald accepted. He summoned the Cabinet Economy Committee for the following day and told it so.

This Committee, composed of MacDonald, Snowden, Henderson, Thomas and Graham, the President of the Board of Trade, had been appointed on 30 July to consider the May Report. It had not expected to reach conclusions before September and had not even arranged to hold its first meeting until 25 August: one of the most remarkable features of the whole affair, indeed, is the initial lack of any sense of urgency on the part of those most directly concerned. Now suddenly told on 11 August that time was running out, most members of the committee were as lost as MacDonald himself. Two of them, Henderson and Graham, argued that the majority recommendations of the May Committee which proposed a cut of £66,500,000 in Unemployment Relief and reductions in the pay of civil servants, teachers and servicemen, went too far and would never be accepted by the general body of the party. But as to what should actually be done in a situation that was, so Snowden now told them, a good deal worse than the May Committee thought (he put the Budget deficit for the current year at £40,000,000 and that for the financial year 1932-33 at probably £170,000,000 instead of the £120,000,000 the May Committee estimated), they had no clearer idea than the rest.

Next day a draft Treasury plan for dealing with the deficit on a fifty-fifty basis, half from economy, half from new taxation, was presented to the Committee. No decision was reached and MacDonald saw Baldwin and Chamberlain. They assured him their one desire was to be helpful, after which, following the best tradition of British politicians at times of crisis, all three went off for the weekend: Mac-Donald to Lossiemouth, Baldwin to Aix-les-Bains, Chamberlain to Scotland to shoot. However, MacDonald did not forget his followers. He gave the *Daily Herald* a message for them. 'I ask them', he told its reporter, 'to remember that we are grappling with this situation with all our ideals unchanged.' Snowden gave a statement to the same paper. 'While a National Government is out of the question,' he said, 'the situation calls for the cooperation of all parties in the House of

Commons because a Government – and especially a Government without a majority – cannot carry through economy proposals of this kind and be attacked afterwards for doing so.'

Refreshed by the weekend break the members of the Cabinet Economy Committee met again on Monday. They found themselves fundamentally divided. Henderson and Graham would not hear of cuts in unemployment benefits. Snowden, that austere defender of Gladstonian principles, was equally hostile to the alternative of a revenue tariff. The one aspect of the subject to which they seem not to have turned their minds was the one that might have been expected to receive most attention from a committee of Socialist Ministers – if that is what they were. This was the question of how far the gold standard itself was a factor in the crisis – in any case at the dollar rate for the pound sentimentally insisted on by Winston Churchill in 1925 and opposed at the time by critics so diverse as Maynard Keynes, Ernest Bevin and Lord Beaverbrook. The gold standard was, in fact, to be abandoned later, to the great benefit of British industry and the national economy, but only after the crisis had destroyed the Labour Government, reduced the standard of living of many millions of ordinary people to a bare susbsistence level and provoked a mutiny in the Royal Navy; indeed, not until a General Election had been fought on the proposition that to abandon gold would bring the nation to ruin and destroy the savings of the people.

For the time being whatever else might be regarded as appropriate for sacrifice the gold standard was sacrosanct. It had been elevated by the convictions of Montagu Norman and the interests of the City of London into a national myth as potent as the flag itself. Rare can have been the occasions in history when a technical instrument of exchange, admirably suited to certain conditions, totally inappropriate to others, had accrued to itself so blind a fidelity.

At this time I was Financial Editor of the *Daily Herald*, and being young and iconoclastic of temperament ventured to ask during a solemn meeting at the Treasury whether everyone was satisfied that we either could or should remain on gold. Only the late Cecil Sprigge, then the brilliant City Editor of the *Manchester Guardian*, was disposed to follow me in this speculation. On the rest of the serious men around the table it produced an effect of frozen horror like that portrayed by H. M. Bateman depicting a guardsman dropping his rifle on parade. Sir Warren Fisher, Permanent Secretary to the Treasury and Head of the Civil Service, was particularly shaken. He found it impossible to remain seated. 'To suggest we should leave the gold standard', he declared rising magisterially to his feet and pacing heavily backward and forwards across the room, 'is an affront not only to the national honour but to the personal honour of every man and woman in the country.' There was nothing for Sprigge and me to do but slink away.

The drama of the financial crisis was thus played to its end like a presentation of *Hamlet* from which not only all reference to the Prince of Denmark has been excluded but to Laertes, Rosencrantz and Osric as well. In these circumstances the turn taken by political events is not surprising. Worldwide in scope, the economic crisis manifested itself at many levels, influencing or influenced by the interaction between a host of diverse factors: the imbalance between industrial output and the production of basic commodities, the postwar instability of economic and financial systems, the rigidity of British industry as a result of the premature return to the gold standard, the unwillingness of the United States to match its responsibilities as an international lender by an acceptance of the lender's obligation to permit foreign imports, the world-wide increase in tariffs, the distortion of international economy by war debts, the universal failure to match the steadily rising power to produce with the ability to consume, and the incompetence of bankers, politicians and industrialists in unaccustomed economic situations. No British Government could have hoped on its own to resolve problems so diverse in cause and so international in scope, though a more socially sensitive one might have done more to cushion the most vulnerable of its citizens against disaster, and a more intelligent might have tried to prime the economic pump by the sort of public works schemes Franklin Roosevelt later went in for.

However, it was not the economic depression as a whole with which the MacDonald Administration was concerned in August 1929 but one aspect or result of it – the run on the pound. Although made more serious by London's position as an international banking and insurance centre this exchange crisis was not unique to Britiain. Nor was it the result of the budget deficit (which was in any event a natural consequence of depression paralleled in practically every other country in the world) although the level of financial illiteracy prevalent among bankers, politicians and civil servants at the time by obscuring the distinction between private and public budgeting naturally made it a factor in accelerating the run on the pound once it had begun.

Unfortunately the Labour Cabinet was peculiarly ill-suited to deal with an exchange crisis of this kind. It possessed neither confidence in itself nor the ability to instil confidence in others. It neither had the City's good will – why should it? – nor the resolution to bend finance to its own purpose. Moreover it was scarcely a Cabinet at all in any real sense. No attempt was made to conduct Cabinet business as a unity. MacDonald, Snowden, Clynes and Thomas, it is true, met once a week during the Parliamentary session. But they met only to consider party tactics in relation to the business before the House not to discuss principles and even to this inner group MacDonald never disclosed his mind in the broad fields of public policy.

Indeed as John P. Mackintosh points out in his admirable study of the British Governmental system, *The British Cabinet*, the Mac-Donald Cabinet stands out among all others for its absence of any effort to concert policy among Ministers. They were expected to stick to their own lasts, not poke their noses into others' business, The Cabinet was not a team but a congeries of disparate and largely antipathetic personalities, each of whom confined himself to his own Department. MacDonald himself was so uninterested in, or incapable of, welding his Administration into a cohesive group, and found personal contact with his party colleagues so unattractive, that even senior Ministers were, as Willie Graham complained, put through a 'sifting process' by secretaries before they were allowed to see the Prime Minister for five minutes. There was only one body MacDonald disliked even more than he did his Cabinet. This was the General Council of the T.U.C., the one organization a Labour Prime Minister needed to be on good terms with in a crisis affecting all industrial workers.

It is possible that at this stage of the Labour Party's political develop-ment no Labour Government could have ridden this particular exchange crisis. Certainly one such as MacDonald's had no chance at all. Bound hand and foot by its orthodox belief that there were only two alternatives to choose from, extreme Government economy or protective tariffs, it could agree on nothing except the disagreeableness of having to do anything.

In such a situation the personalities of MacDonald and Snowden took on a peculiar importance. They did not like each other. But they disliked their colleagues more, and in their meetings with Conservative and Liberal leaders assumed from the start the role not of representatives of the Cabinet but of reporters on its obduracy. As Chamberlain noted in his diary after one such meeting at which he criticized what the Cabinet had in mind: 'In effect the Prime Minister and Snowden gave us to understand that they quite agreed.'

A meeting with the Labour Party Executive and the T.U.C. General Council brought matters no further. Neither body was prepared to accept the cut in unemployment benefit which MacDonald and Snowden now regarded as inevitable – although Snowden for some reason failed to make plain to the trade union leaders the fact that he did so, an omission that subsequently led to accusations of bad faith on both sides. Within the Cabinet Snowden was more explicit. In the absence of economies of at least £76,000,000 and a ten per cent cut in unemployment benefit there was, he stated, no chance of the further American and French credits without which a moratorium was unavoidable. This news shook the financially orthodox Labour Cabinet badly, so much so, in fact, that even those who had previously been most adamant in their rejection of a cut in unemployment benefit agreed that Opposition leaders should be asked what they considered necessary – without prejudice to the Cabinet's right to make up its own mind. The Opposition leaders replied that first they must know what the Bank of England thought. But the Bank of England did not think. It asked for time to find out the American view from Mr Harrison, Chairman of the Federal Reserve Bank. Thereupon MacDonald decided that it might also be prudent to ask J. P. Morgan and Co., the Government's financial agents in New York, and the Cabinet sat back to see what Wall Street required of it.

Ministers were now in almost complete disarray. Henderson, Graham, Alexander, Lansbury and Greenwood were still firm against cuts in unemployment pay but at least nine, and probably ten, of the others (the exact number is hard to fix for there were several denials and counter denials later and a good deal of protective lying) were at this stage ready to fall in behind MacDonald and Snowden. But for the tone of J. P. Morgan's reply when it arrived their number might have increased. However, the Morgan reply proved of a nature affronting even to such tattered dignity as the Cabinet still possessed. So far as Wall Street was concerned, said Morgan, the credit of the British Government would depend on whether its programme could be shown to have 'the sincere approval and support of the Bank of England and the City generally'. This was too much for the waverers. They remembered they were supposed to be the leaders of a British Government – and socialists to boot. Any hope MacDonald may have had – in any event small and not much cherished – of keeping his Cabinet together was over. He departed for Buckingham Palace to hand in his Cabinet's resignation and his own to the King.

So far MacDonald can be said to have acted with propriety if not with vigour or intelligence. Now, however, he took a course unique in British politics. Politicians had changed sides before. But a Prime Minister had never previously left his party during a traumatic crisis in its affairs to put himself at the head of its political enemies and lead a campaign of unparalleled vituperation against his recent colleagues.

Thousands of ordinary Labour supporters had believed in their innocence that MacDonald's talent for oratory was the reflection of a pure socialist soul. When they heard that although the Labour Government had fallen its leader was to remain as head of a predominantly Conservative 'National' Government they could not help but feel he had betrayed them. Not so the majority of the electors. Touchingly anxious, as the British always are, to believe that men set in authority over them know best – until they are found out – even those about to be sacrificed embraced with ardour the vision of MacDonald as one who put principle above party and nation above personal interest. Perhaps he did. Possibly this was what he honestly believed himself to be doing. In any event his reward was great. Never in his wildest dreams can he have expected to find himself conducted to a plinth so majestic as that to which he was now transported by the fond enthusiasm of the British people. Even Baldwin had never enjoyed such acclaim.

Although several of his former colleagues, including Snowden, subsequently believed it to be so, there is no hard evidence that while still Prime Minister of a Labour Government MacDonald conspired to make himself leader of a National one. But the idea in no way surprised him when it came along. It appeared a natural culmination of his beliefs about himself. Like Baldwin, although without Baldwin's strong sense of party, he could not help but think he had a universal talent for healing society.

'Tomorrow every Duchess in London will be wanting to kiss me', he told Snowden when he came back from the Palace. It was a pleasing thought for one who had for so long longed to be invited inside. Nor – so immunized from ordinary contacts had he become – did he appreciate the effect of these antics upon his erstwhile comrades and disciples in the Labour Party. Although he told junior Ministers with a weary Titan's gesture that he did not expect them to make similar sacrifices to his own – indeed he would scarcely have known what to do with them if they had – he seems to have been confident that at least a hundred members of the Parliamentary Labour Party would follow him. In fact, only eleven did – including Snowden, Thomas and his son Malcolm. Moreover he seems to have thought the breach with his Party temporary only. It would, he thought, all turn out rather like the war. At the end of hostilities he would be welcomed back to a party which, chastened by a realization of how badly it had let him down, would appreciate him all the more.

He had been a professional politician for thirty years. Not only had he given most of his adult life to building a political party, been present at its birth, its nurse as it emerged from infancy, its leader as it reached adult years, but his whole career had been one of practising the art of politics in government or opposition. If any man should have understood that political power is rooted in party organization and that the Party struggle derives from and finds its justification in the representation of particular interests and principles, it was he. Despite his voices and his self-imposed mission to unite the country Baldwin never forgot this, even in his loftiest moments. Nor did Bonar Law. And indeed to pretend that the conflict of interest and principle expressed through political parties does not matter – and except in war when questions of sheer national survival are at issue cannot be set aside without damage to the democratic system – is to display a degree of political illiteracy scarcely to be explained in an amateur of politics, indefensible in a mature professional politician.

Yet it was exactly this of which MacDonald was now guilty. He seemed determined to persuade himself that he could opt out of politics; naïvely convinced that he could become a benign non-party presence brooding over the national welfare; a personalized pie in the sky uncontaminated by connection with the purveyors of ordinary foodstuffs.

Lord Parmoor observed in his memoirs that although he had previously always accepted Bagehot's interpretation of the Cabinet as occupying the central place in British government 'if this position is to be held by the Cabinet it is not consistent with the treatment of the Cabinet in August 1931 by the Prime Minister'. Constitutionally the moves that led to the formation of the National Government must be regarded as very odd indeed. Not only did the King go against all modern practice in inviting MacDonald to remain as Prime Minister when his Government resigned but MacDonald accepted and decided the balance of parties in his new Government without any word to the Cabinet or party of which he was still leader.

This exclusion of his Cabinet from knowledge of the negotiations preceding so startling a change in the political scene expressed in part MacDonald's habitual contempt for his colleagues but even more his settled conception of himself as outside and above party. He had long ceased to regard himself as a representative leader bound by the general will of his party. According to Iain Macleod, Neville Chamberlain's papers indicate that from early July MacDonald 'had been confiding to "leaky vessels" ' his taste for some form of National Government in which he might perhaps serve as Foreign Secretary under Baldwin. The impression that it would be no great task to detach him from his own administration was conveyed even more strongly to Conservative leaders quite early in the discussions of the financial crisis. It is possible he deceived himself – his powers of self-deception were great – and genuinely believed that a 'Government of individuals' could be established which would leave the structure of the parties unaffected. If so he deceived no one else, certainly not Chamberlain who wrote jubilantly to his sister Ida after talking to MacDonald and Snowden: 'The only way the economy figures could be raised is by cutting the dole and if we could once fasten that on the Labour Party they would be irrevocably split. R. M.'s proposal therefore suited me down to the ground.'

The natural course for a Party leader in the situation in which MacDonald found himself was to face the House of Commons and if defeated to resign and make way for someone else. If he had done so he would have kept his party intact and in a position to fight an election with some hope of success. Nor is it absolutely certain he would have been defeated on a Commons vote. Churchill was not alone when he said on the morrow of the National Government's formation: 'Some may think that it would have been better to have given the most complete assurances of support to the Socialist Administration in respect of all the economies and financial measures they were willing to take', adding that he was not at all sure that 'they might not have got through their own difficulties themselves without bringing this extraordinary political disturbance upon the country'.

However, MacDonald was no longer interested in keeping his administration. He embraced with honest enthusiasm the idea that it was his duty to save his country by wrecking his party. This came easier to him because essentially he was politically rootless. It was historical accident only that had made him the leader of the Labour Party and he had never wished to identify himself with the interests it represented because he longed to be accepted by all interests. The blurring of economic and social divisions in society was for him not a matter of expediency but the means to a dream of universal appeasement with himself as its classless symbol. Although it seems incredible in the mature survivor of thirty years of parliamentary in-fighting, he may have honestly believed that the party struggle could be briefly suspended and then return to what it was before.

He made his first broadcast to the British people as Prime Minister of a National Government on the evening of 25 August.

'It is not', he told them, 'a Coalition Government. I would take no part in that. It is not a Government which compels any party to it to change its principles or subordinate its distinctive individuality. I would take no part in that either. It is a Government, as has been described, of individuals. It has been formed to do this work. If the work takes a little time the life of the Government will be short. When that life is finished, the work of the House of Commons and the general political situation will return to where they were last week and those who have taken risks will receive either our punishment or our reward. The election which will follow will not be fought by the Government. There will be no coupons and I hope no illegitimate prejudices....'

Everything he said was to prove wrong. It was bound to do so by the very nature of politics.

But when he said it he believed it. It had to be true because he wanted it to be.

It had always been the drama of politics not their administration that engaged his deepest interest. Cast now for a superb dramatic role he soon found it assuming, as such roles often do, a life of its own, compelling him to courses he had not initially contemplated, and from some of which he might have faltered. The press acclaimed him, the public idolized him, society flattered him. Never before had a politician been swept so high by a single act: not until Munich was one to be carried so high again. The scepticism of his former political friends was drowned in what appeared an almost universal enthusiasm. Even a man more immune from popularity than he could have been forgiven for losing his balance.

It would, perhaps, have been different if the crisis had been quickly solved. But instead of responding to the magic of national unity the crisis got worse. The moment for triumphal retirement refused to arrive.

Ten days after MacDonald had become a folk hero by abandoning his party his new Government produced its solutions. Many of them were harsh. The wages of teachers, police and men in the Services were cut, the standard rates of unemployment benefit reduced from the already pitifully low figure of 17s a week for men and 15s for women to 15s and 13s 6d respectively. An estimated saving of £70,000,000 was promised. This was £14,000,000 more than the Labour Government had provisionally accepted three weeks before. It seemed a small prize for so large a turmoil. To Keynes the means chosen seemed 'replete with folly and injustice', bound, in their entirety, to accentuate deflation and unemployment, representing in so far as they contained anything positive 'the triumph of the Treasury view in its narrowest form'. But although Keynes's economic thinking was to provide Franklin Roosevelt with the means to overcome a crisis far worse than Britain's, the Government did not feel obliged to take any notice of him.

It was less easy to ignore the practical consequences of its decisions. There were demonstrations of protests by teachers, clashes between unemployed and police and finally, on 14 September, mutiny in the Royal Navy.

Weeks previously A. V. Alexander, First Lord of the Admiralty in the Labour Government, had warned MacDonald that if Service cuts were contemplated they must be accompanied by the firm promise of machinery to investigate all cases of hardship, and officers must be briefed in advance so that they could deal sympathetically with the anxieties of their men. Nothing of this sort was done. All the naval ratings affected were long-service men who had joined before 1925 and had for the most part entered into family and other commitments based on scales and allowances they had every reason to expect to be permanent. Yet the first they heard of what was now to be done to them was on a B.B.C. news bulletin on the evening of 13 September. Their officers, with whom their relations remained good throughout the mutiny, had no more information than they had. After angry but orderly meetings on that day and the day following ratings of the Atlantic Fleet on shore leave at Invergordon therefore dispatched a letter to The Lords Commissioners of the Admiralty, urgently requesting them to review the position of 'the lowest paid men of the lower deck' since 'it is evident to all concerned that this cut is the forerunner of tragedy, misery and immorality amongst the families of the lower deck'. The letter concluded: 'Unless a guaranteed written agreement is received from the Admiralty and confirmed by Parliament stating that our pay will be revised we are resolved to remain as one unit refusing to sail under the new rates of pay. The men are quite agreeable to accept a cut which they consider reasonable.'

That this was not merely a demonstration by Communist-inspired dissidents, the explanation naturally first advanced, was made clear when on 15 September ratings of all the ships at Invergordon refused to muster and the Admiral-in-Command was compelled to cancel all sailing orders and recall vessels of the Atlantic Fleet already at sea. It was an unpropitious start for an Administration ostensibly formed to restore national unity, and for a Prime Minister whose own background ought to have made him particularly sensitive in such matters. Worse was avoided only by a hasty announcement that the Commanders-in-Chief, along with Admiralty representatives, would investigate all cases of hardship without delay and the promise that in no case would there be cuts of more than ten per cent.

The Invergordon Mutiny provides a classic example of stupidity and shortsightedness in government but there is no evidence that it materially affected the course of the financial crisis. It shocked national and world opinion, persuading many nervous foreigners that if the Royal Navy refused to sail Britain must indeed be near its last gasp, and when characteristically enough the Admiralty subsequently dismissed from the Service those most active in putting the men's case it helped to increase active working-class distrust of the Government and widen the division between classes. But the exchange crisis was already moving to its foredoomed climax before the mutiny. The events of Invergordon may have advanced it by two or three days. They did no more.

Four days after the mutiny, three and a half weeks after the National Government had been formed to save the pound, MacDonald received a sombre communication from the Bank of England. The credits of $200,000,000, and 5 milliard francs, respectively advanced by the Central Banks of New York and Paris on the assurance that the new Government had 'the sincere approval and support of the Bank of England and the City generally', were exhausted. As a result the Bank felt compelled to ask to be relieved of its obligation to sell gold under the provisions of Section (1) Sub-Section (2) of the Gold Standard Act – in other words suspend the gold standard. Ministers were called back from those country weekends, apparently so essential to ministerial efficiency, to which they had just departed, and the financial editors of the national press, so recently assured by the Treasury that even to contemplate leaving the gold standard was an affront to the national honour, were invited to a private meeting at Hoare's Bank in Fleet Street. There on 20 September 1931 they were told by an eminent conclave of bankers and Treasury officials that all would now be well – Britain was to be freed from gold.

The political crisis imposed on the country to save the gold standard was thus shown to have been unnecessary. The gold standard was beyond saving and even if it could have been saved it would, it was now made plain, have been against the national interest to save it. Everyone had been victims of a vast non-confidence trick, the more compelling because deluded and deluders alike had equally been taken in. In so far as anyone was to blame, explained the bankers, it was not the fault of any Government, not even the Labour Government, nor of any man or institution in Britain itself but, as so often before, of the foreigner. 'Those who like to look for political causes of financial movements', declared the *Quarterly Review* published by the eminent firm of London merchant bankers, J. Henry Schroder and Co., 'have found in the Continental drain of gold material for attacks on the Government and the "thriftless conduct of British finance" . . . the real cause seems to have been the highly nervous state of mind prevalent on the Continent. . . .' 'The crisis', amplified the *Westminster Bank Review*, 'grew out of the distrust by many nations of their own position as regards their international obligations and in consequence it is an open question whether the pound could have been saved even had the internal policy of Great Britain been conducted with the wisdom of Diogenes, the statesmanship of Pericles and the strength of Caesar.'

The Labour Government, which could claim no such marriage of talents, was given a free pardon. It was allowed no mitigation of sentence – which was perhaps about right since not even its friends could argue that it had acted with much intelligence or courage at any stage of the proceedings. Nor, for that matter, had the National Government. This, however, in no way diminished its popularity. It had been formed in the wrong way for the wrong reasons to apply the wrong remedy to the wrong disease, but it had given the British their moment of high drama and they loved it with all the force of their romantic natures.

It was therefore with a pure heart and the comforting sense that he had the people on his side as well as those ladies of title who were so charmingly ready to relieve the tedium of office by entertaining him to their dinner parties that MacDonald, who had previously assured the electorate that he would have no part in a long-term Coalition and that the National Government would never fight a coupon election, announced on 6 October that Parliament would be dissolved the following day and a general election take place twenty days later.

It was, said Lloyd George – no mean authority on such matters – 'the most wanton and unpatriotic election into which this country has ever been plunged', and shaking an angry northern finger the *Manchester Guardian* warned the country that the 'National' Government if returned 'will be a Tory Government and those who expect to co-operate with it on any other basis will sooner or later have a painful awakening.... Taking as it does increasingly every day the form of an alliance against Labour it is perhaps the greatest threat to national unity we have.'

These were Liberal voices. But there were Conservatives like L. S. Amery who felt much the same. They distrusted 'the whole humbug about a National Government above Party' and feared that 'a clear national verdict for the causes for which I had worked for so long would be weakened and frittered away in order to hold together a Coalition which had no other object than to perpetuate its own unnecessary existence'.

Members of the Conservative Business Committee took a more pragmatic view. They were, Neville Chamberlain recorded, 'in favour of the national appeal by a national Government under MacDonald, *provided the programme embodied the full tariff.* All agreed that the election should be at the earliest moment. All agreed that if we went to election with R. M. as P.M. we must accept him as P.M. when we came back.' Musingly Chamberlain asked himself in his diary: 'What would have been the astonishment of the Socialist Executive if it could have overheard the Conservative Executive agreeing to allow the man, who has all his life actively opposed them, now to have the credit of carrying out their own policy just when the whole country has come round to it?' 'Truly,' he added complacently, 'the Conservative Party is a wonderful embodiment of good sense, patriotism and honesty.'

It looked otherwise to Labour. To them it seemed that a man who, despite his inconsistencies and egotism, they had long regarded as a custodian of socialist principle was lending himself to a Conservative manœuvre by agreeing to go to the country on behalf of a Coalition in which the Conservatives outnumbered the rest by more than eight to one – even though, contrary to the Business Conservative Committee's expectation, the Liberal and 'National Labour' elements jibbed at tariffs and the Coalition was compelled to base its appeal on the curious principle that Ministers were free to advocate divergent policies.

MacDonald can scarcely have deceived himself as to where the real power lay. But one suspects he no longer cared. The revolutionary singing bird had been confined in a cage of his own making and it was golden: the pomp and circumstance of national leadership were reward enough for what he was required to do. With his pocket stuffed with worthless German marks for waving before the electors to show what would happen to *their* money if his comrades of more than thirty years of political endeavour were allowed to rule the country, he departed for his constituency to ask – and obtain in overwhelming measure – the support of the Seaham miners and their wives. Meanwhile over the air Snowden – who was not well enough for physical campaigning and had already decided to leave the Commons for the Lords – spat venom at his former Labour colleagues in a broadcast of unsurpassed malice. ('I was', wrote Amery, 'sickened by the sadistic malignity of Snowden's horribly effective broadcast attacks upon his old colleagues.') Nor was even this enough. When Walter Runciman announced the 'discovery' of a Labour plot to confiscate the savings of the poor by using deposits in the Post Office Savings Bank to pay for the dole, MacDonald and Snowden – forgetting no doubt that they had been members of the Government accused – eagerly endorsed the charge.

Not all the malice or invention were on the National Government's side. It was a dirty election and the Labour Party threw its share of the dirt. Its leaders, however, had more inhibitions than Snowden and Runciman, lacked MacDonald's assurance that they were God, and had smaller election funds. There was nothing much open to them but to refuse to lose like gentlemen.

It was a political massacre. There had been 289 Labour M.P.s at the dissolution. Now there were 46. Of the Labour Cabinet only George Lansbury survived. Henderson, Clynes, Alexander, Greenwood, Dalton, Morrison, Addison, Margaret Bondfield, Shinwell, Graham, all these along with many others had been swept away. As the *Economist* said, it was 'the greatest electoral tide in the whole story of British democratic politics', establishing 'in the average size of Government candidates' majorities and in the almost complete submergence of all the leading spokesmen of one of the great parties of the State' a record 'which has never been approached and in all human probability will never be equalled again'.

For this result the chief credit must go to MacDonald. No doubt, as Amery and others argued, the Tories could have won without him fighting under their own banner and their own leader. But they could scarcely have done so in such measure and of all the personal triumphs in the election his own, with a majority of 5,951 at Seaham, was the greatest.

There was, of course, plenty of hysteria about, the *Manchester Guardian* spoke no more than the plain truth when it said: 'By the side of the scare about the pound the cry of "Hang the Kaiser" and the Red Letter appear almost respectable.' Nevertheless for millions of ordinary men and women, including many who would normally have voted Labour, the appeal of the National Government was genuinely an appeal to self-sacrifice in the national interest, whereas that of the Labour Party seemed merely one for a vote against cuts in wages and unemployment benefit. They voted, as Mary Agnes Hamilton – herself a victim of the electoral slaughter – observed, out of 'a passion for abstract justice'. The centre of this appeal to what was noble and idealistic in their natures, this call to abstract justice, was MacDonald. Snowden was the executioner, deft in the use of the poisoned dart, the bow string and the dagger in the back. But Mac-Donald was the totem and the magical symbol. He knew now the ecstasy of a total acceptance far beyond the wildest dreams of the little illegitimate boy in the two-roomed Lossiemouth cottage or the ambitious secretary of a Liberal candidate; and beyond, too, anything the uneasy Fabian or the idol of the 'phraseologists' of the I.L.P., the detested pacifist, or even the Labour Prime Minister, could have imagined. He was thus the first of the three Prime Ministers whose careers composed so curiously similar a pattern in the 'twenties and 'thirties of this century to reach the high plateau of a public adulation that went far beyond the normal frontiers of party loyalty.

The role of national saviour was to prove as much beyond his capacity as it was to be beyond that of Baldwin and Chamberlain in their turn. Yet on three separate occasions in the two decades between the wars the British people allowed themselves to fall into the illusion that a national saviour was what they needed. Why did they? The British have, of course, an endemic hankering after the appearance of national unity. Normally, however, the emotional safeguard provided by a monarchy which can be worshipped without much danger of positive political – although some social – harm enables them to under-take without too much pain the democratic duty to be critical of those who rule them, and to accept as natural the fact that these rulers will rarely, if ever, represent the interest of much more than half the nation. They like to pretend to themselves, especially if they are Conservatives, that in Britain, unlike other countries, economic and social self-interest have no part in politics and that the class struggle does not exist, or at any rate is not the sort of thing a gentleman admits to knowing. But the British do not in the usual course of affairs allow this illusion to get in the way of practical politics, the practitioners of which, while dutifully saying the opposite, accept conflict as natural, and gain both pleasure and profit from party friction while pretending it is all the fault of the other side.

Except in war when the instincts of self-preservation compel the normal processes of political controversy to be submerged the British rarely make the mistake of finding universal merit in a Prime Minister. When they do it is a sure sign of the onset of political disaster. It was so now.

6. *Death of a Wraith*

THE electorate sent the National Government back in triumph but no one, certainly not MacDonald, could keep it together. Within six weeks Snowden was protesting: 'I cannot go on sacrificing beliefs and principles, bit by bit, until none are left.'

It was very inconsiderate of him, but then Snowden had always been inconsiderate. MacDonald was forced to meet him and other Free Trade Ministers. 'We talked for half an hour', Snowden recorded. 'The Prime Minister as usual was discursive and incoherent and when we left the meeting we asked each other what he had said and where he stood but none of us could give the answers to these questions.'

By January 1932 four senior Ministers, Snowden, Samuel, Sinclair, Maclean and seven junior Ministers had reached the point of resignation. Again they met MacDonald, this time at Snowden's house, for the situation was critical and MacDonald did not insist on protocol. He informed them that after the most anxious searching of conscience he had been forced to the conclusion that his duty to the nation would require him to remain as Prime Minister even if they went, but that their resignations would put him in an embarrassing and humiliating situation as he would be forced to replace them by Conservatives and he therefore hoped they would reconsider their positions. Could they not, he asked, agree to disagree, suspending for the time being the doctrine of collective Cabinet responsbility and leaving each Minister with the right to promote in public as well as in private the policies each believed in? The proposal understandably struck Snowden, Samuel and the others as both impractical and unconstitutional and they rejected it – only to accept it at Cabinet the following day when the first Lord Hailsham came up with it on MacDonald's behalf, after Neville Chamberlain, who thought the whole proceedings very odd, had made it plain that he would not abandon his advocacy of protection whatever happened.

For MacDonald himself political doctrines, even principles, had ceased to be important except in so far as they could be expressed in vague generalities of goodwill. All that moved him was the conviction of his own indispenability as a symbol of British unity: the socialist Conservatives trusted, or at any rate needed. Even the Ottawa Conference which brought the actual resignation of Snowden, Samuel and the others (they had swallowed much but this draught was beyond them), shook him only temporarily. He contemplated resignation, not because he wanted to resign but because he did not see how he could stay. However, it did not take long to change his mind.

'What', he wrote to Baldwin on holiday at Aix, 'what will the new Government be? Party? How can it be National? How can I remain? What will be the effect on the country? There must be a return to pure party fighting and the National unity is disrupted. The Leader of the House of Commons under such conditions should be a party man and so should the Prime Minister.' And then in a passage very significant of his conviction that by his actions he had raised Britain to a position politically above that of the common run of nations, he asked: 'What will be the effect of that again upon the country in relation to the world? Quite honestly I think it will be bad. It is our internal union which has produced our external strength. When we become as other countries are much of our strength goes and for one or two of us to puff ourselves out and try to make the outside world believe that we are the difference between a party and a national government belongs to the order of comedy. . . .

It was a comedy to which he soon adjusted himself. He was easily reassured by Baldwin (who found it unnecessary to do as MacDonald asked and return to London: 'A sudden return makes everyone yell crisis') that his duty was clear. 'You must stick to the ship till we are in calmer waters.' Happy again, he remained on the bridge of a vessel now manned almost exclusively by officers of a different persuasion to his own, sailing to a port in whose choice he had no part. He was still Prime Minister. He could visit Roosevelt, call on Mussolini, go to Locarno, preside over the World Economic Conference (although that came to little), lend the grace of his presence to Geneva, inspire the nation by speeches ('On and on and on and up and up and up') that, as Winston Churchill cruelly said, compressed 'the largest number of words into the smallest amount of thought'.

Words had always been the breath of his being, the reality of his existence lay in them not in action. But whereas he had formerly often brought to international affairs a skill and lucidity of mind absent in his philosophic musings on domestic relationships even here his mind now seemed clouded by his intoxication with words. He was like an alcoholic, driven by inner compulsion to keep on drinking.

He thought it a triumph when Mussolini turned his visit to Rome into a Fascist holiday whose outcome was a Four Power Pact that for the first time made obeisance to the idea of a directorate of Europe by means of which Britain, France, Germany and Italy, with Russia excluded, would take over from the Council of the League of Nations the task of pacifying the Continent. 'The time has gone by', he told the House of Commons in what was, even for him, a somewhat incoherent passage, 'when, by a combination of any Powers any European people can be kept down by obligations which it regards as being inconsistent with its self-respect and its honour and we have now to make it perfectly clear that the obligations that are to be placed upon the nations of Europe are to be obligations of honour and moral responsibility.... Part of the responsibility of any Government which claims to be pursuing peace and making certain moral claims upon the consideration of nations is to make a contribution to the proper tranquillity of mind of those nations to enable them to do the right thing. . . .

It was Baldwin's peculiar contribution to the history of the 'thirties that by what Professor Trevor-Roper has called his 'ostentatious apathy' towards what was happening in the rest of the world he induced in the popular mind a sympathetic slumber. It was MacDonald's in this latter phase that by clothing international problems in meaningless words he often actually succeeded in making them meaningless to ordinary people. By his aspirations to 'tranquillity' he blurred, not only for himself but for them also, the true significance of what was happening in Europe. Thus a proposal for parity of armaments between Germany and France, which may well have been wise – or at any rate acceptable as a risk – when offered to the Germany of Bruening as a buttress to the internal prestige of the last German Government to have any real hope of establishing a firm democratic constitution, seemed to him no less praiseworthy when it was not Bruening but Hitler with whom he had to deal.

It was to a Germany led by Hitler sworn to revenge for defeat in war, and already far gone along the road to the elimination of all other political parties and the liquidation of the trade unions, that the MacDonald Plan for rearmament at the same level of military strength as France was offered as a prize for returning to the Disarmament Conference, from which Hitler's envoys had rudely stamped out a short time before. A victory for tranquillity no doubt. But one which even MacDonald himself was forced to admit had within less than two years turned into an 'ambush'. Yet he was sustained in what he did by general approval. He set the signals of appeasement but he did so with popular endorsement. Churchill might warn the House of Commons against the danger of pressing the MacDonald Plan on the French and declare that 'as surely as Germany acquires full military equality with her neighbours while her own grievances are unredressed and while she is in the temper we have unhappily seen, so surely shall we see ourselves within a measurable distance of the renewal of general European war'. There were few others to agree with him among either MacDonald's supporters or opponents.

In the area of foreign affairs which most interested him MacDonald did, in the first two years of the National Government, at least assume the posture of a Prime Minister. He was often platitudinous, as Prime Minister's often are, and some of his platitudes were full of menace for the future, but he was not a figure to excite contempt. This unfortunately soon ceased to be the case in domestic affairs. Whatever had been the motives – and they included some, at any rate, that were patriotic and honourable – that persuaded him to tear up his political roots, abandon the Party he had helped to create, and finally become the captive Prime Minister of a massive Conservative majority, the effect upon him personally was traumatic: he had depended more upon socialism – even if his brand of it was misty and imprecise – than he realized.

He had always lived by words and words had often served him well. Even when they could not be certain exactly what he meant, his hearers in earlier days could feel that the phrases rolling so magnificently from his tongue were rooted in something constant and important, an attitude of mind, a philosophy of life, an ideology of some sort or another that, though imprecise, was so not because it lacked meaning but because it had many different layers of meaning through which he was asking them to tunnel with him in search of ultimate verities. 'There is one kind of truth and there is another kind of truth. They may both be true but it all depends upon how they are meant to be used', he retorted, angry and muddled when hard-pressed by Sir Stafford Cripps on one occasion in 1931. It brought a contemptuous laugh from the benches opposite, an embarrassed silence from those behind. Yet perhaps it deserved neither. He had always been preoccupied with the many-sidedness of truth and was trying to express something that was very real to him. But the man who is aware that truth can have several facets – and it is not an awareness profession-ally advantageous to a politician – must at least, if he is to benefit from it, have a sense of firm ground somewhere under his feet and a guiding rope to hold on to when the way is darkest. MacDonald lost both when he abandoned his Party. As the National Government was divested of even the clothes of an all party Coalition and became more and more a straight Conservative administration he found himself increasingly required to meet the bill of premiership in oratorical coin of an alien currency. Macneill Weir, his former Parliamentary Private Secretary, in commenting on the decline in MacDonald's powers as a parliamentary speaker after 1931, shrewdly observed that when a man has been preaching a gospel for forty years he falls into a habit of fluency in idioms congenial to his audiences that, if not quite a sub-stitute for thought yet provides it with an easily put on and instantly recognizable clothing. But when he 'renounces the faith of a lifetime and goes over to the other side he has to learn a different language, discard the old phylacteries and get acquainted with new liturgies'.

This need, greater in domestic affairs than foreign ones where the differences between the two parties were not so large, was all the more compulsive for MacDonald because of the necessity not to admit, even to himself, that he had changed sides. Had he made a considered and deliberate decision to change parties – as men have sometimes done – the moral and intellectual conflict preceding such a change might well, by compelling him to look at his political assumptions afresh, have clarified both his thought and his expression of it. But he had made no such deliberate choice. He still felt himself to be a socialist – indeed the noblest socialist of them all – but as nominal head of a predominantly Conservative administration he was compelled to propound or defend policies which not only were not his own, but were in many instances opposed to those he had advocated during most of his political life.

The ambiguity of his speech reflected the ambiguity of his position. It was not so much that he could not master new idioms or learn to intone new liturgies as that he dare not admit even to himself that such learning was called for. He was compelled to distort the old idioms to new purposes not only because they tripped most easily off his tongue and saved him from the pain of thinking, but because by this means he was able to pretend that he had not changed at all. He retreated into incoherency because incoherency had become more bearable than lucidity. Thus one finds in his defence of the unemployment policy of the National Government all the signs of a confused and tired mind trying to find vague philosophic arguments to support an attitude which, to those who had formerly followed him, could not but seem inhuman in its practical implications: 'Schemes must be devised, policies must be devised, if it is humanly possible to take that section (that is those unemployed who are unlikely shortly to be reabsorbed into industry) and to regard them not as wastrels, not as hopeless people, but as people for whom occupation must be provided some-how or other, and that occupation, although it may not be in the regular factory or in large-scale industrial groups, nevertheless will be quite as effective for themselves mentally, morally, spiritually and physically than perhaps if they were included in this enormous mechanism of humanity which is not always producing the best results and which, to a very large extent, fails in producing the good results that so many of us expect to see from a higher civilization based upon national wealth, which is the problem to be faced.'

When one listened to him on such occasions it was, as a distinguished American newspaperman was later to say of Eisenhower, sometimes just possible to believe that he might mean something, until one looked at a transcript of what he had actually said. The organ sounded. It made increasingly little sense to the hearers, but it comforted the organist.

He continued to preside over the Cabinet. But with the exception of Baldwin, who remained kind, his colleagues scarcely troubled any longer to hide their disdain. His health and mental powers were both failing. 'He reigned', as Churchill said in *The Gathering Storm*, 'in increasing decrepitude at the summit of the British system – a man for whom the springs of action had broken.'

When Snowden in his resignation speech in the Lords had spoken of MacDonald's 'constitutional inability to make any clear and understandable statement on any question' and had added waspishly, 'I would suggest that the Cabinet should look into the case of the Prime Minister, not only in his own interests but in the interests of the country; for it is a positive danger to the country that its affairs should be in the hands of a man who every time he speaks exposes his ignorance or incapacity', it was still just possible to dismiss the jibe as no more than Philip's little way. As MacDonald's mental and psychological deterioration increased with every passing month, it became less easy to do so. Suffered by his Conservative colleagues in the Cabinet only because his status as a national image was still felt by Baldwin to be of value, mocked in the Commons, joked about in clubs and finally derided in the country, he was a sorry remnant of his former self.

Except for the glowing interlude of his marriage he had always been a lonely man. Now he ceased to have even any curiosity value as a social lion at the great houses that had welcomed him so avidly in the first days of the National Government when 'every duchess in London had been anxious to embrace him'. He surrounded himself with a retinue of secretaries grotesquely in excess of the normal requirement, a Principal Private Secretary, a Deputy Principal Private Secretary, three other Private Secretaries, two Personal Private Secretaries, one Press Secretary and two Parliamentary Private Secretaries – a stage court of ten to assure him that he was still a star. He spent longer and longer weekends at Chequers where, dressed in tweeds, he could stroll in the gardens or relax in his study and imagine himself a true inheritor of the English aristocratic tradition, a country gentleman and a man of letters, with his daughter Ishbel to supervise his comforts and act as his hostess, and Ethel, 'the wonderful parlourmaid' in her chocolate-coloured uniform, to surround him with the benediction of her loyalty and deference, her flattering refusal to take any time off when the master was at home.

Only Baldwin's kindness, or perhaps his indolence, kept MacDonald Prime Minister so long. However, even Baldwin could not contemplate – and certainly could not persuade the Conservative Party to contemplate – fighting another election under him. In June 1935, after being permitted the reflected glory of the Royal Jubilee celebrations, he was persuaded, not without difficulty, that it was time for him to step down. Only by doing so, said Baldwin, delicately appealing to his parental feelings, would it be possible to avoid a revolt of the younger Conservatives that might not only unseat him but ruin his son Malcolm's hopes of a political career. On the other hand if there were an exchange of offices – Baldwin to the Premiership, MacDonald to be Lord President – it might well be possible to promote Malcolm in the Cabinet reconstruction that followed. Baldwin was as good as his word. The two leaders having exchanged places, Malcolm MacDonald was brought into the Cabinet as Secretary of State for the Dominions, a promotion thoroughly justified on his own merits. In November the Government went to the country, still under the name 'National'. To speed it on its way and rally the anxious, the Foreign Secretary, Sir Samuel Hoare, issued 'a revivalist appeal' (his own words) to the League of Nations, and Baldwin gave a firm assurance (soon to be broken) that it stood behind the League in the policy of sanctions against Italy.

For the Conservative Party it was a glorious – or perhaps, in the light of what was soon to follow when the Hoare-Laval pact to buy Italy off with Abyssinian territory was disclosed, an inglorious – victory. For them but not for poor MacDonald. The Government was returned with a majority of 247. The Lord President was contemptuously rejected by the electorate. In 1931 the miners of Seaham and their wives had sent him to Parliament as Leader of a National Government with a majority of 6,000. Now they dismissed him with a Labour majority of more than 20,000 against him. At Bassetlaw his son Malcolm was also defeated. They were the only two Ministers to lose their seats.

MacDonald's political life was effectively over. But he was not to be spared further humiliation. Although his National Labour Party had shrunk to eight and was soon to be diminished further by J. H. Thomas's parliamentary resignation after a Budget leak scandal, it was still considered a necessary, if tiny, part of the crumbling façade of National unity. Somehow MacDonald had to be found a seat. But how? No industrial constituency could be trusted to do its duty by the National Government on his behalf. Nor were there any holders of safe Conservative seats to be found ready to resign and give him the succession. However, at this stage one of the Conservative members for the Combined Scottish Universities conveniently died.

MacDonald had opposed separate university franchise all his political life. As recently as 1931 he had sought to abolish it. Now he was requested to make use of it to crawl back to Parliament. Although the seat was Conservative, there would, Baldwin blandly assured him, be no unpleasantness – after all it was a postal vote. He had spoken too confidently. When MacDonald's nomination was announced the university political associations protested in unison against what they regarded as a debasement of the standard of university representation for purposes of gerrymandering. So did the Scottish press. 'Mr Mac-Donald', said one Glasgow newspaper, 'is an unsuitable candidate in every respect and it seems to us that the way in which he has been practically forced upon the Universities is deplorable.' 'It is indeed fortunate', said another sardonically, 'that neither of the two Labour Governments over which he presided was able to end the existence of University seats; otherwise there would be no haven of refuge for the man who was rejected by the workers of Seaham Harbour, whose chances of winning any other industrial seat in the land are nil, and who can only be sure of winning even the Scottish Universities' seat provided that the Tory electors are prepared to rally to Mr Baldwin's call.'

It soon became clear that they were by no means eager to do so and Baldwin was compelled to go to extraordinary lengths to persuade them. A list of all Scottish graduates entitled to vote was compiled by Conservative Central Office and local Conservative agents in every part of the United Kingdom were instructed to track them down and appeal to them in the Baldwin name to vote for MacDonald. Nor was this sufficient. Baldwin was forced to journey to Scotland to make a personal appeal to the leaders of the Conservative Association and tell them that this was not a matter in which their individual opinions – however understandable – could be allowed to count. He expected them to work, if not with enthusiasm at least with efficiency, to ensure that MacDonald was returned. Only after the whole weight of the Conservative political machine had for the first time in history been brought to bear with compelling professional force on a university constituency could a sufficient number of the graduates of the Scottish universities be persuaded to do as they were told. MacDonald was returned; a pathetic political hostage robbed of the last illusion of independence.

It was a far cry from the day when he had been the hero of his country, fêted wherever he went. Such political gratitude as was due to him had run its course. He had become a man without a party or prestige greeted with contemptuous silence in the House of Commons where he had so long sat, rejected by Labour, slighted by Conservative members, his only intimate, J. H. Thomas, soon to be driven in disgrace from office and the House.

But he still had the Lord Presidency. To that he clung. 'He floats around like a wraith', Baldwin told Tom Jones over breakfast at Chequers. 'He held on as P.M. till the Jubilee and will hold on now as Lord President till the Coronation. I have heard of carrying on with a sack of flour fastened to your back. Ramsay is an eiderdown round my head.'

When Baldwin's day ended in a transient blaze of glory after the abdication the day of the eiderdown ended too. 'Ramsay ought to have retired in 1933, he was already failing', Baldwin said to a friend, but he had to the last to put up with his presence in the Cabinet out of a sense of loyalty and a sense, too, that perhaps he still had some small value as a shield against those winds of national dissension which he so much deplored. Neville Chamberlain had no such feelings. The leader of the National Labour Party was returned to the back benchers.

It was the moment for departure. But MacDonald could not bring himself to go. Perhaps he was, as Baldwin said, 'too tired to clear out'. Perhaps he could not think what else to do but live in the shadows where once he had been a great man. Lonely, virtually ignored, he sat listlessly through debates in a House that no longer wished to listen to him. There had always been behind his egotism a lively sensitivity. Unable now to pretend any longer even to himself he broke down. He went to Canada to recuperate, came back no better, and after one last appearance at a Burns' dinner, sailed on a cruise to South America with his daughter Sheila in a pathetic search for health and rest. He died on the voyage.

His body was brought back on a warship to be buried at Lossiemouth to the strain of the pipes. At Westminster Abbey the great, now that he was safely dead, gathered to pay him tribute: Neville Chamberlain, Baldwin and Montagu Norman among them. They were right to do so for they had a debt to repay. He had kept the winds of change away from them and saved their pound. He had achieved all he had ever longed for, a supreme moment of universal acceptance far beyond the hopes of the little lost boy from Lossiemouth clinging to the apron strings of his mother and grandmother and the benign approval of the village Dominie. He had been on the outside and had been invited in where he longed to be. It was like a fairy story in which every wish is granted only to crumble into dust. He had achieved the triumph his soul longed for. But he had paid for it a price too heavy even for the comfort of his enemies. It was past time for him to go.

Neville Chamberlain

Born 1869; son of Joseph Chamberlain, politician; educated at Rugby and Mason College, Birmingham; entered Birmingham City Council 1911; Lord Mayor of Birmingham 1915-16; Director-General of National Service 1916-17; Unionist M.P. for the Ladywood Division of Birmingham 1918-29; Postmaster-General 1922-23; Paymaster-General 1923; Minister of Health 1923; Chancellor of the Exchequer 1923-24; Minister of Health 1924-29; Unionist M.P. for the Edgbaston Division of Birmingham 1929-40; Chairman of Unionist Party 1930-31; Minister of Health 1931; Chancellor of the Exchequer 1931-37; Prime Minister 1937-40; Lord President of the Council 1940; died 1940.

1. *Solitary in Andros*

HOWEVER regrettable the consequences, it is not hard to see the qualities in Baldwin and MacDonald that exerted a peculiar fascination on their countrymen. Neville Chamberlain, on the other hand, seems even now the most unlikely of candidates for hero worship.

Thin of voice, bleak of phraseology he had none of the command of public oratory that both Baldwin and MacDonald at their best and after their own fashion possessed. His public personality, and indeed, except in the most intimate relationships, his private one also, was frigid and condescending. Contemptuous of emotion, which he thought of as sentimentality, and of the half-educated fools with whom he felt himself surrounded, he gave the impression of being painstaking, methodical, but unhumorous and implacable in his dislikes, arrogant and narrow minded. Black-haired, heavily moustached and corvine in profile, it was his misfortune that even when he most wished to be amiable his face seemed to wear a sneer. To an extent extraordinary in one of his antecedents he was incurably provincial; a radio set, as Attlee said, tuned to Midland Regional. One can understand why Baldwin and MacDonald should attract myths to themselves. What was synthetic in them, no less than what was genuine, was a magnet for illusion. They offered magnificent substitutes for the real thing, more comforting than reality ever is. But it is hard to see what made the British people fall in love with Neville Chamberlain.

He was born at the exact mid-point of Queen Victoria's reign, the eldest child of Joseph Chamberlain by his second wife. The death of his mother in childbirth when he was six robbed him not only of a mother but also separated him from his father. Joseph Chamberlain, twice widowed before he was forty, sold his interests in the Birmingham screw manufacturing firm of Nettlefold and Chamberlain for £120,000 and went into Parliament, seeking in public ambition a solace to private sorrow and becoming with each step in power and popular acclaim a more remote figure to his younger children, admired and feared but not capable of being loved: not their's but history's. Neville himself was packed off to a preparatory school at the earliest possible moment. He hated it, only to hate Rugby even more when he was sent there in the footsteps of his brilliant half brother Austen – so much so, indeed, that he refused every invitation to revisit it when he was a man.

He left Rugby to find his future already decided for him by his father. He was to be the Martha to Austen's Mary. Austen was to be trained for politics. After an excellent start at Cambridge he had been sent to Berlin and Paris to widen his mind, had helped his father in the general election of 1886, and was in line for selection as a parliamentary candidate. Cambridge, Berlin, Paris, the excitements of the political life were not, however, for Neville. He was destined for business. He was packed off to study mathematics, engineering and metallurgy as a day student at Mason College, Birmingham (the subjects were not of his chosing, he came bottom of the list in all of them), and then apprenticed to a Birmingham firm of Chartered Accountants.

In the ugly Victorian-Gothic mansion built by his father at Highbury on the outskirts of Birmingham there was to be found when the head of the family was at home some of the best political conversation and most stimulating political company in the world. It was the centre of the most efficient political machine in Britain, the drawing office for great imperial policies and radical domestic reforms. In such gatherings Neville took little part. He preferred (and who shall blame him?) hunting moths to listening to the great, bird songs to political talk. Mary Endicott, Joseph Chamberlain's third wife, was impressed by his 'extreme immaturity' when she first met him, although he was only a year or two younger than herself, and in the records of this ebullient household he strikes a curiously muted note. He seems to have been left almost completely untouched by the greatness around him. However, he could not escape his father's energy. At the age of twenty-two it transplanted him to the barren island of Andros in the Bahamas to restore the family fortunes by growing sisal.

The saga of this young man of 'extreme immaturity', dumped with a salary of £200 a year on an arid and desolate island, with the impossible task before him of pioneering in totally unsuitable surroundings the large-scale commercial growing of sisal in order to replace the capital Joseph Chamberlain had lost by over-optimistic investment in South African shares, compels admiration. Originally it had been assumed that a yearly visit of a few months at a time would be enough for the efficient management of the estate, which would, so the Governor of the Bahamas, a gentleman given to rich fancies, had assured Joseph Chamberlain, undoubtedly bring in a return of at least thirty per cent per annum. In fact, Neville had to stay there with scarcely a break for five years, living alone most of the time with no European companion except a white overseer with whom his relationship was strictly that of superior to subordinate and who, as the youthful Neville Chamberlain priggishly told him, forfeited his confidence permanently when he allowed himself to be seen on one occasion after his wife's death slightly the worse for drink.

By the end of four years Neville had cleared 6,000 acres of bush, planted it, built roads, houses, stores, a shop and a wharf, and was in control of a native labour force of 800. Machinery for turning the sisal into commercial fibre had been ordered from Cuba and he was laying a railway from the processing sheds to the wharf for easier shipping of the finished product. He had had a hard time and had often been bitterly lonely, condemned to a life, as he wrote in a letter home, 'of total solitude, mentally if not physically'. He was twenty-five. At home in England his father had just become Secretary of State for the Colonies. Austen was nursing a constituency.

Nevertheless life on Andros was not without some compensations. In the evening when he walked to the wharf from the spacious red-roofed house with a Union Jack flying at the masthead he had built for himself ('as good as any in Nassau'), and smoked his cigar amid roses and hibiscus, coleus, vineas gloxinia, and golden rod imported from Highbury, he could feel himself king of no mean realm. He had horses to ride, a schooner to sail. He could watch birds. He could organize the lives of his Negro workers like a benevolent deity. Above all he could see everywhere around him the results of his labours and had enough practical business to see to to keep him occupied every minute of the day.

Unfortunately the whole of this immense effort was founded on illusion. What Neville had described to his father when he arrived as 'the best site in the Bahamas' turned out to be quite useless as a sisal plantation. It was in fact quite impossible to grow sisal commercially anywhere in the Bahamas, though a few bushes grew wild.

Realization came reluctantly. The young man from Birmingham refused to believe what he did not want to believe. It was less disturbing not to look ahead too far, simpler to keep on with the work at hand, which each day brought its own satisfactions and gave him an excuse to put disagreeable thoughts aside. By January 1895, however, even he could no longer escape the facts. He was compelled to write to his father and warn him that of the 6,000 acres he had planted no more than 300 were likely to yield a crop that summer. 'Anxiety weighs on me day and night', he wrote.

A spell of rain revived his hopes: they were always easily raised. He bought 500,000 more plants and flung himself into work once more: work was better than thought. By the end of another year even work could not keep truth away. Not only were the crops negligible in size but they were so poor in quality that the samples he sent to the American market were rejected out of hand as unsaleable. He wrote despairingly to his father: 'The plants don't grow ... all the order and discipline that I have worked up will be lost, all the people will go away....'

The scale of the impending disaster shook even Joseph Chamberlain's buoyant spirit. 'This would indeed be a catastrophe', he wrote when he understood that Neville actually proposed the entire abandonment of a venture in which he had by this time sunk some £50,000 – more than a third of his fortune – and for which he had also unwisely raised additional outside capital to an amount of £20,000 in the form of a debenture issue by the Andros Fibre Company. But the catastrophe was not to be avoided. Not only were there no crops that year, it was plain that there was no good reason to expect anything better in the future. The enterprise had been misjudged from the start. There was no possibility of turning the estate into a fertile plantation. 'I can no longer see any chance of making the investment pay', Neville confessed to his father. 'I cannot blame myself too much for my want of judgment.'

He went home for a family conclave and offered to do anything his father asked of him to put things right, go back to Andros for ten years if necessary. It was a brave but useless gesture. There was nothing for it but to write off the work of nearly six years as a total loss. The machinery was knocked down to a solitary bidder for £560. For the estate itself there was no offer. It lay abandoned for twenty-five years. Then it was sold for £200. That was all that was saved from the investment of £70,000 and the years of labour.

It is not difficult to find in the young man on the island of Andros some of the virtues and defects that were later to be seen in the Prime Minister: the virtues of tenacity and courage, the defects of obstinacy and refusal to recognize any fact that did not fit in with his own hopes. But if the years on Andros revealed character, they also shaped it. Driven in upon himself by this solitary life, without intellectual equals with whom to exchange ideas, and with no near neighbours other than missionaries whose 'unctuous ways' he despised with all the force of his inherited Unitarianism, working with one white overseer whom he regarded as his inferior and with primitive native labourers who were taught to regard him almost as a supreme being ('I keep tightening the reins of discipline', he told his father, and he treasured, perhaps only half humorously, a note from one worker he had punished for smoking near the engine room: 'Mr Lord Chamberlain Dear Sir as the Lord Jesus is above the earth so is you above me'), elements of egotism and coldness that had already begun to manifest themselves at Highbury became, as his diary and letters show, deeply ingrained in his character. He imposed order on his small community with an increasingly exasperated contempt for the general incompetence of humanity, so incapable of appreciating what was good for it, so unwilling to do what it was told, and was forced by the conditions of his life into a habit of inordinate dependence upon his own solitary judgment. And because constant activity was so necessary to keep loneliness away he became permanently distrustful of thought unrelated to immediate practical decision: 'A day without incessant action', as his official biographer, Sir Keith Feiling, comments, 'seemed a day wasted.'

Such a life might have been expected to leave little taste for the humdrum routine of a Birmingham business career but on his return home Neville Chamberlain merged into the Birmingham background as though he had never left it. 'Having chucked away a competence – you know where – I am going to toil and moil, until I grab it back again', he wrote to a friend. He was twenty-eight and without conventional business experience. However, there were plenty of Chamberlains, Martineaus and Kenricks to give him a hand. A directorship in the copper and brass manufacturing firm of Elliott's and a controlling interest in a private company manufacturing the metal parts of cabin berths for ships were bought for him. For fourteen years he immersed himself wholly in the life of a middling size manufacturer in the metal trade without sign of other ambition.

One of his name could hardly, of course, avoid getting mixed up in politics occasionally. But when he did so it was from the outside; urging Austen to fight for the successorship when Balfour was thrown out of the Conservative leadership in 1911; arranging a Birmingham meeting for Carson whose 'strong action' in organizing armed resistance in Ulster to the Irish Home Rule Bill he admired; denouncing the Old Age Pension Bill as 'a scandalous attempt to catch votes – a direct discouragement of thrift'; taking the chair for the Navy League at a meeting to demand eight new battleships ('We want eight and we won't wait' was the popular cry); and generally attacking the 'accursed, mischievous, cowardly' Liberal Government for its numerous sins. But he did not allow public ambition to move him personally until he was forty and had made certain of a secure competence in business: and even then only as far as Birmingham Town Hall. Nor did he marry until he was forty-two although then very happily and with sincere affection on both sides.

Winston Churchill was later to describe him as 'a good Lord Mayor of Birmingham – in a lean year'. But although Birmingham Town Hall was almost a family preserve (four of his relations were already in residence on the City Council when he arrived there and ten of his family, including his father, had been Lord Mayors before him) his success in municipal politics had nothing to do with nepotism. The running of an efficient and well established City administration exactly suited him. Narrow and ignorant in world affairs he had inherited from his father a reforming zeal in local ones and although he could not stomach the idea that the Council's workmen should be given a wage of 30s a week, or tolerate the Lloyd George measure for levying a rate on land values (it was nothing but socialism, he said), he was prominent in housing developments, in the building of a university, and in the launching of a municipal bank. In business his contemporaries found him competent but not outstanding, a careful, buttoned-up man singularly lacking in his father's fire and his brother's cosmopolitan enthusiasms, determined to get value for money in all his dealings but active in the Chamber of Commerce and the Unitarian Sunday School, and a good employer to those he regarded as 'loyal'.

Even his private diaries stick mostly to prosaic facts: on one rare occasion when after an unfortunate love affair he allowed emotion to break in, he later, as his official biographer records, cut out the page.

Yet although his main energies went in business and municipal affairs he was not without other interests. He read much: Carlyle, Romanes, T. H. Green, Admiral Mahan, Darwin, W. H. Hudson, Jane Austen, Samuel Butler, Henry James, Conrad especially, and conducted a long, detailed, intelligent correspondence with the Shakespearean scholar Dover Wilson on *Hamlet*. He was a passionate gardener, a respectable collector of china, a botanist of merit, a knowledgeable entomologist (he bequeathed his notebooks on insects and butterflies to Birmingham), an enthusiastic and patient bird watcher, and a keen fisherman. He liked listening to classical music (his knowledge of Beethoven according to Sir Hugh Allen was greater than that of most professional musicians) and to drawing-room ballads, but was made uncomfortable by anything he thought vulgar (the present writer once had the searing experience of being in his company when the exigencies of official business compelled him to sit through an after-dinner performance by Miss Nellie Wallace at her admirable ripest). Although so inhibited and cold in public he was capable of great private warmth in his family circle and even of inspiring something approaching idolatry, as he did in his young cousin Norman Chamberlain, who wrote of him that he was 'one of the very few people who roused in me all the sensations of a willing and enthusiastic follower'. Norman's death in action in France was a sorrow from which he took long to recover. Chords of eloquence and sensitivity mute in most of his human relationships were touched, too, by the contemplation of natural beauty, so that he found delight in describing in his private journal 'a larch which seems like a ball of golden gauze in the sun it is so soft and luminous', or telling of a walk beside a river 'through the long grass with the buttercups up to your knee, till you get to the last bend before the weir where the stream runs dark and slow under big elms'.

Such emotion had no part in his life at the Town Hall. There he wanted facts, precision, correctitude, the limited approach to limited problems offering the possibility of limited solutions, the company of those who would do faithfully what they were told. Lacking both the virtues and insincerities that commonly make for success in political management he seemed a most unlikely candidate for the wider political life. Even when war came he would have been well content to see it through in the industrious exercise of his civic responsibilities as Lord Mayor of Birmingham had not his 'd—d well-meaning brother' Austen considered it a filial act to suggest his name to Lloyd George in 1917, when that statesman was looking for a Director-General of National Service to quieten press and parliamentary criticism of the inefficient use of manpower in the services and industry.

It seemed a job ideally suited to his abilities, yet he failed disastrously at it. Given charge of a settled Department he might well have succeeded brilliantly. But this was a new Department and Lloyd George believed in flinging his appointees into the jungle of wartime White-hall to cut their own paths, fight their own battles, and carve out their own empires – in much the same spirit as Northcliffe when he appointed two men to the same positions on his newspapers and waited for the toughest to come out on top: L. G. saw no reason to present his subordinates with blue prints for success.

In such a situation Neville Chamberlain was lost. He had no capacity for imposing his own terms on chaos. Nor did he improve matters by insisting on appointing an ex-Town Clerk of Birmingham as his second in command and other municipal officials from Birmingham as departmental chiefs. Lloyd George's offer had reached him as he sat in the Birmingham train at Euston enjoying a cigar with the City Treasurer after negotiating with their brokers the terms for a new issue of municipal bonds. He seems not to have asked any questions or inquired what powers the Director-General of National Service would have, no doubt because he was confident of his own. 'It is an appalling responsibility', he wrote in his diary, adding, 'But the outcome of the war may depend on what I do.'

Installed in unsuitable quarters in the St Ermin's Hotel he issued grandiose promises of quick success and rushed (if such a word is appropriate to so pedestrian a character) about the country making statements that he subsequently found he had no power to implement, pursued throughout by the hostility of the Ministry of Labour, the Ministry of Munitions, the Admiralty and the War Office, all of whom were determined not to allow this upstart Department to encroach on any of their preserves. It was all very unlike Birmingham Town Hall.

The flower of the British Expeditionary Force had been destroyed in the fighting on the Somme, the French Army had been decimated at Verdun, Russia was out of the war. The need for manpower in the Services and the munitions industries was desperate. Yet two months after the new Department had been established and a small army of officials appointed to cover the country, and after more than £60,000 had been spent on publicity, a parliamentary question elicited that fewer than 3,000 men had been placed in employment as a result of its activities. Three months later a Select Committee of the House commented critically that the Department's results 'were not commensurate with the preparations made and the heavy preliminary outlay of money'.

It was the Bahamas all over again. Indeed he ruefully acknowledged as much in the privacy of his journal: 'Now I am in a position that reminds me of the Bahamas when the plants didn't grow.'

There were daily stories in the newspapers of men who had thrown up their work or closed down their own small business on the instructions of the Director of National Service only to find themselves waiting week after week, idle and without money, for the war work for which they had been told they were required. The total number enrolled for essential war work by the new Department was less than a third of the number expected. Yet even so three-fifths turned out on investigation to be already engaged on work of national importance from which they could not be released and less than half of the rest proved suitable for employment in the munitions industries. The St Ermin's Hotel, the press angrily proclaimed, was 'a palace of make-believe'.

Not all the fault was Chamberlain's, any more than it had been in that earlier venture. The conditions in which Lloyd George compelled him to operate would have been almost impossible for any man. But he made sure of failure by the climate of self-deception with which he surrounded himself, behaving exactly as he had in his youth in the Bahamas when he shied away from every unpalatable fact and constantly embraced hopes founded on illusion. When a Cabinet Committee was set up to help him he refused to look at its recommendations, since he considered that anything it might say must seem an aspersion on his own competence. Every attempt at reform foundered on what Lloyd George – not, of course, a wholly unbiased witness – described as 'a vein of self-sufficient obstinacy ... that baffled all our endeavours'. It was a task calling, as Lloyd George said, for 'a great breadth and boldness of conception, a remorseless energy and thoroughness of exertion and for the exercise of supreme tact'. Instead the ex-Lord Mayor of Birmingham turned out to be 'a man of rigid competency ... lost in an emergency or in creative tasks at any time'. At the end of seven months Lloyd George sacked him.

For his earlier failure twenty-five years before Neville Chamberlain had blamed himself too much. For this one he found it hardly possible to blame himself at all. He preferred to put the blame on the jealousy of politicians and above all on Lloyd George, for whom his hatred never diminished and whom he did everything he could in later years to keep out of public life. It was in this mood that, eighteen months off his fiftieth birthday, he decided to get into the House of Commons – but only, of course, for a Birmingham constituency.

He had no great expectations of the parliamentary life. He went into it, as Saki said of Latimer Springfield, 'as other people might go into half mourning', determined only to prove to himself that he was as good as the politicians who despised him. It was political therapy he was engaged on, and he embarked on it with a good deal of loathing. 'A feeling of almost irresistible nausea and revulsion comes over me at the thought of all the drudgery, the humiliation, the meanness and pettiness of that life …' he recorded in his diary. And again: 'My career is broken. How can a man of nearly 50, entering the House with this stigma upon him hope to achieve anything?'

Few future Prime Ministers have entered upon a parliamentary career in so dubious a mood, with so uncertain an aim, and with so few obvious qualifications for the political life.

As he brooded in Birmingham neither he nor anyone else could have envisaged that he would outstrip both his father and step-brother in political attainment, be idolized by a great nation and repeat for a third time, but on a far vaster scale, the pattern of Andros and the St Ermin's Hotel.

2. Businessman in Politics

ALTHOUGH thwarted in his determination to come at once to grips with the House of Commons by the intransigence of the sitting Conservative Members for Birmingham, none of whom proved ready to do their duty and resign when asked to make way for a Chamberlain, and forced instead to make do with an invitation to fight the new constituency of Ladywood at the general election, Neville Chamberlain did not waste his time. Once he had made up his mind that only success in national politics could expunge the shame of failure he showed his father's aptitude for getting his hands on the levers of power. The Birmingham constituencies were to be increased from seven to twelve at the general election, and the Tory Party appointed a Committee to consider what changes in party organization were needed to meet this situation. He became its Chairman, and at a meeting of Birmingham M.P.s and candidates in Austen's room at the House of Commons managed to push through, despite some strong opposition, a proposal that in future all the Divisions should come under central control and subscriptions go to a central fund instead of as formerly to individual constituencies. 'Of course as I am Chairman this decision practically places the direction of Unionist politics in my hands', he wrote to his sister Hilda, adding with firm satisfaction, 'I am not sure whether all those present perceived this; I didn't mention it.'

Modesty had never been one of his failings and he did not allow it to inhibit him when he finally reached Westminster in February 1919 as a member of that first postwar House of Commons of 'hard-faced men who looked as if they had done well out of the war' that so distressed Baldwin's more sensitive spirit. Even to himself he could not pretend the possession of great debating skill or mastery over words. But he had other qualities that could be turned to good use in the political life. He had always lived through action rather than thought, it was the practical that appealed to him. By dint of taking what others did not want he acquired within a few months an impressive collection of Committees ranging from Unhealthy Areas to Canals and Waterways, Members' Salaries and Anti-Dumping. He was a good committeeman – the ink of bureaucracy ran relentlessly through his true blue veins – and with control of the Birmingham party machine to add weight to his opinions, and the Chamberlain name to help him, it is not surprising that before long his reputation stood high as an influential back bencher. He was elected to the Tory Reconstruction Committee – predecessor of the 1922 Committee – from which vantage point he had the pleasure of reprimanding his old enemy, Lloyd George, for his too frequent and too extended absences from the House; and though without the graces that make a man generally popular or the talents that pack the benches was accepted as a good House of Commons man whose spectacular failure as Director of National Service soon ceased to be remembered by anyone but himself. Within a year he could have had office (Bonar Law who appreciated his virtues because they were so like his own, suggested the Parliamentary Secretaryship to the Ministry of Health). But he could not bring himself to serve under Lloyd George. His enmities ran deep and constant; he even arranged to be away on holiday when

Lloyd George, 'the little beast' as he called him in letters, was given the freedom of Birmingham.

His influence among Tory back-benchers might have been expected to make him prominent in the movement to get rid of the Prime Minister. Caution and family loyalty to his step-brother Austen restrained him. He refused the chairmanship of the Conservative Reconstruction Committee because a revolt against Austen as leader might, he thought, be necessary and he did not want to lead it. In any event he had no great esteem for Bonar Law who had, he later told a friend with his customary aptitude for denigration, returned to the leadership with 'extraordinary ideas of his own importance'.

By bad, or perhaps good, timing he was in Canada when Austen was routed at the battle of the Carlton Club and Bonar Law, the reluctant leader, put in his place. He returned to take office as Postmaster-General under the new Prime Minister, a decision Austen took badly. It is typical of his insensitivity to the feeling of others that it surprised him that Austen should feel hurt by his brother's ready acceptance of office from the man who had beaten him. When Austen made his feelings known he replied brusquely that if it was going to affect their personal relations he would refuse the job but in such an event he would consider his political career ended. 'I said this,' he recorded, 'in justice to myself not as an argument. However, it proved too much for him.'

He cannot, of course, be blamed for looking to his own interests in this matter. Those who are untimely picked for Marthadom cannot be expected to put Mary's feelings first all their lives. And, as he told Hilda, he found Austen 'unprogressive and prejudiced'. Moreover he had a genuine urge to public service and combined a strong conviction of his own merits with a continuing need to wipe away the hurt of his wartime failure. Ministerial office, even of a modest sort, was a necessary first step in the programme of rehabilitation on which he had embarked with such distaste in August 1919.

There was no further looking back. Scarcely had he settled in at the Post Office before Bonar Law, desperately short of talent, moved him to the Ministry of Health. There he remained when Baldwin of whom he had no very high opinion either (he would have preferred Curzon) succeeded.

Health was of all Departments the one most suited to his abilities and interests. To it he brought much knowledge of local government, a deep, if rather nineteen-centuryish passion for social reform inherited from his father, a formidable memory for detail and a talent for close administration that won him the well-justified respect of his officials. Within his own rigid and moralist terms of reference he was a considerable success, even though these at times led him, as Beatrice Webb complained, to a callous application of the principles of 1834 in dealing with relief. (Odd to think what might have been the consequences on British political history if her tentative romance with Joseph Chamberlain as a young woman had led to matrimony.) He left it with regret when Baldwin, unable to find a Chancellor, moved him to the Treasury after only a few months and returned to it of his own choice after the interlude of the first MacDonald Administration, recognizing, as he said, with a clarity about his abilities that did not always stay with him: 'I am likely to be a great Minister of Health but am not likely to be more than a second-rate Chancellor.'

Yet even at the Ministry of Health, in the most creative period of his political life, defects of character that were, in the end, to mar so much of what was positive and valuable in his attitude to politics began to emerge. The finger of Andros and the St Ermin's Hotel was heavy on him: he could not bear opposition or find it possible to reconcile criticism of himself and his projects with honesty on the part of those who criticized. Ironclad in his own rectitude, even the normal courtesies of debate were often beyond him. The freemasonry of the Commons, which encourages friendship and respect between men of very different opinions, was not for him. Like Bonar Law and Baldwin he had been brought up in the ethics of Victorian business but unlike Baldwin, the reluctant businessman, he had little aptitude for adjusting himself to changing democratic relationships, perhaps because his experience of business was mainly confined to privately owned concerns in which the owner was the undisputed master. I remember Hore-Belisha saying to me later that to sit under Chamberlain in Cabinet was like being a departmental manager in a firm in which the Chairman owned all the shares, and from the beginning the vigour of parliamentary debate angered him. He could not disguise his immeasurable exasperation with those who seemed to wish to thwart him, his contempt for the oafs on the other side who dared to disagree with him. Baldwin found it necessary to beg him to remember that he was addressing a meeting of gentlemen. He always gave the impression, he said, that he looked on the Labour Party as dirt. It was not advice that Neville Chamberlain found it easy to take. Self-righteously he noted in his journal a little later that it was his opponents' 'utter inability to appreciate a reasonable argument' that embittered his soul. 'If I seem hard and unsympathetic to them it is the reaction brought about by their own attitude.'

Despite his genuine radicalism in some areas of social legislation and the substantial administrative reforms produced by his massive Local Government Act – the most durable of his political achievements in so far as anything in the 'twenties was durable – he was extraordinarily insensitive to the plight of individuals. He could think of and legislate for a social problem in the abstract, and within his own terms of reference cared much for the welfare of humanity in the mass. But he had the soul of a bureaucrat. It was the machinery of administration, tidy, efficient, free of corruption, that quickened his imagination and held his loyalty; he had no sympathy for personal emotion in such matters. For this reason he was implacable in his hatred of Poplarism, wholly incapable of understanding, still less of sympathizing with, the motives that made George Lansbury ('where reason reigns he has no place') and other Poor Law Guardians ready to defy what they regarded as unjust orders from Whitehall in order to relieve the individual suffering of the poor and unemployed. Even the Webbs, who shared many of his bureaucratic enthusiams, found themselves compelled to ask, 'Have we exaggerated in our *History* – especially in the last chapter – the evil of "proletarianism" and minimized the evil of strict administration insisted on by Neville Chamberlain?' and to add anxiously 'certainly it is a public scandal that the Poor Law has not relieved destitution in South Wales and that it has had to be supplemented by this demoralizing and inept appeal for charitable funds dispensed by hastily organized local committees'.

Chamberlain suffered no such humane doubts. He could write complacently in his diary during the miners' lock-out that followed the General Strike (in which naturally enough he had been one of the chief advocates of smashing the unions): 'They [the miners] are not within sight of starvation, hardly of under-nutrition, so well are they looked after by the guardians ... they are living not too uncomfortably at the expense of the ratepayer while the nation is gradually overcome by creeping paralysis.' At a later date a friendly commentator, Sir Arthur Salter, reviewing Chamberlain's international policy, was to observe, that although his desire to avoid the sufferings of a general conflict was unquestionable 'the individual distresses of those who fall by the wayside, in Czechoslovakia, or China or Spain do not often visibly touch his emotions. And what he does not feel he does not profess to feel.' The Minister of Health was the father of the Prime Minister.

All this time he was growing in stature and self-assurance. Although unwilling to join actively in the growing intrigues against Baldwin, which, especially after the loss of power in the 1929 election, reached a venom exceptional even for the Conservative Party in such matters and would have unseated any leader less adroit in keeping a hold on public affection, Chamberlain made no secret in the privacy of his diary of his belief that he was the only Tory who 'might bring about S. B.'s retirement'. And on resuming his activities in the House after serving as Chairman of the Party Organization for a year he was soon recording complacently 'I have, I believe, recovered the second position in the Party'. He had a firm conviction of his own uniqueness. Just as, when accepting the makeshift and personally disastrous appointment of Director of National Service, he had confided, 'the outcome of the war may depend on what I do', so he noted when taking over the Party chairmanship, 'I believe it is true that I can render a service which is possible to no one else.'

As one studies his letters and diaries one finds oneself, indeed, constantly astounded by the immense private egotism hidden behind the rather dull and unexciting exterior he presented to the world. It was not the egotism, open, flamboyant and even appealing, of the great actors of politics but the hoarded egotism of a man driven in upon himself; one is conscious of the effects not only of Andros and the Ministry of National Service but also of his father's choice of Austen as the favoured inheritor of the family's political fortunes and of the consequences, too, of being for too long a large frog in a municipal pond. This impenetrable core of self-satisfaction of which one was aware whenever one met him had perhaps been at the beginning no more than the defence of one who felt himself rated at less than his real value and subjected to unmerited failure. But it prevented him from broadening and growing as many men do with new experience. Instead of stretching the muscles of mind and imagination to encompass the challenge of new demands, he sought to constrict each problem to his own stature. He carried a Procrustean bed on his back wherever he went, armoured against fate by a narrow obstinacy that grew more self-sufficient with each passing year.

But he was efficient and he was a man of action. The dock and the railway got built even though the sisal for which they were intended had no prospect of growing. Such a man could not help but appeal to Baldwin's indolence. 'He left a final message for me that he was most grateful to me for sparing him the necessity of returning and would "back me to the end" ', he wrote to Hilda during the 1931 crisis, after reporting that Baldwin, who 'I think would agree that crises of this sort are not his forte, had apparently given no thought to the situation, asked no intelligent questions, made no helpful suggestion and was chiefly anxious to get away before he was drawn into something.' He had all the virtues of political application that Baldwin lacked. In such a climate of leadership it was impossible that power should not accrue to him. If only he had been capable of growing with it how different things might have been. But he was not. Possibly George V appreciated this when after the victory of the National Government at the polls he urged that Chamberlain should remain at the Ministry of Health where he had been 'so good', and not be translated to the Treasury where he was bound to be suspected for his ultra-protectionist views. But the wisdom of the King was ignored. It was to the Treasury he went. He was now, next to Baldwin himself, the leading figure in the Conservative Party. His influence on it, and through it on the world, was to become steadily more decisive.

His policy as Chancellor from 1931 until he became Prime Minister provides a key not only to his own character but also to the forces in public life he particularly represented.

He was confronted by a complex financial and economic situation which had been created in part by a breakdown of international financial confidence due to over lending and fears of political instability, in part by the failure of effective consuming power to keep pace with productive power, and in part by the immense burden of political debts imposed by the war. He saw it almost entirely in the simple terms of a nineteenth-century business moralist denouncing extravagance. In a time of severe industrial depression largely created by the system's failure to enable consumers to consume what expanding industrial power could produce he set himself to reduce the ability of the mass of the people to buy by a policy of rigid economy and curtailment of social expenditure. All schemes for public spending with the double object of breaking the spiral of depression and reducing the social evils of over-crowding were rejected. He opposed every proposal for monetary expansion to increase total consuming power, or to put men to work by encouraging industrial expansion through Government guarantees. Instead he adopted a rigidly deflationary policy. He refused even to examine the arguments for alternative courses, defending his restrictionist policy with a grim puritanical fervour through which there echoed the tones of long dead speeches in the mechanical institutes of the industrial towns of half a century ago, with their naïve conviction that success and happiness would accrue inevitably from a life of careful toil and careful saving, their moral assumption that it is always good for people to have to tighten their belts.

To Keynes's *Treatise on Money* and the whole of that body of new economic thinking that was to find its superb expression in *The General Theory of Employment, Interest and Money* he replied with the works of the late Samuel Smiles. At a time when the damaging effects of excessive saving on an industrial system geared for mass production and demanding for its success a high rate of spending by the mass of the people had been disclosed by economists of standing all over the world, he urged the ordinary people of Britain to save harder than ever. When State planning of public works to reduce unemployment had been recognized as necessary in almost every other country in the world, he remained convinced that the free working of uncontrolled private enterprise as inherited from the golden period of nineteenth-century liberalism had an absolute moral value of its own with which it would be blasphemous to interfere, and seemed to share with nineteenth-century liberalism the belief that the poor in the main poor through their own fault. In a period when the great need was for an expansion of world trade, and when the abandonment of the gold standard had in any event made protection irrelevant, he forced through a policy of imperial preference on 'the greatest day of his life'. As Sir Roy Harrod remarks in his *Life of Keynes*: 'Britain went off the Gold Standard which removed the need for Protection and had Protection also and then failed to give any lead to international reconstruction.' Chamberlain gained acceptance in the public mind because he represented a mood which was to possess a large number of British people for some years.

The boom of 1929 had been followed by a crash which left millions of the middle and lower middle classes bewildered and anchorless. They had been brought up under the shadow of that English non-conformist tradition of which Neville Chamberlain, the Unitarian, was so loyal a representative, holding that if a man worked steadily, put money by for a rainy day and did not dissipate his talents in rich living, he could confidently expect to achieve a respectable and solid position in the world and enjoy that position to the end of his days.

And then, suddenly, the depression came and threatened to sweep away, and in many cases did sweep away, all this assured security. It made no distinction between the respectable hard-working citizen and the irresponsible follower of his own pleasures. It brought before the middle classes the stark and terrible fact that all their carefully planned stability could be destroyed overnight by forces outside their personal control that could fling them into the ranks of the 'lower classes' or even of the 'unemployed' without compunction. As men do at such times they tried to find comfort in an emotional feeling of national unity. They were not fully articulate but they were frightened. They wanted the assurance that they were members of a tight community – hence their uncritical support for a National Government for reasons comparable to, but of a milder form than, those which made millions of Germans support National Socialism when confronted with personal economic disaster. And they wanted the assurance that the standards by which they had set their lives were valid and would survive. Neville Chamberlain gave them this assurance. It was not justified. But he believed it. The narrow integrity expressed in his Budget, of a kind he shared with another nineteenth-century liberal, Snowden, restored their confidence in the foundations of their middle-class morality. His economic nationalism satisfied their instinctive reaction towards insularity in time of crisis. He did not perceive, any more than they did, the consequences of this nationalism, nor the international fruits of a reversal of British fiscal policy. With the best intentions he was concerned only with the interests of British business as he saw them. For these interests he regarded as the interests of the nation.

When in May 1937 he became Prime Minister he carried the same values into the wider sphere of international affairs. He had been the businessman at the Treasury. Now he became the businessman at 10 Downing Street, rejecting not only the true traditions of the British people but those of the Conservative Party itself, which is always at its best when most romantic.

3. Diplomacy by Bigamy

THE tragedy of world policy from 1918 to 1940 was the recurring failure to achieve adjustment between national policies and international needs.

Politically, men's mind in 1918 embraced, however tentatively, a new conception of international justice and security embodied in the ideal of the League of Nations. Under its spur they accepted responsibilities only capable of being wholly fulfilled if national policies were closely related to international obligations. It was not simply a matter of readiness to honour engagements of a larger scope and wider application than those undertaken in prewar treaties. It was even more a matter of considering the international consequences of all policies contemplated for national purposes.

Economically a similar adjustment between national and international obligations was necessary to world stability. This was the more so since some parts of the economic system were already international in scope while others were almost exclusively national in their conception. The danger of maladjustment was constant. It could have been avoided only by the most careful coordination of national and international policies.

The world, it is frequently said, grows smaller. But that is true only in certain ways. One can cable from London to Hong Kong in a few seconds and ring up from New York to talk to a friend in Rome in a matter of minutes. But most Londoners in fact know nobody in Hong Kong to cable to and only a minority in New York have anyone to ring up in Rome. It is a mistake to think, that the physical fact of increased speed of communication in the world has of itself increased understanding between nations or made men and women in a London suburb feel any closer in spirit to an Indian peasant. There is great danger, indeed, that we shall come to think of ourselves as internationally-minded because television has taught us what other peoples and countries look like, and because we know it to be possible to fly round the world in a time counted in hours, whereas in fact, on matters much more fundamental, we remain circumscribed in our thoughts by national boundaries. The outward vision may embrace the whole world. The eyes of the spirit remain obstinately centred on the interests of the group to which one belongs.

The financial structure of the world after the first world war had become almost completely international involving all major nations in a network of financial obligations some political, some commercial. A worldwide machinery of credit transmitted a stress felt in one centre almost instantaneously to every other. The cable and the telephone had made it possible for credits to be negotiated, to be withdrawn from this country to that, to be transferred from one end of the world to another in a matter of moments. But the physical realities of commerce, the exchange of commodities, the buying and selling of the products of men's labour which such credit decisions affected remained relatively slow of consummation. A financial decision taken in New York or London and flashed around the world before those making it has gone to lunch could and did involve changes in the balance of trade of Germany or France or Britain, or in the standard of living of millions of Europeans, Asians or Africans, which by the nature of things took months to adjust. Moreover, the consequences of such financial decisions were observable and had their effect on men's minds and on their confidence before the slower moving economic machine could prepare itself to meet the strain or alter its operations to suit new circumstances.

The economic system was thus open to nervous shocks to which it was impossible for it to adapt itself in the time available. This was one of the chief causes of the monetary and credit crises which distinguished these years, and which had their economic effect in unemployment and industrial instability, and their political effect in the development of nationalist policies designed, for the most part unavailingly, to insulate national economic systems from the financial and economic stresses of the international system. These crises might have been avoided, or at least their severity much reduced, if those responsible for decisions had been thoroughly international in outlook. But they were not. They were twenty-five per cent internationally minded, seventy-five per cent bound by national horizons in their determination of policy.

The same was true politically. The circumstances of the postwar world, and particularly the international obligations entered into by members of the League of Nations, required a world mind which did not exist save in a very few instances. This was a period of transition in which it was essential that there should be a careful examination of the international consequence of national policies if a pattern composed of an internationalised credit system, a partially internationalised economic system, and independent national political systems linked by a new set of international rules, was to be effective. It was necessary to decide in what spheres of political, economic and financial activity national sovereignty could properly remain paramount, and in which it ought to submit itself to the overriding claims of the world community. Translated into world terms it was the recurring problem which faces democracy as a practical political system: that of establishing a correct relationship between the individual and the community, of striking a proper balance between man's freedom as a person and his responsibility to society, and of securing a harmonious correlation

NEVILLE CHAMBERLAIN

between his duty to himself and his family, his duty as a member of an economic or class group, and his duty as a member of a wider national society.

The failure of the democracies in the interwar years was that while talking internationally they proved incapable of so widening their conception of democracy as to make it work internationally. Perhaps it was too much to expect that they would even in the best of circumstances, but failure was made doubly sure by the hostility of key individuals like Chamberlain to principles alien to their outlook and tradition. They feared, and because they feared did not understand, the necessities of international democracy. They were neither nationalist nor internationalist, but kept an unsteady foot in either camp.

The authoritarian countries attempted no such compromise. They were logical enough to see that it was impossible successfully to balance permanently between two opposing systems. They did not believe in democracy either as a national or as an international creed. They were despotic and nationalist. Having decided on despotism and nationalism they saw that it was necessary to withdraw economically as well as politically from the international system and became economic nationalists as well as political ones, setting themselves to create an economic autarchy which, by making them as nearly self-sufficient as possible, would insulate them against the stresses of the international exchange. They did not try to conduct their affairs on two planes but brought every part of their society – political, economic, financial – down to one plane. They thus secured a cohesion of purpose and a single-mindedness of policy which the democracies, wavering between two conceptions of world society, did not possess. The dictatorships saw where they were going. The democracies were like men with a bad squint. They rarely focused both eyes on the same objective at the same time.

This confusion and debility of purpose, this unwillingness to consider the long-term consequences of political and economic acts, runs through all the interwar policies of the major democracies. It explains the failure of the United States to adapt itself to the responsibilities brought by its postwar position as an international lender, and its unwillingness to accept trading policies which would allow its debtors to keep solvent. It explains the failure of the British Government to comprehend, until industrial disorganization and loss of export markets demonstrated them, the economic consequences, national and international, of its return to the gold standard at too high a level in 1925 for reasons of banking prestige. It explains its failure to appreciate until too late the extent to which international economic policies, by producing a serious shrinkage of world markets, drove Japan to her war of expansion in Manchuria, and of how substantially the Ottawa agreements, by closing valuable colonial markets to Japanese goods, still further stimulated the drive for military conquest. And it explains the failure of the Allied Governments to understand until too late either the economic consequences of the Versailles Treaty or the political effects on Germany and Middle Europe of the economic depression of the late 'twenties and 'thirties and to evolve any political programme to mitigate these consequences. The treaty-makers at Versailles forgot economics. The statesmen of the post-Versailles period forgot that economic policies have political as well as economic consequences, international as well as national effects.

Moreover the League of Nations, which was to have been the framework of the new international order, suffered from the beginning from the fact that its architects were statesmen of nations and classes to whose advantage it was that the world should remain very much as it was. Because their internationalist ideals were imposed, not very firmly, upon nationalist conceptions, and because they represented the nations they did, they planned for a static, not a dynamic, society.

Foreign policy is always an extension and expression of home policy. The men who made peace in 1918 were concerned with avoiding social upheaval at home. Some of them were mild reformists. They wanted to be good so long as it did not cost too much. But they did not want a new order of society and were hagridden by the fear of socialist revolution to such a degree that again and again it blinded them to the much more pressing danger of fascism.

Their conception of the new world which the League of Nations was to help bring into being was similar to that of the domestic society they wished painlessly to evolve. It was to be a just world – if justice means only the absence of violence. It was to be a stable world – if stability means only the prevention of change. It was to be a world of international law – if international law has nothing to do with the resignation of national sovereignty when it conflicts with the requirements of world order.

Internationalist aspirations and nationalist convictions of a mutually incompatible kind were thus driven in tandem. And since nationalist convictions went deepest it was the international aspirations that suffered when the incompatibility was made manifest by events.

In no country was this confusion of aim more pronounced than in
Britain, a country peculiarly addicted to mixed motives and to the
attempt to combine moral ideals with practical expediency. Public
support of the ideal of an international world was mixed up with
policies, political, economic and financial, as insoluble with it as oil
with water.

The two MacDonald Governments were, it is true, vaguely – and
sometimes even positively – international in political outlook. As
representatives of a movement of social change they could hardly help
being receptive to the conception of the League of Nations as an
instrument of international change. Nor did the idea of associating
together for collective security seem strange to those who had long
been used to practising it in their trade union organizations. But they
did not understand enough economics to see how closely economic
and political action were related, and were too afraid of being thought
wild men to go very far in promoting either national or international
change – even if they had had the power. The Conservatives, although
polite to the League so long as politeness was the fashion, never seriously
considered it as a positive instrument of international policy because
apart from a few eccentrics they were not interested in trying to
organize a new world order. Their concern was to prevent radical
change whether at home or abroad. What they most wanted, in fact
is something that it is impossible ever to secure – a static world. They
were sincerely anxious to avoid war. The senseless mass slaughter of
1914-18 had knocked all the romance out of fighting and nauseated
every man and woman of any sensibility. In any event war is
throughly bad business for an established and satiated imperialism. But
they were equally anxious to avoid doing anything that might affect
their privileged domestic position or seem to endorse social revolution
in Russia or elsewhere. As a result successive British Governments
followed a foreign policy which combined in bewildering confusion
a wish to help the League of Nations build a New Jerusalem so long
as it did not cost anything, a strong determination to maintain the
status quo – and distrust of any alliance with Russia for any purpose
whatever.

In the decisive years from 1931 to 1939 Britain was thus prey to a
kind of diplomatic bigamy which proved peculiarly damaging to her
moral pretensions. Those in control of her policies shilly-shallied between the League of Nations and power politics without coming
firmly to rest on the breast of either. Privately disenchanted with the

League, they lacked the will to set up new combinations of power and, like businessmen on the edge of bankruptcy, scrambled through each new crisis without plan for the future, sustained only, as men in such condition often are, by bursts of unreasoning optimism.

Although opportunism on the defensive reached its climax under Chamberlain it had begun more than five years before when, convinced that no one could stop successful Japanese aggression in Manchuria and that the United States, although anxious to condemn, would be unwilling to act, the National Government decided that British financial and commercial interests in Singapore required the 'major postulate' of Far Eastern policy to be 'the maintenance of really cordial relations with Japan' with an attempt to reach solutions through the League very much 'a secondary function'. By October 1935 when Italian troops invaded Abyssinia it had been adopted as settled official policy, only to be hurriedly, if temporarily, dropped in favour of moral indignation when questions began to be asked about the purpose of Britain's membership of the League of Nations: questions which so surprised Baldwin that he confessed he had not been expecting 'that deeper feeling manifested by many of my hon. friends and friends in many parts of the country on what I may call the grounds of conscience and honour'. The outcome was the reluctant imposition of economic sanctions insufficient to prevent, or even seriously hamper, Italy's aggressive purpose but onerous enough to convince her that Britain was primarily inspired by jealousy of her claim to be a Great Power: a policy of hypocrisy restrained by fear.

Forgetting Canning's maxim that the worst kind of diplomacy is uncertain diplomacy and that the foundation of successful power politics is that, on the rare occasions when intervention is undertaken, it shall be undertaken with overwhelming force, Britain thus embarked on a policy capable of bringing her neither advantage nor honour. One of its more bizarre accompaniments was a whispering campaign that Mussolini had gone mad and if provoked might lead a suicide air squadron to bomb the British Mediterranean Fleet, whose presence in a place of danger was, it now appeared, to be regarded as a liability and not, as had previously been supposed, a substantial asset.

When Neville Chamberlain presented the world with the judgment that sanctions were 'midsummer madness', the *Berliner Tageblatt* had no difficulty in pointing the moral for National Socialists: 'Whoever is ready to stake his existence has still today a great advantage over somebody much stronger than himself who is not yet ready to risk his life.' Nor did Hitler delay in acting on it. Even before Mussolini had completed his Abyssinian conquest, German troops marched into the Rhineland. At this stage they could easily have been compelled to withdraw as France wished. They were allowed to remain because remorse for the Treaty of Versailles had the British by the throat. Determined to think the best of Germany in order to make up for having thought the worst of her, they were not interested in the warning of Germany's military ambitions provided by the Rhineland adventure. Yet even before the march into the Rhineland the nature of these ambitions had become clear. It was not, for example, difficult to discover from official statistics still available that Hitler had spent in the neighbourhood of £1,140,000,000 on armaments in the previous three years and was by now spending at the rate of well over £500,000,000 a year. I myself published one such estimate. It was quoted by Winston Churchill in the House of Commons. But it had no noticeable effect on public opinion and still less on Baldwin, whose policy it was to swim with the tide, slowly, with a great appearance of good humour, and on his back.

The uncertain purpose of British diplomacy was made even plainer during the Spanish Civil War. An uneasy feeling that a democratically elected government of liberal character ought to be helped to resist a military coup clashed head on with the fear of Communism and the desire to avoid another quarrel with Italy, to produce a policy that made Fascist victory certain and offered the German and Italian dictators an attractive dress rehearsal for future world war.

This sequence of Japanese aggression in Manchuria, Italian aggression in Abyssinia, German occupation in the Rhineland and Italian-German intervention in Spain as Britain alternated between shaking her fists and wringing her hands, could not help but consolidate Hitler's confidence in the policy of aggression he had already laid down in *Mein Kampf*.

It was in such an atmosphere and as the willing inheritor of a policy which as the strongest member of the MacDonald and Baldwin national administrations he had done much to formulate that Chamberlain became Prime Minister in May 1937.

4. *The Age of the Old Men*

THIS was the age of old men. Baldwin at seventy handed over to Chamberlain less than three years younger. Not since 1905 had so old a resident arrived at 10 Downing Street for the first time. He was in every aspect of his character a Victorian: 'In small things and great', to quote one of the most sympathetic of his biographers, Iain Macleod, 'very much a product of the years in which he grew to manhood. The fastidiousness and formality of his dress recalled his father and his father's day but so did the cast of his mind.'

His step-brother Austen had died a few months before, his last years spent, in Lord Vansittart's phrase, 'in straits and a small flat', from which he emerged for luncheon with his friends 'immaculate in frayed white shirt and shiny tail coat'. The ugly duckling had outstripped both father and favourite son. Now he entered into his kingdom with the confident aplomb of one who takes over an estate long due to him. Five years before he had written to Hilda, 'It amuses me to find a new policy for each of my colleagues in turn', and a year or two after that, 'I am more and more carrying the Government on my back.' 'I have', he confided, 'become a sort of acting P.M. – only without the actual power of the P.M.'

Now the power was his to do as he liked with. The provincial Lord Mayor who had entered the House of Commons loathing 'the drudgery, the humiliation, the meanness and pettiness' of the life he felt compelled to undertake in order to rehabilitate himself, and who had asked, 'How can a man of nearly fifty entering the House with this stigma upon him hope to achieve anything?' had risen to the chief place and had the destiny of the nation, and indeed in large measure of the world, in his hands.

In political terms his success was merited. He had worked hard. Combining the office of Chancellor of the Exchequer with that of Chairman of the Conservative Research Department – the Party's thinking machine – he had brought influence to bear on every aspect of policy, and served his Party well. To do him justice he had seldom, like Baldwin, closed his eyes to ugly facts. In so far as the Government had a defence policy it was his. His hand had largely drafted the Defence White Paper of 1936. It was largely his initiative that had produced a Ministry for the Co-ordination of Defence, although significantly when it came to choosing a Minister he had black-balled Winston Churchill on the grounds that he had a European reputation which would make it dangerous to add him to the Cabinet at a critical moment and had instead backed Inskip. 'He would', he said, 'excite no enthusiasm but he would involve us in no fresh perplexities.' Nor did he, as Baldwin seemed to do, try to close his eyes to the nature of

Hitlerism. He had 'loathed Germans' since before the Boer War; Nazi Germany, he considered, was again 'instigating, suggesting, encouraging bloodshed and assassination for her own selfish aggrandizement and pride'.

Such a man, practical, competent, given to action rather than thought, sedulous in the reading of reports and firm in decision, might have seemed ideally suited to respond to the dangers that faced his country and the world. In fact by temperament and attitude, and by those flaws of character which it is not illogical to see as deriving from the forces that had shaped him in early youth and manhood, he was as unsuited for the tasks before him as a man could well be. Although energetic in the conduct of Cabinet business he regarded his minsters not as joint architects of policy but as executive officers called together from time to time to report what they were doing and receive their instructions. He expected them to have ideas on administration but to accept implicitly his authority on general policy, and he had the obstinacy and the egotism which is to be found in many men who have controlled successful private businesses and have been used to working with subordinates whose economic dependence makes them unlikely to criticize the policy decisions of the man who controls the purse-strings. He determined his foreign policy himself by the light of values he had followed at the Treasury.

Because he was the son of Joseph Chamberlain, and because he more than anyone else killed British free trade, he is sometimes thought of as an imperialist. But he was not an imperialist in any dynamic sense of that word. He was a businessman and as such, contrary to Marxist conceptions of capitalism, was anxious above all else to avoid war which disorganizes markets and disrupts orderly trade expansion. In the past, it is true, wars had sometimes been fought to secure control of markets. But Britain and the interests in Britain Chamberlain represented had long outgrown that stage of capitalist imperialism. For them peace and the opportunity to consolidate and improve their favoured position by legitimate methods of commerce was the natural objective of foreign policy. They were old enough, established enough, experienced enough, to know that in the usual run of things more can be secured by bargaining than by fighting.

As a product of that class and that attitude of mind Chamberlain saw the problem of meeting Nazi aggression in the same terms as negotiating an agreement in industry. It was by no accident that he chose Sir Horace Wilson, the Industrial Adviser to the Government, whom he had first learnt to value as a lieutenant in the Ottawa trade talks, as his chief companion and consultant in international diplomacy. He thought of diplomatic negotiations with Hitler as a combination of discussions with a business competitor who, though not the sort of person one would invite to one's house, could, with patience and compromise, be brought to see that a sales agreement was better than cut-throat competition, and negotiations with dissatisfied trade union-ists threatening a strike but glad to talk round a table if their employers would meet them part way. Sir Horace Wilson who had smoothed out many industrial difficulties in his time was the obvious man to help – and unlikely to upset his Chairman's vanity by too inconvenient a knowledge of international history.

And so these two innocents set out on the journey that was to lead to Munich and from Munich to war. They were anxious, almost obsessively so, about the weaknesses in the British and French military positions, less ready to consider evidence of Germany's, almost wholly uninterested in the forces of world conscience. Like Stalin when he asked how many divisions the Pope deployed Chamberlain did not believe in intangibles. During the years of appeasement he was to do many things that seemed to a large number of his fellow-countrymen unjust and dishonourable. But he was never conscious of sin.

As a private citizen he deplored the beastliness and cruelty of the Nazi régime. But so long as there was a possibility of coming to what he considered a legitimate arrangement with this régime he did not allow its crimes to concern him. When one is anxious to come to a business arrangement with a troublesome competitor one cannot set oneself up as a judge of his moral standards or of the way he treats his employees. It is best to avoid knowledge of such matters.

This was less difficult for him than for many others because he possessed to a high degree the insular British inability to think of foreigners as human beings. His references to the Japanese war against China, which he saw always in terms of its effect on British business interests in the East rather than those of the sufferings of the Chinese people, to the Spanish Civil War, and to the people of Czechoslovakia on the eve of Munich, the startling detachment of his mood when he informed the House of Commons of the seizure of Prague, all these indicated a congenital incapacity for warmth and sympathy towards men and women of distant nations. The cry of the hurt and the defeated produced in him none of the quick response that gives fire and warmth to statesmanship.

Certainly at no time was he affected in his policy by the knowledge of the Nazi attitude to the civilized virtues of kindness and common human decency. He was aware of the loathsome facts later published in the White Paper on the treatment of German Nationals. These facts were not new. Many of them were published in British newspapers – and Chamberlain, unlike Baldwin, was a constant newspaper reader. But they awoke no passion of hatred against cruelty and injustice in his soul. He was concerned not with sentiment but with business.

Yet it is amazing that if they did not touch his heart they rang no warning bell in his mind. The policy of appeasement was a business man's policy of seeking to come to an arrangement. But negotiations undertaken with a business competitor rest on the assumption that he will, if assured that they will be advanced by agreement, make an agreement.

Deeply suspicious of Soviet Communism for this very reason of disparity of interests and very conscious that the moral values of Stalin had no conjunction with those of a Unitarian businessman he recoiled from a Soviet alliance. Perhaps he was right to do so. But he did not recoil from a Nazi alliance. He sought it avidly. He could not bring himself to sup with the Communist devil but invited the Nazi one to dinner.

Indeed throughout his policy of appeasement he showed hardly any conception of the wide gulf between the standards of Hitler and a respectable businessman or British trade unionist.

Precisely because of his disinterestedness in political principles, he was incapable of understanding the true nature of the forces with which he was trying to deal. He suffered, of course, from the natural disadvantage of any civilized man in trying to negotiate with those who have put the values of civilization aside. But the civilized man is not necessarily incapacitated from recognizing roguery when he meets it. The startling fact is that again and again the British Prime Minister seemed incapable of appreciating that he was dealing with barbarians because his own lack of understanding of the political purposes, the human ideals, the loyalty to abstract causes, out of which civilization has grown, was so inadequate. Because he himself had little interest in political philosophy he failed to recognize in National Socialism a philosophy wholly antagonistic to his own comfortable materialism. Like any simple Marxist he saw in it no more than a new form of capitalism. He thought it after the same sort of things as himself and

WOULD YOU OBLIGE ME WITH A MATCH PLEASE?

Evening Standard, 25 February 1938

as such open to compromise. He knew little of 'world theories' but was obsessed by a distrust of Russia, fearing Stalinism not so much for the good reason that it was an oppressor of human liberty – for such considerations did not in his mind rule out the possibility of friendly arrangements with the Fascism of Germany and Italy, or affect the benevolence of his attitude towards General Franco – as for the bad one that it was against private enterprise economy, whereas he could persuade himself that Fascism was not.

His inability to comprehend the moral nature of the forces he was up against might not have mattered so much if he had been open to advice, or had ever allowed himself to be touched by self doubt. But neither of these would his nature permit. He prepared to repeat on a world scale the disastrous patterns of Andros and the Ministry of National Service. With the same obstinate confidence as then in his own judgment and a similarly implacable concentration on the practical task at hand, he closed his mind to everything he did not want to believe and found in action an escape from thought.

In so doing, it is only fair to say, he brought to British foreign policy a consistency it had not previously had. He ended the bigamous arrangements which had for so long clouded its intentions, showed the League of Nations the door, and embraced power politics with determined if inexperienced ardour.

Unfortunately, as on the two previous occasions when, head high, he had advanced with inflexible courage on disaster, his consistency was not matched by any understanding of what he was up against. Rather he had a wilful determination not to understand.

He was Prime Minister for only three years. It was not long to achieve with so much rectitude and so high-minded a devotion to duty so complete a subservience of the true interests of his nation and Western civilization to the ambitions of a half-mad dictator. But the tone was set early. Before he had been at Downing Street a year he was publicly asking 'What country in Europe if threatened by a larger one can rely upon the League of Nations to give it protection?' and answering 'None'. It thus came as no surprise when Hitler proved him right and invaded Austria four days later, securing without the loss of a single man territory whose independence the League had pledged itself to protect. Yet when Russia asked that in the light of this evidence of the League's incapacity there should be immediate Anglo-French-Soviet talks on joint resistance to any future aggression he replied that they would be 'inopportune'.

It was an oddly chosen word, for if the League still had any place in future arrangements it was obviously desirable to determine the role of the great powers in its affairs and restore, if possible, the morale of those small but strategically important countries who had been badly shaken by seeing what could happen to one of their number. If power politics was the choice, then there was no less advantage in seeking a clear understanding between Britain, France and Russia and much to be gained by doing so when Russia felt her own interests threatened by the German advance to the borders of Czechoslovakia, with which, like France, she was in alliance. But though Chamberlain saw the weaknesses of the League – how should he not: he had helped to produce them – he could not bring himself to think in terms of a power bloc that included Russia, as Churchill, for example, though no less anti-Communist than he, was ready to do in face of the more immediate threat of German ambitions.

The Austrian coup strengthened Germany both militarily and financially. It increased her reserves of manpower for military purposes by ten per cent and brought vast additions to her reserves of raw materials and money. But he persuaded himself that this might be an advantage in the long run. Mussolini, for whose sake he had by then already got rid of his Foreign Secretary, Anthony Eden, could scarcely, he thought, face with equanimity the presence of German troops on the Brenner. It would therefore now be easier to divide Italy from Germany. More disastrously still, he persuaded himself that by satisfying some of Hitler's ambitions the annexation of Austria would make him more willing to renounce others: for a Shakespearean scholar he showed surprisingly little understanding of the nature of vaulting ambition.

He had by now so convinced himself of the unassailable correctness of his own and Sir Horace Wilson's innocent view of the world that he would not recognize any fact that ran counter to it. The sisal would grow because he wanted it to – to think otherwise was to betray the most fundamental need of his character. When unpleasant facts forced themselves upon even his consciousness he became irritated by them. Thus when Hitler, pursuing a technique increasingly familiar, turned from Austria to Czechoslovakia and promoted trouble in the Sudeten area, his reaction was that what happened in this distant land on the other side of Europe was no concern of Britain's. For the Czechs themselves he could, as for the Austrians, find no sympathy. They made irritating spots on the glass of the binoculars through which he viewed with such pleasure the distant prospects of Anglo-German rapprochement.

In this instance French pressure compelled him to affirm publicly the solidarity of Britain and France and their common interest in the peace of Europe and to declare that 'if war broke out it would be impossible to say where it would end'. But he was an honest man. He could not long pretend what he did not feel. Any effect his public declaration may have had on German ambitions was dissipated when he informed newspaper correspondents at a private lunch at which he was the chief guest that in his opinion neither France nor Russia would be prepared to go to war over Czechoslovakia. Although not published in the British press this observation could scarcely be kept secret. It became an immediate topic of speculation in diplomatic and newspaper circles and was naturally communicated to Berlin, whereupon Hitler moved troops to the Czech border; whether as a preparation for invasion or, as was later claimed, a normal part of manœuvres, was not clear. Probably though not yet committed to war Hitler was concerned to be in a position to take advantage of any opportunity British policy might open to him.

In the event a partial mobilization by the Czechs, who called up reservists and manned frontier posts, and a French declaration that, 'If Germany crosses the Czechoslovak border that will automatically start war and France will help to the uttermost', persuaded Hitler that it might be prudent to wait a little longer. He was, as A. J. P. Taylor has pointed out, an opportunist of aggression. He knew what he wanted but not yet whether he could get it at a price he could pay. As the evidence now available from German sources shows it is incorrect to assume that every detail of his policy was planned in advance and irrevocable. He was still probing. The major part of the responsibility for the war that lay ahead was to be his. But it was not his only. His was the ambition. But the activation came from the opportunities offered him by the misjudgments and irresolution of others. Among them Chamberlain must be numbered high.

To Chamberlain at this stage the obstinacy of Daladier and the readiness of the Czechs to fight alike seemed an intolerable interference with his plans. The day after the call-up of Czech reservists, Sir Nevile Henderson, the nervous British Ambassador in Berlin, assured Ribbentrop: 'We should only have patience and I am certain that all would end well and that Germany would win all along the line. If only this Sudeten German problem were shifted out of the way conversations would then be continued on all subjects.' Two days later Henderson communicated to Ribbentrop the contents of a telegram from Eden's successor as Foreign Secretary, Lord Halifax, urging calmness and declaring, 'We should not let it [the Czech situation] get out of hand for then the only ones to profit would be the Communists.' Indeed Chamberlain's main interest, as was made clear by various inter-mediaries, was to find a means of helping Germany to satisfy her Sudeten demands so that this minor obstacle, as he felt it, to the agree-ment he had set himself so blindly and so stubbornly to secure, could be swept away.

He had nothing but contempt for those who allowed emotions of humanity to influence their attitude towards German ambitions. When Lord Woolton, then head of Lewis's, the departmental chain store, felt impelled after the annexation of Austria to make 'the small protest that a private citizen could' against Nazi policy and instructed his buyers in Germany 'to close their books, honourably to fulfil all their contracts and to return home', he was summoned to 10 Downing Street to be told by Sir Horace Wilson of Chamberlain's 'strong dis-approval' of such a boycott, and sharply informed that he had 'no right to interfere in this manner in the foreign policy of the country'. Newspaper editors, the present writer among them, were under constant official pressure on themselves and their publishers – fortun-ately for the most part resisted – to tone down comments on Nazi policy and abstain from publishing cartoons or articles that Hitler might not like.

But when pressed to inform the Prime Minister of the exact extent of his claims Hitler remained reticent: he had everything to gain from leaving Chamberlain in a state of mind that allowed Germany to probe deeper and deeper into the weaknesses of those who stood in the path of his ambitions. Nor is it to be wondered at that he was lavish in private assurances of friendliness to Britain, having seen how patheti-cally eager to be deceived Chamberlain was.

In June he sent his aide-de-camp, Captain Wiedemann, to London to help on the process. Wiedemann had the happiness of two long talks with Chamberlain and Halifax. In the course of these, according to his own account – although he may have gilded the lily a little – Halifax assured him that 'he would like to see, as the culmination of his work, the Führer entering London at the side of the English King, amid the acclamation of the English people'. For his own part Wiede-mann assured his English hosts of Hitler's firm desire for friendship with Britain, his willingness to negotiate an air pact between the two countries and his readiness to be good for ever after if only allowed to have his way in Czechoslovakia. Glowing with the combined optimism of his leader and himself Halifax took advantage of a State visit to Paris by the King and Queen to convey, in a suitably cordial atmosphere, the good news to the more sceptical French, and to urge them to persuade their Allies, the Czechs, to make concessions to Germany.

No feeling for democratic principle, no sympathy for the Czech people, no appreciation of the moral case for supporting a small, highly civilized country in its opposition to dictation from a powerful and brutal neighbour, seem to have stirred Chamberlain at this time. It was not that he was incapable of such emotions. But his view was entirely concentrated on an arrangement with Germany. Nothing that might weaken this concentration was permitted to obtrude. If human charity interfered it had to be dismissed from audience. No doubt this seemed to him one of those cases where if a small firm got in the way of two big ones it had no one to blame but itself for what happened to it. And since it was a matter of business he decided to send a business-man to settle it. So off to Prague went Lord Runciman, whose capacities as a wealthy and able business negotiator were recognized by all, although his qualities as a statesman did not receive such universal endorsement.

He went as a 'mediator'. Chamberlain had originally tried to get the Czechs to accept him as an arbitrator but this with the support of the French they had rejected. Nevertheless, with that strange disregard for the strict letter of the truth which at this time only too frequently distinguished Chamberlain's public utterances despite his high standards of personal honesty – a distinction between public and private morality not infrequently to be found in men grown fanatical in their belief in their own rightness – he contrived to put a misleading gloss on the situation by declaring that Runciman was going 'in response to a request from the Government of Czechoslovakia', although in fact the Czechoslovakian Government had only agreed under duress.

It is typical also of the state of mind into which Chamberlain had by now persuaded himself that the decision to send Lord Runciman to 'mediate' having been made, he at once assumed that this unfortunate business was as good as settled. This at any rate can be his only justification for telling the House of Commons: 'The atmosphere is lighter. Throughout the Continent there is a relaxation of the sense of tension which three months ago was present.'

With this completely baseless interpretation of the situation to hearten it the British public turned its mind to thoughts of holiday, oblivious of the massing of German troops along the southern, western and northern frontiers of Czechoslovakia which continued throughout July and August.

Only if the extent to which public opinion was misled that summer by official optimism is appreciated can the popular reaction to Munich be properly understood. The crisis of September 1938 came to the British public, if not out of a clear sky, at least out of one whose half-light they had been led to believe was that of the dawn. With Chamberlain's unfounded confidence as its guide the great mass of the Government press – *The Observer* under J. L. Garvin and the *Yorkshire Post* under Arthur Mann were honourable exceptions – felt entitled to be optimistic, although none of the others went so far as Lord Beaverbrook's *Daily Express*, which in a daily exhortation to cheerfulness informed its readers: 'There will be no war this year or next year either.' The great advertising concerns, which had a vested interest in optimism, brought their influence to bear to persuade others to take a similar view. No doubt they had convinced themselves, as men are apt to do, that what best served their interests must also be true. To tell the truth about the international situation in the press, as some insisted on doing, was not only unpopular: it was felt to be rather disgraceful.

It was into this hotchpotch of optimism that the September crisis burst with calamitous effect upon public morale.

Lord Runciman, the businessman mediator, had laboured conscientiously in Prague. By the end of August he had succeeded in persuading the Czechoslovak Government to concede practically all the demands made by Hitler's mouthpiece Henlein, leader of the Sudeten German National Socialists. These demands went much further than justice to a minority group required. But at least agreement to them opened the possibility of a compromise settlement that would leave Czechoslovakian independence, although impaired, not mortally affected. If there had been any basis for the confidence Chamberlain had expressed in Hitler's intentions the agreement would have been accepted. But of course it was not. Any doubts Hitler may have had as to his ability to get more were removed by a leading article in *The Times*, whose editor, Geoffrey Dawson, was known to be one of Chamberlain's most intimate supporters. It argued that the local self-government proposed for the Sudeten Germans under the Runciman Plan did not go far enough, and that the Czech Government might be better advised to cede to Germany the whole of the Sudeten area. This meant, in effect, that she should not only give up large areas of territory, but abandon also her carefully prepared frontier fortifications. The effect of the leader was immediate. A number of incidents were provoked on the Czech-German frontier and five days later in a violent speech at Nuremberg Hitler denounced President Beneš and the Czech nation in terms which made clear both his determination to crush Czechoslovakia and his confidence that he could do so without hindrance from outside.

The *Times* leader was not directly inspired by Chamberlain, though most of the world assumed that it had been, including the Czechs themselves. I myself well remember the reaction of a group of Czech trade union leaders, who had flown to England as unofficial emissaries of their Government to take advantage of the annual Trade Union Congress at Blackpool for urgent talks with Labour and trade union leaders at which I was also present as the then Editor of the *Daily Herald*. I was able to assure them after a call to the Foreign Office that the Foreign Office knew nothing of the *Times* leader before its publication and proposed publicly to disassociate itself from its terms. They remained unconvinced. They were aware, as everyone else by now was, that one of the most significant features of British policy as then organized was that the Prime Minister had ceased to consult senior officials of the Foreign Office or even inform them of his private negotiations. The Foreign Office might be surprised and shocked by what *The Times* suggested. But this no longer had relevance. The Czech trade union leaders replied sombrely: 'Mr Chamberlain has made up his mind. This means war. A war in which Czechoslovakia will be required to fight alone. But do not doubt that we will fight.'

In fact Geoffrey Dawson had composed his notorious leading article after returning to Printing House Square from a month's holiday at Langcliffe Hall, Settle, Yorkshire, which he had inherited from an aunt. Here he liked to play the local squire and join shooting parties with his friend and not very distant neighbour, Lord Halifax. But if not written after direct consultation it was composed with a full knowledge of Chamberlain's general attitude and that of Halifax, his loyal hench-man, and it was soon to be shown to represent this very faithfully. Indeed on the very morning that it appeared Dawson was able to record in his diary, as quoted by Evelyn Wrench in his memorial volume, *Geoffrey Dawson and our Times*: 'There was a hubbub as I fully expected, over the morning's leader – reactions in Prague and Berlin, and the Foreign Office went up through the roof – Not so, however, the Foreign Secretary who came and lunched with me at the Travellers' and had a long talk.'

In fact the decision to compel the Czechs to dismember their country if Hitler so desired and if it seemed helpful to an Anglo-German Agreement had been brewing for some time. In early August Crolla, the Counsellor of the Italian Embassy in London, had been in a position to advise a German newspaper friend with whom he discussed the Czech crisis that 'Great Britain was prepared for any solution by peaceful methods', and a week later Horace Wilson was assuring a member of the German Embassy, Theo Kordt, that he would 'see to it that the British Government was prepared for the time when Runciman's Mission might fail'. When Kordt informed him that Hitler would not agree to a solution that left the Czechoslovak State intact, Wilson replied blandly that 'if we two, Great Britain and Germany, can come to an agreement regarding the settlement of the Czech problem we should simply brush aside the resistance that France or Czechoslovakia herself may offer to the decision'.

There was nothing, therefore, to surprise or disconcert Chamberlain in the *Times* leader – or in Hitler's reaction to it. It was otherwise with the British people. To them it seemed as though the smoke screen of official optimism behind which they and Parliament had been sent off on their summer holidays had been dispersed by a lightning flash of war. Shocked and frightened – though not yet so frightened as they were later to become – by this inexplicable change in the international temperature, they received with relief and delight the news that the Prime Minister had decided to fly to Berchtesgaden to confront Hitler personally. He had never flown before. That at the age of nearly seventy he should be ready to fly for the first time filled the sentimental British with admiration. As he left from Heston with his umbrella and Sir Horace Wilson they felt that this tough and resolute old man must be worthy of their trust and would justify it. They believed his purpose was to force Hitler to realize that if he attacked Czechoslovakia Britain would defend her. Indeed he had already privately assured the leaders of the Opposition of his intention to do so when advising them of his decision to go to Berchtesgaden. This was in keeping with the mood of most of the British people. The National Executive of the Labour Party and the General Council of the T.U.C. – both carrying a heavy load of responsibility for the degree to which their opposition to defence expenditure had given the Government an excuse for appeasement – had just issued a joint declaration from Blackpool calling on the British Government 'to leave no doubt in the mind of the German Government that they will unite with the French and Soviet Governments to resist any attack on Czechoslovakia'. In so doing they had expressed an attitude that by now went far beyond their own members or that minority in the Conservative party headed by Winston Churchill who had for so long, so brilliantly, and so un-availingly sought to rouse Conservative and national opinion to the dangers of appeasement.

None of this had importance to Chamberlain. He was beyond influence or advice: a prudent and honourable man driven by the compulsive force of his profound egotism to set aside both honour and prudence in pursuit of a policy that had long since lost touch with reality.

Three years before, Sir Robert Vansittart, then still Permanent Under-Secretary at the Foreign Office, had written to King George V in response to a request for his opinion as to whether there was any possibility of a firm understanding with Nazi Germany. He had ex-pressed his firm conviction that it was quite unprofitable 'to undertake any serious attempt for an agreement with Germany until our own national re-equipment is under way', and had then gone on to say: 'Any attempt at giving Germany a free hand to annex other people's property in Central or Eastern Europe is both absolutely immoral and completely contrary to all the principles of the League which form the background of the policy of this country. Any British Government that attempted to do a deal would almost certainly be brought down in ignominy – and deservedly.' It was on such a course that Chamberlain was now set.

It is probable that even yet he did not realize where it would lead him. He had an infinite capacity for self-deception. Just as he had convinced himself when Director of National Service that the Service Departments who were bent on his destruction were on his side so now he was confident that a private talk between Hitler and himself would remove all difficulties. He had allowed himself to be driven by ignorance and obstinacy to a policy which although originally well intentioned was no longer justified either by morality or expediency. He would not turn back.

Nor was he prepared even to play the cards others put into his hands. At the beginning of September, a fortnight before the flight to Berch-tesgaden, Ernst Weizsäcker, State Secretary of the German Foreign

Ministry, went privately to see Burckhardt, the League Commissioner in Danzig, then in Berlin. He advised him in the strictest confidence that Hitler planned to overrun Czechoslovakia in six weeks. The only method of stopping him, he said, was for the British Prime Minister to warn him in the strongest terms that 'if an attack were made by Germany on Czechoslovakia a war would start in which Great Britain would inevitably be on the opposite side to Germany'. This Weizsäcker did, at obvious risk to himself, as a German patriot acting for military, official and business groups in Germany who were appalled by the course Hitler was taking. He asked Burckhardt to act as their intermediary with the British Government. Burchkardt accepted the commission and drove 900 kilometres to Berne to see the British Minister there, George Warner, whom he knew well and felt he could safely confide in. That evening Warner transmitted Weizsäcker's message to Halifax. Its arrival coincided with a visit to Halifax and Horace Wilson from Theo Kordt, the German Chargé d'Affaires in London, on a similar errand 'as spokesman of political and military circles in Berlin who desire by every means to prevent war ... and who see no other way out of the dilemma except in close cooperation with the British Government'. The démarche from the Prime Minister could not, declared Kordt, 'be too unequivocal and firm for the purpose in question'. Similar confidential appeals for firm British action were reaching London newspapers, including my own, from German businessmen and prominent officials in Berlin, Cologne and other German cities. They were at once passed on to the Foreign Office and provided evidence of an impressive kind of the weakness of Hitler's position in relation to his own military, Civil Service and commercial interests.

In the light of this knowledge Halifax finally brought himself to draft a strongly worded memorandum on the consequences of aggression against Czechoslovakia. It was transmitted to Nevile Henderson to pass to Hitler before the Nuremberg rally. But when Henderson, who was already at Nuremberg with Hitler and in a highly hysterical state, urged that he should not be required to deliver it because it might annoy the German leader, Chamberlain at once agreed. At a Cabinet meeting called, apparently deliberately, too late to do anything before Hitler delivered his Nuremberg speech, he told his colleagues that it was vital that Britain should do nothing to upset Hitler on the eve of an important utterance. The warning was therefore never delivered. Nor did Chamberlain take any advantage of this insight into

Germany's internal situation when he met Hitler at Berchtesgaden. He was not much impressed by Hitler when he met him. 'The commonest little dog', he told the Cabinet when he returned, and to his sister Ida in one of those long family letters he always found time to write, however pressing the demands of State business, he observed loftily, 'You would take him for the house painter he once was.' However, business was business and he returned confident that he had impressed the common little dog and had him where he wanted him. He told the French that he was convinced 'he would be better rather than worse than his word', and to his sisters wrote: 'I got the impression that here was a man who could be relied upon when he had given his word.' It was to prove a disastrous misjudgment.

Even if Hitler had been ready to stick to his word there could be no doubt left in anyone's mind that he was out to end the existence of Czechoslovakia as a viable independent state. To Chamberlain this was a small price to pay for his goodwill; he returned to London with renewed optimism. Yet Hitler had not only demanded that Czechoslovakia should be required to end her military alliance with Russia, which 'threatened' him, but after a long harangue on racial unity and his success in 'incorporating' the Austrian people into the Reich, had stated that the three million Sudeten Germans must similarly be 'incorporated' and all other minorities in Czechoslovakia likewise allowed to secede. This, he declared according to the British version of the talks, would leave Czechoslovakia so small that 'he would not bother his head about it', according to the official German version, in such a position that 'it would in any event cease to exist after a time'.

With this Chamberlain returned to London convinced – despite the strong evidence in his possession of the opposition to Hitler's policy in Germany itself – that 'with the German troops in the positions they then occupied there was nothing that anybody could do that would prevent that invasion unless the right of self-determination were granted to the Sudeten Germans and that quickly'. The Czechs must be told to submit. Yet at this time the Germans had only forty divisions, one armoured, while the Czechs alone had thirty-six, four armoured. The French had eighty-two against which Hitler immediately was in a position to send only two to defend his Western frontier with another two to follow. The French were less easy to convince than the British Prime Minister. It took Chamberlain six hours to bring them to a proper state of mind. But, resolute in argument with his friends if not his enemies, he succeeded. At two o'clock the following morning Dr Beneš was dragged from his bed by the British and French Ministers in Prague to be told that unless his Government accepted Germany's demands immediately Britain and France would leave his country to its fate. Before a pressure Beneš correctly described as 'unprecedented in history' Czechoslovakia, perhaps unwisely, capitulated. Hitler's war of nerves had paid off. He had judged his man correctly.

It is interesting to conjecture what would have happened if when Hitler delivered his ultimatum at Berchtesgaden Chamberlain, instead of accepting it and returning proudly to London with the minor concession that Hitler would not act until there had been an opportunity to inform the French and the Czechs, had announced that in that case he proposed to fly not to London but to Moscow to concert Anglo-French and Soviet strategy. The Russians were still pressing for joint action. They might not have been prepared to implement their words which may have been only propaganda. No one can be sure. But in view of the weighty opposition to Hitler inside Germany (one of his Generals, Beck, had as Chamberlain knew from Foreign Office telegrams, actually already resigned rather than carry out orders for an attack on a friendly State), might not such a warning even at this late stage have been effective?

But Chamberlain was not interested in such a possibility. He preferred to sacrifice Czechoslovakian national integrity rather than save it with Russian aid. He was concerned only to see that what Hitler required was done, confident that, if it were, this man 'who could be relied upon when he had given his word' would be only too flattered to fall in with his own plans for an Anglo-German Agreement. After all, had he not said, or so it was tactfully reported, that he had been 'much impressed' by Chamberlain himself, an indication surely that the 'common little dog' was not wholly lacking in judgment.

The French persuaded and the Czechs intimidated, Chamberlain prepared to fly back to Germany – this time to Bad Godesberg with the faithful Horace Wilson and Strang and Malkin of the Foreign Office to accompany him. Geoffrey Dawson of *The Times*, whose leading article had so faithfully reflected the shape of things to come, saw him off at the airport: 'I think he was glad to see me', Dawson wrote in his diary, 'and was very appreciative of the support of *The Times*.'

It is clear that Chamberlain was still far from understanding – one suspects because he did not wish to understand – the nature of the man he was negotiating with. He expected thanks. He got abuse, confessing later that the situation placed him 'in some perplexity'. Reinforced in confidence by the course of events since the Berchtesgaden meeting, Hitler delivered another ultimatum. The Anglo-French plan, he said, was 'too dilatory'. The Czechs must now agree within a week to clear out of all the areas marked on a map by Hitler – and defined mainly for strategical and economic, not racial purposes – and hand over all military and other material including livestock within these areas without compensation.

This new ultimatum meant that not only the Sudeten German areas but also territory inhabited by more than 800,000 Czechs was to be handed over to Germany at once, and that Germany was to be given, without payment of compensation, fortifications and armaments costing over £50,000,000, and to receive, again without payment of compensation, railways and rolling stock, wireless stations, army stores and public buildings of enormous value. It meant that within a few days all those in these areas who did not wish to live under the tyranny of National Socialism must flee from their homes and take not the smallest part of their possessions; the peasant must leave his cow; the shopkeeper his goods, the ordinary family all their belonging save those they could pile hurriedly into a motor car or a hand-cart. It meant the severing of Prague from the industrial areas of Eastern Moravia and the creation of a state with no future ahead of it but economic bankruptcy and, before long, political slavery. Even Chamberlain was 'profoundly shocked'. He undertook to transmit but not recommend these terms to the Czech Government and flew back to London.

His sense of shock did not long remain. When the Cabinet met that evening he ended an hour's report, in which he told his colleagues how he had 'snorted with indignation' when he first heard Hitler's proposals, by concluding that they should accept them and advise the Czechs to do so. He then suggested that the Cabinet should adjourn. To this Duff Cooper, First Lord of the Admiralty retorted, according to his own account in *Old Men Forget*, that it appeared from what the Prime Minister had said that the Germans were still convinced that in no circumstances would Britain fight, and that there existed one method and one method only of persuading them to the contrary and that was by instantly declaring full mobilization. He added that the Chiefs of Staff had reported on the previous day that immediate mobilization was of urgent and vital importance and one day those present might have to explain why they had disregarded this advice.

This made Chamberlain angry. Duff Cooper had omitted to say, he snapped, that this advice had been given on the assumption that there was danger of war with Germany within the next few days. The retort amazed Duff Cooper, who did not see how such a danger could be denied. He then suggested that, at the very least, preliminary measures should be put in hand for the protection of the Suez Canal, one of the most vital and vulnerable of imperial links. No one, he thought, could object to this. On the contrary, said Chamberlain, he objected very strongly. 'It all depends', he added, 'on whether we can trust Hitler.' Arrived home, Duff Cooper recorded in his diary, 'I believe Hitler has cast a spell over Neville.' It is hard not to agree.

The following day Jan Masaryk, the Czechoslovak Minister in London, made known his Government's response to Hitler's terms. As was to be expected it found them absolutely and unconditionally unacceptable: 'a *de facto* ultimatum of the sort usually presented to a vanquished nation and not a proposition to a sovereign state which has shown the greatest readiness to make sacrifices for the appeasement of Europe.' To the Foreign Office this reply seemed 'premature' and efforts were made to prevent its publication. In Downing Street, Chamberlain and other Ministers met Daladier and Bonnet to discuss what should be done if Hitler refused to withdraw his ultimatum. 'Each of us,' replied Daladier, 'would have to do his duty.' This reply enraged Chamberlain and Sir John Simon, whose 'unrivalled skill at cross-examination' was, according to the account of the meeting later published by Sir Samuel Hoare, of great value to the British at this time, took over: his purpose to force the French Ministers to admit that there was no direct assistance they could give the Czechs. Daladier readily admitted it. He had, he pointed out, made it clear more than five months before that France could not send help directly to Czechoslovakia by land. But, he added, with a resolution that the British Ministers found unsympathetic and that his colleague M. Bonnet manifestly did not share, she 'could materially assist Czechoslavkia by diverting the greater part of the German Army against France' and this she would do. Under a cross-examination by Simon of a kind normally reserved for those accused in a Court of Law he finally agreed that alone France could probably do little more than hold the Maginot Line, attempt probing offensives against the Siegfried Line and make some demonstrations in the air. This admission seems to have made Chamberlain feel better: confirming him no doubt in his conviction that the price of resisting Hitler was now too high to be an acceptable business proposition and that the resolution of Daladier was no more than a piece of romantic folly for which the French people as a whole were unlikely to have any enthusiasm. And, indeed, it must in fairness be said that by now the French attitude was no less equivocal than the British. Daladier remained staunch but appeasement was gaining ground and Bonnet for one was ready to pay any price in another nation's money to buy off Hitler.

Outside, the British people prepared for a war they now assumed to be inevitable. In the parks and open spaces air raid shelter trenches were hurriedly dug all day and by the light of acetylene flares at night and long queues gathered outside schools and public buildings to receive gas masks. It was a demonstration of ill-preparedness that might have been – and in the eyes of some informed observers was – deliberately designed to undermine courage.

Inside the Cabinet, opinion, despite Chamberlain, hardened against further appeasement. Horace Wilson was despatched to Germany with a message asking that details of the transfer of Czech territory should be settled by an International Commission of Germans, British and Czechs and with instructions to warn Hitler, if he refused, that France and Britain would both fight for Czechoslovakia. He found Hitler in a bad mood and did not deliver the second part of his message, and in London Chamberlain, broadcasting to the British people, found it possible in a notorious phrase to say: 'How horrible, fantastic, incredible, it is that we should be digging trenches and trying on gas masks here because of a quarrel in a faraway country between people of whom we know nothing.' The broadcast contained no word of sympathy for Czechoslovakia, but only for Hitler whose feelings about the Sudetenland Chamberlain remarked he could well understand. It must not, he added, be thought that Britain would 'in all circumstances' be prepared to go to war on Czechoslovakia's account.

To those with political experience it was at once clear that there would be no defence of Czechoslovakia. In my own office in the *Herald* my staff had gathered to listen. As the broadcast ended I said to them, 'We are backing down.' We turned wearily to remake the paper. Nothing remained but to hope that even yet the Prime Minister would summon enough resolution to gain some concessions before the sacrifice was made.

He had, in fact, already written to Hitler to suggest a third meeting. Next day he rose in the House of Commons to recount a story of broken pledges and ultimatums, dramatically interrupted in the middle by a piece of paper passed to him by Simon who had received it from Halifax in the Peers' Gallery. He paused in his speech, read it and then turned again to the House, smiling, to say: 'That is not all. I have something further to say to the House yet. I have now been informed by Herr Hitler that he invites me to meet him at Munich tomorrow morning. He has also invited Signor Mussolini and M. Daladier. Signor Mussolini has accepted and I have no doubt M. Daldier will accept. I need not say what my answer will be.'

In the immediate relief from strain almost the entire House rose to him. The Leaders of the Labour and Liberal oppositions wished him well. They could scarcely do otherwise although Attlee insisted that peace must be secured without sacrifice of principle and Sinclair that it should give Czechoslovakia an independent life in its new frontiers – words soon to be forgotten by the Prime Minister, if ever noted.

The background for Munich had been set.

The consummation was not long in coming. Next day Chamberlain flew off from Heston, accompanied as always by the faithful Horace Wilson, and by his P.P.S. Lord Dunglass (Sir Alec Douglas-Home) and Strang and Ashton-Gwatkin of the Foreign Office. To the crowd that came to see him off, including the whole of the Cabinet, he recited the nursery rhyme, 'If at first you don't succeed, try, try again', and told them in Hotspur's words, 'Out of this nettle, danger, we pluck this flower, safety.' Arrived in Munich he, Daladier and Mussolini met Hitler. After some argument and one or two outbursts from Hitler, they agreed with business-like dispatch on terms which gave Hitler even more than he had originally demanded at Bad Godesberg, with the one improvement that the Czechs were given seven days – seven days! – to evacuate completely the areas they were required to surrender, although they were allowed only two days to withdraw from the frontier areas. Perhaps characteristically Chamberlain spent most time arguing over questions of compensation for Czech-owned property in the Sudetenland and other financial and currency questions.

The Czech Ministers who had been summoned to Munich to hear their fate were not consulted. They were not even treated with the courtesy granted to those defeated in war of being present when their fate was decided. They were allowed neither plea nor argument but put in an anteroom until their masters had finished. 'It was', said Jan Masaryk, 'explained to us in a sufficiently clear manner that it was a matter of condemnation without appeal.'

This accomplished, Chamberlain went to bed. Next morning he

rose refreshed and apparently in the best of spirits, with no indication that he felt any regret for Czechoslovakia's fate or responsibility for it. One macabre footnote remained. In the frontier lands of Czechoslovakia the betrayed peoples bundled their belongings together and started out on the long trek to seek safety from the coming Nazi terror. In Prague the Czechoslovak Cabinet met to review a future which held, they knew, the end of their country; British and French journalists were advised for their own safety not to show themselves on the streets. But Chamberlain had other things on his mind. He awakened early and instructed Strang to draft a statement on Anglo-German relations for presentation to Hitler. Strang did so. Chamberlain found it unsatisfactory and rewrote it. He wanted a reference to the symbolic importance of the Anglo-German Naval Agreement and when Strang replied that this 'was not a thing to be proud of' retorted that on the contrary it was just the type of agreement they should now try to reach with Germany. Nor would he agree to show what he had drafted to the French.

With this paper in his pocket, he went to Hitler's private flat 'in a tenement where the other floors are occupied by ordinary citizens', as he naïvely told his sisters in the long letter he wrote them. Hitler received him cordially – he had much to be cordial about – and they had 'a very friendly and pleasant talk' about Spain (where the Non-Intervention Committee had collapsed and Franco was racing to victory with the aid of German and Italian bombing planes), the economics of south-east Europe, and disarmament. They even spoke of Czechoslovakia, Chamberlain observing that it was still possible that the Czechs might 'be mad enough to refuse the terms' and even to 'attempt resistance'. In such an event, he said, he appreciated that Hitler would have to invade, but hoped that it would not be necessary to bomb Prague and that it would be possible to avoid 'the killing of women and children by attacks from the air'. Hitler assured him that he hated 'the thought of little children being killed by gas bombs'. These courtesies concluded and in an atmosphere now thoroughly harmonious, Chamberlain produced his paper and read it aloud. As he did so, Hitler several times ejaculated 'Ja, ja', and when Chamberlain had finished they together went to a writing table where they signed what was to prove one of the emptiest documents in international history: a declaration that they regarded 'the agreement signed last night and the Anglo-German Naval Agreement as symbolic of the desire of our two peoples never to go to war with one another again' and were 'resolved that the method of consultation shall be the method adopted to deal with any other question that may concern our two countries'.

This done Chamberlain flew home. At Heston airport he waved his piece of paper in front of the reporters who had gathered to interview him and then broadcast its terms to the nation before driving to Downing Street. There a great crowd had already gathered to welcome him. To them, speaking from an upper window, he said: 'This is the second time in our history that there has come back from Germany to Downing Street peace with honour. I believe it is peace for our time', and hysterical with relief from tension and fear they roared their happiness. From the Foreign Office across the way Strang watched with bitterness and disgust. 'For all the fun and cheers,' he said, 'you might think they were celebrating a major victory over an enemy instead of the betrayal of an ally.'

Chamberlain had climbed to the high place earlier occupied by MacDonald and Baldwin. He had become the idol of the British people.

5. Peace Not in Our Time

MUNICH was the culmination and the crown of a policy of expediency on the defensive. It was also the peculiar and inevitable achievement of Chamberlain's inflexible talent for excluding from the range of his vision anything he did not wish to see.

The responsibility was not his alone, of course. It was shared by the two Prime Ministers who had preceded him, and especially Baldwin. Nor can the Labour Party escape its part. Its internal disunity following MacDonald's 'betrayal', its desperate desire not to alienate too wholly the pacifist emotion in its own ranks, the rigidity of its loyalty to the League of Nations, which it employed as a cloak against unpleasant decisions even when the League had manifestly become incapable of the role planned for it, the clumsiness of its Parliamentary technique which led it to choose a vote against rearmament as a means of seeking to censure a foreign policy which it rightly distrusted: all these contributed to the climate in which appeasement blossomed. Labour's responsibility is all the greater because, though bedevilled, as almost the whole of British public opinion was, by a sense of guilt about the Treaty of Versailles, it never made the mistake, as Chamberlain and many other Conservatives did, of underestimating the moral horror of Nazism and Fascism, or the nature of their aggressive intentions. Yet despite this, and despite their well justified suspicion of British foreign policy from Manchuria onwards, its leaders, with one or two exceptions allowed their party's tradition of pacifism, so painfully sloughed off after so much internal anguish, and their own belief in collective security, dangerously to debilitate and misdirect the force of their attack upon a Government whose policies it was their duty to expose.

But although the anomalies of Labour's attitude – clear-sighted in appreciation of the danger, confused in response to it – provide, and justifiably enough, debating points for the defenders of appeasement, they do little more. With only 154 members in the House of Commons Labour was in any event in no position to divert a policy supported throughout by an inert mass of Conservative back-benchers, who remained totally unmoved even by the sustained criticism of those in their own party whose background and experience made them most worthy of trust in such matters. Whether for praise or blame the main responsibility for British policy must rest with those in whose hands power resided.

There has, of course, to be taken into account the natural repulsion of civilized people from the thought of war, a repulsion Chamberlain wholly shared. War seemed so incredible, so illogical, so insane that it was not easy for the people of Britain or France to adjust themselves to the thought of it. But the devastating effect in September of the realization that there might be war in a few days was immensely enhanced by the previous campaign of officially inspired optimism. There is no greater disservice that a democratic statesman can do to his countrymen than to withhold from them advance knowledge of grave peril, for it is only by such knowledge that they can steel themselves to meet it when it comes. This great disservice Chamberlain had done. The British public was almost totally unprepared for the task of bracing itself against the impact of threatened war. Momentarily it was knocked off its balance. The effect of the crisis was, moreover, heightened by the minor but unfortunate coincidence that H. G. Wells's film, *The Shape of Things to Come*, had a little time previously implanted in the minds of many hundreds of thousands of impressionable people a belief that modern air warfare would bring in its train a devastation nothing could withstand, and had provided them with a visual picture of this devastation which they carried with them all through the anxious days of that September. The Munich Agreement came, therefore, as an escape from nightmare. Men and women reacted to it with a frenzy of relief that momentarily drove from the minds of most of them any consideration of consequences.

And so Chamberlain had his hour. It remained for Churchill to utter the truer verdict: 'We have suffered total and unmitigated defeat.'

The cheering crowds, the humble writers of the thousands of letters of praise and thanksgiving could be forgiven. For them what mattered was that war had been terribly near and had been averted by the journeyings of this ageing statesman. It is less easy to forgive the man whose naïve egotism had brought them so far along this road.

Of course he was hampered by the military weakness of Britain and France. But, as Iain Macleod claimed in his biography of him, he not only dominated his own Cabinet but the last Administration of Ramsay MacDonald and Baldwin. He cannot therefore escape responsibility for British deficiency in this respect. Nor can the argument that by appeasement he bought badly needed time hold up. The loss of Austria and Czechoslovakia, the refusal, however understandable his doubts, seriously to explore at any stage the possibility of a Russian alliance, the continuous diminution in French morale under British pressure and the consequent strengthening of the most reactionary elements in French life, all reduced the military power of the Western Alliance and increased that of Germany to a greater degree than was compensated for in the late build-up in British strength. The seeds of disaster lay not in his circumstances but in his character – so honourable, so public spirited yet so fatally flawed.

The crowds who applauded him had little or no means of knowing how far his own complacency had contributed to the position in which they had found themselves. They would surely have been astonished if they had known, for example, that in January of that year Sumner Welles, the American Under-Secretary of State, had called on the British Ambassador in Washington with a secret and confidential message from President Roosevelt to the Prime Minister, offering to take the initiative in bringing together in Washington representatives of the Governments of Britain, France, Germany and Italy to seek some settlement of the grave international situation, and that this offer, holding such momentous possibilities of bringing the weight of American power on the side of the European democracies, had been rejected by Chamberlain without even a word to his then Foreign Secretary, Eden – because it 'might irritate the Dictators'.

Even at this distance of time, as Winston Churchill wrote in *The Gathering Storm*, it is hard 'to reconstruct the state of mind which would render such gestures possible'. Difficult, also, not to agree that: 'If only British people could have known and realized that, having neglected our air defences and sought to diminish the defences of France, we were now disengaging ourselves, one after the other, from two mighty nations whose extreme efforts were needed to save our lives and their own, history might have taken a different turn.'

But they did not know. Chamberlain was in command. He saw no reason either to tell them or to change his mind. The scrap of paper brought back from Munich was to him an historic document guaranteeing long term goodwill for no better reason than it was a promise made to him personally. Hitler had made many promises before, and broken them. But none of them had been to Chamberlain. This was the difference.

It was a comfortable belief. He closed his mind to everything that might make him question it. When Germany's demands at the Ambassadors' Conference which had the task of carrying through the Munich Agreement far exceeded even those made at Munich he did not even instruct the British Ambassador to make a formal protest. Nor was he interested when President Beneš, whose conduct throughout the crisis had been exemplary, was forced to resign and leave the country in whose history he had played so notable a part.

Even the launching only six weeks after the meeting at Munich of a pogrom against the whole Jewish community of the Greater Reich on a scale greater than anything hitherto known and exceeding all previous anti-Jewish atrocities in its obscenities, its brutalities, its frankly financial purpose of taking from the Jewish community nearly all it possessed, appears hardly to have aroused his interest. Certainly it did not, so far as the outside world was privileged to see, stir him to any indignation. He remained convinced that the appeasement of men capable of such horrors was an honourable and practical policy. With a heart full of innocence and loving kindness he travelled to Rome in January 1939 where he found Mussolini 'straightforward and considerate in his behaviour to us, and moreover he has a sense of humour which is quite attractive'. In February he was noting in his diary, 'I think we ought to be able to establish excellent relations with Franco who seems well disposed to us. . . .' The world was full of friendly dictators.

Early in March his optimism about the world reached a level higher even than that which had lulled the British people into a false sense of security before the crisis of the previous September. Every responsible newspaper other than *The Times*, whose Editor, like Chamberlain, did not want to know, was aware from the accumulating evidence of its correspondents in Berlin and Prague that Hitler was preparing for a fresh and probably final act of aggression against what remained of Czechoslovakia and that an early military invasion and occupation of Prague – which in fact took place on 15 March – was probable. These warnings were not confined to the Labour and Liberal press. The Conservative *Daily Telegraph* played a leading and most honourable part in telling the public the truth. Yet on 9 March the political correspondents of the British newspapers were called to an off-the-record conference with the Prime Minister at 10 Downing Street and told by him that the international situation had now taken so remarkable a turn for the better that he expected a disarmament conference to be arranged by the end of the year. He went on to inform his startled listeners that the betterment in the European situation since Munich had so out-paced all expectations that there was every likelihood of achieving, that year, political and economic agreements which would bring permanent peace to Europe.

I can well remember the amazement with which, sitting in my office studying the cables which told of mounting tension throughout Europe, I was told of the Downing Street conference. Other newspaper editors were similarly baffled. Our amazement was, we discovered, shared by the Foreign Office, which had neither been consulted on, nor informed of, the Premier's decision to meet the Political Correspondents and discuss the international situation with them, and which completely disagreed with his view of European prospects. Nor could it understand the references to the possibility of a disarmament conference – a mystery which, indeed, remains unsolved to this day. Even Halifax felt compelled to protest.

Six days later Hitler demonstrated the reliability of the Prime Minister's judgment by marching into Prague, annexing what remained of Czechoslovakia and tearing up even the remnants of the Munich Agreement.

It seemed at first as though Chamberlain was going to find it possible to ignore even this. His first references to the matter were cold and detached. He informed the House that the Anglo-French guarantees that had been given to what was left of Czechoslovakia as conscience money at Munich had moral but not legal force and could not in the circumstances be expected to apply, and added that until he received further information he did not wish to associate himself with any charge against Hitler of bad faith.

This time, however, the fuller information when it arrived did at last convince him. Speaking at Birmingham the following day he declared that his 'somewhat cool and objective statement' in the House of Commons had given rise to a 'misapprehension' as to his real feelings. He continued to defend appeasement and the Munich agreement. But he felt himself compelled to ask whether Hitler's latest move was 'a step in the direction of an attempt to dominate the world by force'.

He was capable of changing the direction but not the quality of his vision. Compelled to do something he lurched from a policy of expediency on the defensive to one of expediency on the offensive. The next object of German attack he decided after a quick innocent look at the map would be Roumania – a view the Roumanians were willing for their own purposes to confirm. This being so Britain must on this occasion be ready to act. But how? She had no common frontier with Roumania. Nor had she allies who had. One must there-fore be found. For this reason negotiations were opened with Poland. She was promised an Anglo-French guarantee in return for a defensive alliance with Roumania but ended with the guarantee and no Rouman-ian alliance – which was what Beck, the Polish Foreign Minister, had intended from the first. The Anglo-French guarantee was given a fortnight after a Russian proposal for a joint Anglo-Soviet initiative in arranging a meeting with representatives of the French, Polish, Turkish and Roumanian Governments in Bucharest to concert measures of resistance to further German aggression had been dismissed by Britain as 'premature'. Yet without Russian support it was impossible – as subsequent events were to confirm – to make the Polish guarantee militarily effective. Every argument advanced as valid against a guarantee to Czechoslovakia and used to excuse inaction during the cross-examination of Daladier in September was equally applicable in this case – and with more force.

By his Polish guarantee Chamberlain threw away what remained of his bargaining power in eastern Europe. No longer was he in a position to say to Russia: 'If you wish to avoid the danger of a German advance to the East which you may have to meet alone you must accept an alliance on terms agreeable to us as well as you' – for a German attack on Russia could only be mounted through Poland and Britain was now committed to defend her anyway. Nor was he in a position to require of the Polish Government some amendment of the bitterly anti-Russian policy which stood in the way of a comprehensive security alliance, for Beck had already got what he wanted, more indeed than he had expected.

Seldom has it been the lot of men to see the business of power politics handled so ineptly. In this world Chamberlain was like a small-town businessman settling down to a game of stud poker in the smoke room of an Atlantic liner with all the confidence of a man much sought after for local whist drives. Without Russia the Polish guarantee, as Lloyd George flatly observed, was 'a reckless gamble'. But expediency on the offensive was in full control. Throwing caution to the winds the gambler at the poker table pulled out his note case and tossed two more guarantees on the table, this time to Roumania and Greece – both nearly as difficult to implement as the Polish one.

Only Russia was ignored. Even in Chamberlain's speech announcing the Roumanian and Greek guarantees there was no reference to her until Labour interventions compelled him to make what Hugh Dalton described as 'a few improvised platitudes of goodwill'. However, later in the debate Dalton did manage by hard pressing to elicit from Simon, who was winding up for the Government, an assurance that the Government had 'no objection in principle' to an Anglo-French-Soviet military alliance. It was not much but it was something. The response was immediate. The following morning Maisky, the Soviet Ambassador, called at the Foreign Office with a message welcoming the statement and offering to assist in the defence of Roumania. Three days later the Russians proposed a Triple Alliance of Britain, France and Russia to resist aggression in Europe against any one of them, to be followed by a military convention and joint guarantees of all the smaller states from the Baltic to the Black Sea.

It seemed that the breakthrough had come. As Winston Churchill – whom even Chamberlain could scarcely dismiss as a pro-Communist – wrote subsequently in *The Gathering Storm:* 'There can be no doubt even in the after light that Britain and France should have accepted the Russian offer, proclaimed the Triple Alliance and left the method by which it could be made effective in case of war to be adjusted between allies engaged against a common foe. . . . When events are moving at such a speed and in such tremendous mass as at this juncture, it is wise to take one step at a time. The Alliance of Britain, France and Russia would have struck deep alarm into the heart of Germany in 1939 and no one can prove that war might not even then have been averted.

The next step would have been taken with superior power on the side of the Allies. The initiative would have been regained by our diplomacy. . . .'

To such a step Chamberlain could not bring himself. He sat on the Russian offer for twenty-two days. At the end of this time he ignored the offer of a Triple Alliance and asked Russia to agree to join in the defence of states on her border without, however, any specific reciprocal Anglo-French undertaking to assist her if she should be involved in war as a result of her own obligations to any eastern European state.

'If you are ready to be an ally of Russia in time of war which is the supreme test, the great occasion of all, if you are ready to join hands with Russia in the defence of Poland, which you have guaranteed, and of Roumania, why', asked Churchill in the House of Commons, 'should you shrink from becoming the ally of Russia now, when you may by that very fact prevent the breaking out of war?' To this there was no answer from Chamberlain. In any event it was too late. Russian suspicions, already acute, had been brought to boiling point by this further delay. Litvinov, the chief Soviet protagonist of a Western Alliance was dismissed and replaced by Molotov, who at once made tentative approaches to the Nazis. Henceforth Stalin's policy, dictated as always by his fear of a German eastward drive, was to play off Britain and Germany against each other and double-cross either as it suited him. Nor had the effect of British tardiness gone unnoticed by Hitler. To the German Ambassador in Moscow went new instructions: 'Contrary to the policy previously planned we have now decided to undertake definite negotiations with the Soviet Union.' The chance of a Triple Alliance against Nazi aggression had been lost, the first step to the German-Soviet pact taken.

It is hard even now to conceive how all this was allowed to come about. The reckless scattering of guarantees rose from the compulsion to do something – anything – to offset Hitler's march into Prague. But why the tardiness of the response to Russia and the repeated rebuffs to her approaches? Without deceiving oneself as to Russia's motives in seeking an alliance it was clear, as Churchill for one pointed out again and again, that an Anglo-French-Soviet Alliance offered the best, indeed probably the only, chance of averting war. But this was one of those facts Chamberlain did not want to see. Even when he was finally forced by events to acknowledge it he could not bring himself to accept the further fact that, as Churchill put it in debate, 'clearly Russia is not going to enter into any agreements unless she is treated as an equal'. It was like asking the company chairman to deal with a shop steward on equal terms. In any event he could not disabuse himself of the belief that there was plenty of time. He had a nineteenth-century picture in his mind of Britain as the rich relation among nations whose invitations were both an honour and a command. There was no need for hurry over Russia. Probably it would be possible to do without her: one sincerely hoped so anyway. If not she would come at a snap of the fingers. He had become so used to turning down Russian offers of co-operation that it never occurred to him that an offer of his own could be refused.

I remember how, when the Anglo-Russian negotiations which dragged on from May to August were going badly, the Premier's entourage would again and again reassure itself with the theory that Stalin was merely standing on his dignity in order to demonstrate to himself and the world that he really was negotiating with Great Britain as an equal. When things got very critical they comforted themselves with the story of Stalin, Lady Astor and the map of the world. According to this story, during Lady Astor's notorious visit to Moscow Stalin took her by the arm, walked over to a map of the world occupying one wall of his room and, pointing to the red of the British Empire, said, 'Tell me, how did such a small nation conquer so much? There must be *something* about the British character.' I was told this story more times than I can remember during those days. Sometimes the cast varied and it was Anthony Eden and not Lady Astor whose arm Stalin took. And on one momentous occasion the point of the story was that he had said it to both Lady Astor and Eden. That seemed to be decisive. Obviously, a man who felt like that about the British would be honoured and delighted to become their ally on their terms. He merely needed a little time to preen his tail feathers before getting down to business. Even the warning light when Litvinov 'resigned' could not cut through such complacency. It needed the German-Soviet agreement, signed while a British Military Mission was actually conducting its leisurely explorations in Moscow, to do that.

With that agreement an attack on Poland and world war became inevitable. Chamberlain had sat out the poker game to the bitter end and lost.

Yet even now he could not quite convince himself. When he appeared before the House of Commons on the afternoon of 2 September, the day after the German attack on Poland, it was not to announce a declaration of war as had been expected and our guarantee required, but to say that 'If the German Government should agree to withdraw their forces then His Majesty's Government would be willing to regard the position as being the same as it was before the German forces crossed the Polish frontier', and to add that in these circumstances 'the way would be open to discussion' between Germany and Poland, with which Britain would be willing to be associated. To M.P.s of all parties it seemed that another Munich was being prepared. Chamberlain sat down without a cheer in a House oozing hostility, returning to his room after a debate of which resentment, apprehension and anger were the most marked features, conscious that almost the whole House was against him. He was joined there by Arthur Greenwood, Acting Leader of the Opposition in Attlee's absence due to illness, who told him without civility that unless the inevitable decision of fight had been taken before Parliament met the next day, Sunday, 'it would be impossible to hold the House'. Yet even at this late hour Horace Wilson was advising the German Chargé d'Affaires that if the Germans would withdraw the British Government would 'be prepared to let bygones be bygones' and start Anglo-German negotiations immediately, apparently without concerning itself with the fact that Germany had invaded a friendly country without even a declaration of war, and had bombed civilian populations for forty-two hours. Even when the Cabinet met at 11 p.m. that night Chamberlain and Halifax, in face of the by now unanimous resistance of their colleagues, still sought for further delay, and in the end so timed their ultimatum as to give the Germans another night and day to advance before it became effective. And even at this stage, in spite of the reports of massive civilian casualties, they found it possible when telegraphing Sir Howard Kennard, the British Ambassador in Warsaw, for further details, to say, 'In the meantime it is accepted Germans are attacking only military objectives.' Illusion indeed died hard.

What is in some ways even more amazing is the extent to which, even after war had been declared, Chamberlain continued to deceive himself as to its nature and possible duration. In November he found it possible to write to his sister Ida: 'I have a "hunch" that the war will be over in the spring. It won't be by defeat in the field but by German realization that they *can't* win and that it isn't worth their while to go on getting thinner and poorer when they might have instant relief and perhaps not have to give up anything they really care about.' And in April 1940 he told the nation that Hitler had 'missed the bus'. He was still as far away as he had ever been from understanding the nature and methods of those he had sought so long to appease; still as convinced as ever that this was a business matter that would be settled by business principles, and that when the Germans paused to consider their position they would, like any sensible business firm looking at its balance sheet, come to the conclusion that it was better to settle than fight; still as unwilling as he had ever been to face any facts that did not conform to his own ideas. When his Secretary of State for War, Hore-Belisha, became too inconsiderate of others' feelings, and especially of those of the General Staff, in his criticism of the inadequacies of the defences and strategy of the British Expeditionary Force, he sacked him. Departmental managers could not be allowed to get uppish.

Even when the defeat in Norway showed that the war was now entering on a phase very different from any he had anticipated, and exposed in startling light the deficiencies of British arms and strategy, he could not bring himself to think that what had happened cast any reflection on his own conduct of affairs. Obstinate to the last he could find nothing better to offer a hostile House than an appeal to 'my friends in the House – and I have friends in the House – to support us in the Lobby tonight.' It might have been a debate on a contentious clause in a Bill from the Ministry of Health, not a matter affecting the survival of the nation.

Even when the Government's majority fell to eighty-one, with twenty-nine Conservatives voting with the Opposition and more than double that number abstaining ('We ought to sing something,' said Harold Macmillan, and Josiah Wedgwood struck up 'Rule Britannia'), he was still capable of seeing the issue largely in personal terms. To Ida, that ever faithful confidante, he wrote: 'The debate was a very painful affair to many besides myself and in particular for its exhibition of personal and Party passion. . . . The Amerys, Duff-Coopers and their lot are consciously or unconsciously swayed by a sense of frustration because they can only look on. . . .' Only Attlee's intimation, after consultation with his chief parliamentary colleagues and with the National Executive of the Labour Party, then meeting in Annual Conference at Bournemouth, that under no circumstances would Labour agree to serve under him, convinced him at last that the time had come to go. He hoped – so far was he even yet from comprehending the mood of those he had led through three disastrous years – that Halifax could succeed him.

He had risen to a pinnacle of public esteem higher even than that climbed by MacDonald and Baldwin and fallen further. But he was in some ways more fortunate than they. He did not have to suffer long years of decline. Magnanimous even at this moment, Churchill whose warnings he had for so long treated so contemptuously, invited him to stay in the new and now truly National Government as Lord President of the Council. He served it well for nearly five months, for four of them in almost constant pain and towards the end under sentence of death from a cancerous growth that he knew was inoperable and incurable and that manifested itself for the first time a month after the collapse of his Government and was perhaps induced by it. During these months he won the esteem of those who had most opposed him and his policies. He was, said Attlee in a conversation with the present writer recorded in *A Prime Minister Remembers*, 'free from any of the rancour he might have felt against us. He worked very hard and well: a good chairman, a good committee man, always very businesslike. You could work with him.' He had indeed most of the qualities of a great public servant except the very highest. Apart from one black spell, when he allowed himself to believe that Britain's defeat was unavoidable and communicated his sentiments to the equally pessimistic American Ambassador, Joseph Kennedy, he remained to the last confident, courageous and complacent. One of his last letters was to Baldwin, who assumed that he had suffered not only a physical but a nervous breakdown – an assumption he was quick to repudiate. 'There has', he wrote, 'never been any question of nerves giving way with me. Nor was I ever conscious of that "terrific strain" which so many of my correspondents assume to be the cause of my breakdown.'

No doubts afflicted him. Or did they? Did he perchance protest too much? 'Never for one single instant', he assured Baldwin, 'have I doubted the rightness of what I did at Munich nor can I believe that it was possible for me to do more than I did to prepare the country for war after Munich, given the violent and persistent opposition I had to fight against. . . . My critics differed from me because they were ignorant, it is only fair to add wilfully ignorant, in many cases. So I regret nothing in the past. . . .'

Three and half weeks later he died. His ashes were buried in Westminster Abbey next to those of Bonar Law of whom he had never thought much. He had been a great municipal administrator, a good Minister of Health, a competent Chancellor and the most disastrous Prime Minister in British history. One cannot help feeling sorry for him. He had worked so hard, sought so ardently for peace, thought so well of himself. He was the Martha who had grown into Mary, the Cinderella who had gone to the ball not realizing that when midnight struck it was the Prince who would turn into a monster. He had many virtues, almost all, indeed, except those of humility and imagination.

But it was a time for greatness and this was not his to offer.

Montagu Norman

Born 1871; son of Frederic Norman, banker; educated at Eton and King's, Cambridge; served with the Bedfordshire Regiment in South Africa 1900-1; partner, Brown, Shipley and Co., Merchant Bankers, 1901-14; elected to Court of the Bank of England 1907; Deputy Governor 1918-20; Governor 1920-44; created Baron Norman of St Clere 1944; died 1950.

1. *Lame Duck in Hell*

BALDWIN, MacDonald, Chamberlain, all so unlikely and so ill prepared, were the main contrivers of Britain's destiny during these desolate and dangerous decades. But two others, a banker and an aristocrat, exercised through much of the time a pervasive influence second only to theirs, and no record of these times is complete without a note on them. Like the three Prime Ministers they too seemed in 1918 wholly unlikely to be touched by the finger of history – or to deserve to be.

The life of politics is one of changes and chances. Although Baldwin and MacDonald were certainly exceptional in the speed of their rise to great power from positions of small expectation, sudden enhancements or reverses of fortune are frequent enough.

They are less so in banking, especially Central Banking. Here men usually increase only slowly in reputation. Those whom Lloyd George called the frozen penguins of the City open their ranks to ambition with extreme caution.

Yet Montagu Norman, who was to be Governor of the Bank of England for twenty-four years, breaking a tradition of short-term Governorship that had existed for more than two centuries, and to reach a position of personal power such as no Governor before or after him has ever achieved, was hardly known even within the City two years before he became Governor.

He was a member by inheritance of the city's ruling caste. Yet in the mid-flight of his career his impact upon his contemporaries in this world in which he was to exercise so unique an influence was so small that when the Bank's Court of Treasury wrote privately to the heads of five of the great joint stock banks in 1918 to ask for their views on changes in the direction of the Bank which included his election to the Deputy Governorship, one of the five replied that he was not acquainted with Mr Norman and therefore could not give an opinion on him, another that Mr Norman was not sufficiently well known in banking circles for a view to be possible and a third that he did not know Mr Norman personally although he had heard well of him. The remaining two made no mention of him in their replies.

In his maturity Norman was striking in appearance beyond most men. His pointed beard, the strong nose with a high bridge, the deep-set, piercing eyes, the sculptured profile, the grace of his bearing and something that seemed wild and reckless in the carriage of his head; these, together with the elegance of his attire, the dark, meticulously valeted, loosely fitting clothes, the magnificent emerald ring through which his tie was threaded, the broad-rimmed black hat worn carelessly at whatever angle it came to rest when he tossed it casually in the air above his head, all combined to give an impression of distinction and vitality. When one met him one was reminded of Joseph Conrad, or Cunninghame Graham. He seemed less a banker than an artist, less a City man than a merchant adventurer – from the Florence of Cosimo Medici, perhaps, or Venice in the days of Enrico Dandolo – and of the most impeccable lineage. His bones were small, his hands delicately shaped. There was something at once steely and feminine in the fascination he was able to exert, with an amused pleasure in its exercise, over nearly everyone he met, something captivating in the mercurial play across his features of an intelligence more intuitive than intellectual. He was at once arrogant and courteous.

In his youth he had been small and undistinguished, so shy and sensitive that conversation was painful both to himself and others. Like his father, his uncles and brother, he was an old Etonian, but unlike them, hated the place: the public schools can hardly be considered fortunate in their relationships with our future rulers at this time. The others of the Norman clan had been robust, popular and successful, each in turn captain of cricket. He was a failure in all things physical, and indescribably bored by almost all school work, a martyr to constant headaches, so timid and highly strung that a change in housemasters shortly after he went to Eton threw him completely off balance, and a transfer from one tutor to another plunged him into a pit of doubt and desolation. Cambridge proved no better. He was sent down from King's after an unhappy and mutinous first year, his tutor observing for his comfort that it did not much matter as he was in any event not the sort of person to get a degree.

To one of Norman's rich and assured milieu, in which Eton and Cambridge were no more than part of a social background, such academic failures mattered less than to nouveau riche industrialists like the Baldwins, for whom school and university could throw long shadows. But the unhappiness persisted. A Continental tour did little to disperse it. Only in the United States, where he was sent to learn his business of banking with the New York associates of the family banking firm of Brown, Shipley and Co., did he apparently find himself at ease. He was already contemptuous of theory, holding action to be the best spur to thought. ('One's so-called happiness', he wrote in words that might have come from Neville Chamberlain, 'depends upon occupation irrespective of place and people.') America in a period of business expansion on an intercontinental scale suited his mood.

Power and fortune were here at command for those with financial skill and daring. Nor was anyone so presumptuous as to expect the rich and successful to be publicly accountable for their actions. As Norman travelled from Boston to New York, Philadelphia, New Orleans, Houston, San Francisco, Denver and elsewhere on this and other visits between 1895 and 1899, he saw many of the new enterprises that were springing to life and came to know many of the bankers who made fortunes out of backing them. They were, he said later, the happiest years of his life.

He thought of settling permanently in the States. Had he done so he would no doubt have become a millionaire, for he had many of the qualities needed in a Wall Street tycoon, including, as he subsequently said of himself, 'a sense of smell where money is concerned and a nose for making a lot of it'. He had also to a high degree the autocratic habit of the very rich, that liking for secrecy, combined with pleasure in personal publicity of his own choosing, that often distinguishes successful money barons; their contempt, also, for values contrary to their own. Although neither would perhaps have cherished the comparison, I often used to think when I talked to him at the Bank of England that the contemporary figure on the British scene of whom he most reminded me was Lord Beaverbrook.

Although the hereditary pull of the City of London was strong and his place in it already laid down for him, he might very probably have remained in the United States but for the Boer War. That settled the question. Those of his relatives who were not bankers were mostly soldiers and the military life with its concentration on action rather than thought had always appealed to him. On coming down from Cambridge he had joined the Militia as a second lieutenant in the 4th Battalion of the Bedfordshire and Hertfordshire Regiment, and he now hurried home to join his battalion. It was dispatched to Kimberley to join the 9th Brigade commanded by his mother's cousin, General Sir Edward Hutton, who put him in command of a company and sent him to administer martial law in a considerable territory around Richmond, and later to Bloemhof, where he established military government over an even larger area of some 900 square miles.

Until forced to withdraw by the Boer advance he found occupation as Governor of an enemy province highly congenial. He was a long way from Headquarters and, subject to very broad instructions, had absolute authority. He wrote home that he hated the Boers but believed he was making them come to respect him. Then, and subsequently in action, he attracted the approval of his senior officers, several of whom were relatives or family friends, and was awarded the D.S.O. The life of activity and decision suited him. Just as he had earlier contemplated settling in America so now he considered the possibility of remaining in South Africa and made enquiries about the prospects of a career in the police force when the war ended. He was a most reluctant recruit to the City. However, it was not easy for one of his family connections to escape. A letter from his father recalled him to his obligations, reminding him that he had already been given the promise of a junior partnership in the family banking firm of Brown, Shipley and Co. of which his maternal grandfather, Sir Mark Collet, former Governor of the Bank of England, was the senior partner. He returned home.

As it turned out the South African experience was to prove an unfortunate prelude to life as a partner in a private banking firm. Being Military Governor of a hostile territory at a youthful age had indulged all that was most autocratic and secretive in his character. Like Neville Chamberlain on his island of Andros, he had been answerable to no one but himself. The obligations of partnership did not come easily to him.

Brown, Shipley and Co. was in a period of transition. Its senior partners, including Collet, were old men ready to retire, and anxious to pass effective control to their juniors. Of these there were two others besides Norman, both senior to him. Although junior in status Norman, however, soon made it plain that he was determined to be first in fact. Such social activities as he had formerly enjoyed were abandoned. Even shooting, which had been his favourite pursuit, was dropped so that he would be left in sole charge when his partners went off to the moors. Nor was he inclined to discuss matters with them even when they were available. Instead he set about overhauling the bank's policy and staff with a neurotic, solitary energy and absence of discrimination that produced sharp clashes of opinion. 'A lonely queer man', one of his banking acquaintances described him.

As time went by it became clear that these difficulties were rooted in something much deeper than a temporary distaste for new conditions of work. He became not less but more solitary and peremptory, shutting himself off from almost all social activities in order to concentrate his energies on dominating the firm of which, constitutionally, he was the most junior partner. In 1907 the hereditary accolade of a directorship of the Bank of England was bestowed on him; it was his family's due. But he betrayed small interest at this time in the affairs of the great institution he was later to dominate so completely, nor did he participate in any of the public or social activities of the City.

Outside Brown, Shipley and Co. he permitted himself one interest only: Thorpe Lodge, Campden Hill, which he bought as a personal residence when he was thirty-two. On this house he spent considerable sums, rebuilding extensively and importing rare timbers, panelling and Italian fireplaces to go with the tapestries and carpets with which he furnished it in harmony with the artistic conceptions of William Morris, whom he greatly admired. He had originally intended to use the house for extensive entertaining but as time passed he found it harder and harder to force himself to make new friends, or even keep up with the old ones. Some society was indispensable to him but for it he relied increasingly upon a few close relatives. Such of his spare time as was left over from his preoccupation with the reconstruction of his house and garden he devoted to reading works on moral philosophy, theology and mysticism in the hope of finding a substitute for the rejected religious faith of his youth, and to an eager but unorganized study of the relationship between mind and health as disclosed by the new science of psychology. In this search his chief guide was a *Manual for Mystics*, written by J. Porter Mills, an American doctor practising in London as a psychological healer without English medical qualifications.

Alone in the library he had designed for himself – and which was perhaps unique among libraries in that no books were to be seen on shelves, all were hidden tidily away in cupboards – Norman jotted down long comments on the books he read, making careful marginal notes in his beautiful handwriting as he tried to find some view of life to help him through the black fits of depression to which he was increasingly subject. His social life was now almost wholly restricted to the circle of his own family and to one or two women friends, wives of his professional associates, who shared his interest in mysticism and his admiration for the writings of Dr J. Porter Mills. Like Ramsay MacDonald he found it easier to talk to women than men and was more at ease with the wives of his professional colleagues than he was with those colleagues themselves. But although he liked women's company he found it impossible in his youth and middle age to make a close personal relationship with any one woman: he did not marry until he was sixty-two.

His relations with his partners had never been good. By 1910 they had worsened dramatically. This was partly due to differences on policy, particularly whether the firm should stick to the acceptance business or develop as an underwriter of new issues as the other partners wished. But the main cause, as all accounts show, lay in Norman's unwillingness or inability to accept the full discussion among equals common in – and indeed essential to – a private banking partnership. Decisions vitally affecting the firm's interests were taken without consultation for reasons which he either could not or would not put into words. When his partners objected he reacted as though they were presumptuous clerks.

As a result of this clash of personalities a period of his life now opened which strikes a strange, almost macabre note when set against the usual background of the successful banker: the idea that such a man would not only become Governor of the Bank of England but be allowed to transform the office into a long term vehicle of personal power on a scale without precedent in banking history would surely have struck his associates at the time as wholly incredible.

At Founders' Court his life was one of almost continuous frustration and boredom, his own conduct increasingly eccentric and uncooperative. Only New York lifted his spirits. 'For work', he wrote, 'and particularly for that kind of work we call business, no place can match it.' His biographer, Sir Henry Clay, quotes him as writing on the way home on one occasion: 'I am filled with dismay, with the feeling of, as it were, going back to gaol.'

The gaol grew darker and more confining as the continuous conflicts between himself and his partners and his baffled rage when he could not have entirely his own way brought him nearer to the edge of a nervous and mental breakdown. The headaches that had crippled him as a boy at Eton returned, making him incapable of meeting or talking to anyone for days at a time. They were followed by severe attacks of eczema. As the black moods grew on him he withdrew more and more into himself, turning his back on all social life and refusing for long periods to see any but intimate relatives.

On 24 September 1911, while staying at his father's house, he had a complete nervous collapse. For two months he could do nothing, remember nothing. 'From that day until now', he wrote to one of his American partners in December, 'I have neither read nor written a letter. Indeed I have been a close prisoner and to me it seems that the prison was constructed on the lines of hell.'

When he recovered sufficiently to move he was sent on a sea voyage. It seemed to do him a little good and he returned to Founders' Court. But the fits of depression and the disabling pains in the head continued. He was now, indeed, in so morbid a state that those closest to him began to fear he would never recover. Finally in April 1913 he was prevailed upon to go to Zürich in the care of his sister-in-law, Lady Florence Norman, to seek the advice of the great psychoanalyst Carl Jung.

Jung had no previous knowledge of Norman and seems at first to have suspected tertiary syphilis. He arranged for tests of his blood and spinal fluid. When these were negative he advised Lady Florence that the only hope for her brother-in-law lay in absolute rest for several months, after which Norman should be brought back to Zürich for a course of treatment – presumably a deep analysis. This, Jung warned, might be prolonged. Nor could he give any guarantee of a successful outcome.

Norman was devastated by the verdict. He had built extravagant hopes on this visit. Their disappointment brought a relapse so severe that his sister-in-law reported that his doctor believed he might not live for more than a few months. For four weeks he lay prostrate in a darkened room nursing a raging head.

At this stage a woman friend suggested that he should go to see another Swiss specialist in nervous diseases, Dr Roger Vittoz of Lausanne, of whom she had heard remarkable accounts. Vittoz's methods were unorthodox. But he was reported sometimes to achieve success where more orthodox practitioners failed. In May, when Norman was at last well enough to leave his room, his brother, who had come to Zürich to look after him, arranged a consultation with Vittoz. Thereafter Norman visited him every alternate day for two months.

Vittoz's system was based on a series of exercises invented by himself which, he claimed, could relieve tension at times of approaching nervous crisis by emptying the mind of emotion. These exercises – or the confidence Vittoz managed to engender, for Norman found him 'clever and very understanding' – had a rapid and marked effect. The nerve storms that had brought Norman to the verge of complete collapse became less frequent and he began to develop new confidence in his ability to face the world, even though, as he wrote to the woman friend who had first recommended Vittoz, it must be 'as a lame duck'. Possibly Vittoz's treatment was one of alleviation rather than fundamental cure. But it gave Norman something to cling to.

As for the future, Vittoz advised that Norman's best hope was to find work so utterly exacting that there would be no room in his mind for other worries. It was not work but fellow workers he had to guard against. A single-minded absorption in work was, Vittoz advised, the one sure means of escape from those problems of personal relationships that made ordinary life difficult for him. But at this very moment news came that the outlet he most needed was to be denied him. His partners at Brown, Shipley and Co. had come to the conclusion that they could no longer put up with him under any circumstances whatever. Attempts at reconciliation were made by some of the American partners of the firm and by mutual friends among the senior partners of some of the London banks with whom they had close connections, but all efforts at mediation failed. By July 1914 it was clear that no agreement was likely; nothing remained but to end the partnership with as little adverse effect on the firm as possible.

The situation between Norman and his partners was so bad that even the outbreak of war could not change it. With the declaration of war he offered to stay on in a purely nominal position under any conditions his partners cared to impose, in order to avoid the possible damage to the firm of a public break at such a moment. But even this was rejected. His partners were not prepared to contemplate anything that meant continued association with him, however slight. At all costs they were determined to see the last of him. On 21 December 1915 his fifteen years' partnership was compulsorily ended – a situation almost unprecedented in the small, closely-knit merchant banking world of that time.

The full facts of Norman's mental illness are difficult to establish at this distance. The details of the medical diagnosis given in the official biography are imprecise and much even of what is given does not fit any known illness. Norman himself told friends that his brain had been found to 'work wrong in a mechanical way' and that there was 'an erratic corner in it which makes all the trouble'. Others who knew him at this time have no more to go on than vague secondhand reports of what was wrong.

But that Norman suffered from a grave psychological illness the causes of which were never completely diagnosed and which was never wholly cured seems not to be in doubt. Absorption in work so complete and unremitting as to shut out almost everything else in life later provided, as Vittoz had said it would, some amelioration of the psychological conflict that had nearly destroyed him. But this dark division in his personality continued to affect his relationships with those who worked with him: even those who, like Benjamin Strong of the Federal Reserve Bank of New York, represented independent powers outside his domination and who were generous in their recognition of his banking ability. To the end of his life he found it almost impossible to accept any situation in which he was not master. He did not go out of his way to usurp the authority of others, but he would brook no restriction on his own. In matters where his colleagues possessed greater knowledge than he did or had enjoyed special experience he was prepared to listen briefly. But his had always to be the final word. The discussion between equals usual in the management of great affairs remained beyond him as it was beyond Chamberlain. He found any request to explain his actions intolerable. He could not, or would not, argue. Secretiveness, sometimes of a quite absurd and childish kind, became a mania with him and he would often go to absurd lengths to preserve it.

Even his closest professional assistants and those of whose loyalty and devotion he was most sure found their dealings with him subject to the hazard of sudden tantrums for which there was no sensible explanation, and to gusts of unreason of a kind unfairly labelled by other men as 'feminine'. Nor could they ignore a streak in his character that was even darker: something implacable and pitiless about him that at times delighted in aggressiveness and cruelty for their own sakes. For the most part those who suffered forgave him. They accepted him as a great man subject to his own rules and not to those that govern the conduct of lesser individuals. Yet he cannot but seem a strange choice for the City, which commonly prides itself so much on managing its affairs by the light of reason, moderation and good sense, to accept as the arbitrator of its destinies for so long.

Such a choice seemed remote indeed at the beginning of the war as he flung himself into a multitude of minor activities in a desperate attempt to fill the gap left by his divorce from Brown, Shipley and Co. and find some escape from the psychological illness that so grievously affected him. He took on almost every job that offered: Financial Adviser to the Cable Censorship, Advisor to the Trading with the Enemy Committee, Chairman of the Committee on Aircraft Insurance, Adviser to the Postal Censorship and to the Ministry of Blockade, a whole host of small appointments that gave him the illusion of being needed and in which, indeed, he did work of great value. In the swirl of these minor activities his recuperative powers proved stronger than had seemed possible in the dark days in Zürich and Lausanne. He began to spend more time at the Bank of England where the Deputy Governor, Brian Cokayne (later Lord Cullen), invited him to 'devil' for him on a number of committees. It was a kindly gesture by Cokayne, made in part, at any rate, for the purpose of providing Norman with some respectable public excuse for his departure from Brown, Shipley. ('The City', Cokayne wrote, 'understands that you have left your firm to devote yourself to public work and if you come here and help me here your action will be more "intelligible" still.') But apart from this the Bank itself was ill fitted to meet the emergencies of war and badly needed more directors it could call on regularly. In approaching Norman Cokayne was compelled, however, to explain that while it had informally given him leave to do so the Court of Treasury had also requested him to make it quite plain that 'you would have no official status nor be put on the Court of Treasury', and that the invitation 'would not in any way imply that you would be nominated as the next Deputy Governor'.

It was an invitation to come in at a side door, but an entrance nevertheless, and once he had his foot in Norman did not falter. Within two years the Deputy Governorship he had been warned not to expect was his. Another two years and on 31 March 1920 he was elected Governor of the Bank for what was to prove the first of twenty-four successive years of office – a tenure so unprecedented as to be beyond anyone's expectations at the time.

He was even then hardly known in the City. Apart from his two years as Deputy Governor of the Bank he had little behind him but a history of personal failure. Moreover, although he had conquered the worst of his mental and emotional difficulties the disharmonies in his personality remained. They were to have a pervasive influence on the history of his age. Secretive, egotistic, suspicious of intellectual ability and almost incapable of normal human relationships, he moved forward from the wreckage of his career to a position of unparalleled economic and financial authority.

2. Autocrat on the Gold Standard

THAT this secretive and tormented man should become the virtual despot of the Bank of England for the best part of a quarter of a century, and through it exercise a dominant role not only in the affairs of the City but on the economic policy of the nation and the lives of many millions of ordinary people, seems all the more remarkable in that he was first elected to the Governorship at a time when the Bank was seeking to break away from a period of personal rule to which it had, perhaps unavoidably, been subjected during the war years. By long hallowed tradition the members of the Bank Court, all drawn from a small circle of merchant banks, were each in turn elected Deputy Governor, in which capacity they served two years, and then Governor for another two, irrespective of merit or qualification. During office they retained their partnerships in their own businesses to which they returned when their term ended. It was, perhaps, not much of a way to run a bank but in the ripe prewar years it had served.

This two-hundred-year-old system had been temporarily suspended during the war when the exigencies of national financial policy and the need for close association with the Treasury in managing credit and mobilizing Britain's overseas financial resources had seemed to make continuity desirable. Lord Cunliffe, Governor when the war broke out, stayed on.

The experiment did not prove an unmitigated success. Jealous of the Bank's status as a private institution, Lord Cunliffe so conducted himself as to bring an almost open breach with the Chancellor of the

Exchequer on several occasions, one of them being so bad as to compel an apology from the Bank and bring a sharp threat from Lloyd George that unless the Bank was prepared to do as it was told – or at the very least inform the Government of what it was doing – he would take it over. What was even more unsatisfactory from the Bank's point of view was that once he had power firmly in his hands Cunliffe virtually ignored the Bank Court and its executive body, the Committee of Treasury, neither consulting nor even informing its members regarding most of the major policy decisions he took. In November 1917 the Committee of Treasury finally reasserted its authority. It refused to renominate Cunliffe, who had wanted and expected to remain in office at least until the end of the war, and replaced him by Cokayne, the Deputy Governor, with Norman as his Deputy.

Apart from the minor breach with former practice represented by the fact that Norman was no longer a partner in a merchant banking house, this was meant to be a return to tradition. So far as Cokayne was concerned it was so. He relinquished his Governorship after the traditional two years and made way for Norman who, in his turn, was expected to hold it no longer.

That he held it instead for twenty-four years, remaining in office for the rest of his active life, was in part due to personality, in part to postwar conditions. The amateur tradition in Central Banking, whatever may or may not have been its justification earlier, was no longer suited to the times; professionalism and continuity were required. At the end of his first two years Norman, with his compulsive need to work and dominate, had already drawn so many of the strings of authority into his own hands that no obvious successor was in sight. This was especially so as his Deputy Governor, H. A. Trotter, was anxious to return to the direction of his own business and most of the other merchant bankers to whom it would have been normal to turn were equally reluctant to be away from their own banks at a time when the emergence of New York as the most powerful banking centre in the world compelled them to fight for international business as never before. Ironically Norman gained advantage from what had earlier seemed his disastrous failure at Brown, Shipley and Co. If he had still been a partner the firm might well have insisted that he go back there. But he was free and available and this and the fact that his compulsive need to immerse himself wholly in his work had turned him into the only truly professional central banker on the Court seemed to make it sensible to ask him to continue.

Even so, many members of the Committee of Treasury agreed only reluctantly, seeing in an extension of his term a dangerous breach of a tradition to which they were anxious to return as quickly as they could. Right up to 1931 he was re-elected on a yearly basis only. The principle that a Governor should normally serve no more than two years was still insisted on. Not until that year did the Court of the Bank bring itself to bow to the inevitable and pass a resolution affirming that 'Subject to Annual election as required by the Charter, the term of office of the present Governor be regarded as not subject to any definite limitation as to time'. Even then it did so only after Norman had rejected as impractical and unacceptable a proposal that he should step down from the Governorship but remain as the Bank's 'Foreign Secretary', advising Governors, as they came and went, on its international activities.

In its long rearguard action against the principle of appointing a permanent Governor the Court believed itself to be fighting a battle not finally lost until after the second world war. Its members were afraid that if the principle of permanency were once publicly accepted the Government would demand a voice in the appointment of the Governor and the way be opened to what had already been accepted as right and proper in every other major country in the world, national control of the Central Bank. In fact, as the more perceptive of the members of the Committee of Treasury had early realized, Norman's continued presence was their strongest safeguard against this. He would brook no interference from outside. To him the Bank was a private empire – and while he was in the full spate of his powers it was not a question of the Government dictating to the Bank, but of the Bank dictating to the Government. He was, as that distinguished financial writer Paul Einzig wrote in 1932, as characteristic a Governor of the Bank of England as Francis Joseph was a Habsburg Emperor.

Some members of the Court – indeed throughout a good deal of the time a majority – might be disturbed about the extent of the power they had inadvertently allowed to pass into the hands of one man, but this power was resolutely used for a purpose they approved: to keep the Bank a nation within a nation, an independent authority equal, if not indeed in some instances superior, to Government. The jagged nerve edges of a personality which had made relationship with him impossible to his partners in Brown, Shipley and Co. were smoothed over by success, retracted beneath a brilliant surface of urbane if sometimes capricious courtesy. But in the Bank itself Norman had and brooked no rival. There was no question here of the problems of partnership he had found so insupportable at Brown, Shipley & Co. Circumstance and his own character, combined ultimately with the prestige of his long tenure of office, enabled him to carve out for himself exactly the position and status his neurotic nature required. Here he could satisfy in full the prescription laid down for him by Vittoz: single-minded absorption in work so exacting that it would free his mind of all other anxieties without requiring of him that compliance with the views of equals that he found impossible.

He was the inheritor on both sides of his family of a long tradition of private banking and as such was, in the dichotomy that so much afflicted British policy in the interwar years, firmly an internationalist – but an internationalist wedded not to the new conceptions that had come to life so hopefully yet so fragilely in the League of Nations but to those that had served Britain in her dominant role as world banker in the nineteenth century. He recognized and sympathised with the vigour of the new world power that had risen financially as well as politically across the Atlantic, and got on well, as he always had, with American bankers whose thrusting faith in the extremist forms of private enterprise and contempt for Government interference he shared. He was prepared to accord them an equal, indeed if there was no help for it, a predominant partnership in running world finance. But his internationalism was one of *realpolitik* not idealism, and in it there was little or no place for considering the impact of the interests he served on the lives of the ordinary people of Britain or on British industry.

Despite his deep and genuine commitment to international re-habilitation, the whole strength of his powerful and twisted personality and all the weight of the despotic power he was able to exercise from the central citadel of the Bank was thus employed to bring back the shape of the past, not to advance to a new future. His influence on events was in the result almost wholly malevolent. It was so not because he lacked fidelity to principle but because his loyalty was to principles which were out of step with the times and because, like Chamberlain in a greater office, he was incapable of tolerating the views of those who saw the world differently from himself. He used his immense abilities in what he believed to be the public interest. But for him the Bank's interests and the nation's were the same, just as for Baldwin the nation and the Tory party were identical.

A man of money, he was concerned with power not money. His

private fortune though adequate was by no means large by the standards of his contemporaries, derisory compared with what he could have made if he had used his 'smell' for money for his own gain. Yet he insisted that the fees of the Governor, unaltered since 1892 and even then fixed merely as a sort of honorarium for someone actively engaged in his own business, should not be revised to his advantage, and that any change should apply only to a successor. Like the others who shaped Britain's destinies so disastrously during these years, he was a disinterested public servant. One is sometimes tempted to think that Britain suffered peculiarly during this time from men of principle. She might have come off better with less high-minded leaders – at least there would have been more chance of their being found out.

Although fundamentally conservative, Norman was by no means a reactionary. His strength derived from a deep traditionalism wedded to a quick eye for change in methodology where the times required it. He gave the Bank an adequate 'civil service' of permanent officials for the first time in its history and even – a thing previously undreamed of – a statistical service. He went so far as to recognize the existence of newspapers other than *The Times*, inviting selected financial editors – of whom he impishly chose the present writer, then financial editor of the *Daily Herald*, as the first – to confidential private talks in which he was, as always, charming and implacable, interested but beyond argument. But although he sponsored many technical innovations he was above all an artist of banking in the great tradition, moved by intuition and feel, not science or economics, as independent and egotistical as a great painter or poet, despising alike the views of industrialists, trade unionists and economists, neither ready nor able, as he showed in his evidence before the Macmillan Committee on Finance and Industry, to explain his actions to those who had the audacity to expect it of him. Even allowing for the fact that he was by nature a bad witness whose powers of explanation fell, as his defenders argue, far short of his powers of insight and decision, he was extraordinarily arrogant to those, on the Macmillan Committee and elsewhere, who so far forgot themselves as to imagine they had a right to question him. Throughout these decisive years British monetary and credit policy was treated as the personal prerogative of a disdainful sphinx fully prepared to sacrifice the economic and industrial interests of Britain for what he believed to be those of the City. He rarely, indeed, seemed to bother his head as to what the interests of industry were. They lay outside the frame of reference by which he felt it proper to govern his actions.

In his overlordship of the Bank he saw no reason to concede even the pretence of being a constitutional monarch. Even when it would have been tactful, he rarely sought to persuade: he was not good at persuasion. But he was a great cajoler, a Ulysses among men who delighted in getting his own way by deception and the exercise of a charm as tantalizing and iridescent as a butterfly's wing. He had, too, as the anonymous author of the appendix, 'The Man', in the Bank's memorial volume regretfully admits in trying to explain Benjamin String's reference to 'certain personal qualities of which I heartily disapprove', a 'tendency to dramatize and over dramatize' and an artist's inclination 'to surprise and shock *pour épater les bourgeois*'.

These qualities of an engaging and quicksilver personality, enabled him to dazzle, beguile and bend to his purpose most of the politicians he had to deal with – not least among them that sea-green incorruptible Snowden, who became his devoted slave. His purpose did not vary. 'The dogs', as he observed in a famous remark at the Mansion House, 'may bark but the caravan moves on.'

There is a revealing passage in Sir Henry Clay's official biography which notes that although the end of the immediate postwar boom brought a catastrophic fall in prices and a rise in unemployment to 17·7 per cent, 'Depression at home which quickly diverted political and commercial interest from Europe and concentrated it on domestic conditions did not figure prominently at this time in the correspondence and notes in his diary which indicate Norman's preoccupations.'

Through his room at the Bank there passed a constant stream of visitors from other banking centres or from merchant banks 'pressed by former continental clients to make some loan, short or long, to meet an emergency, or whose own position was jeopardized by the inability of Central European customers to meet their obligations on prewar acceptance credits'. But there was rarely an industrialist and never a trade unionist.

The Government had in August 1918 appointed a Committee under Lord Cunliffe, the former Governor of the Bank, to consider currency and foreign exchange policy after the war. Taking its line very much from a memorandum prepared by Norman this Committee reported in favour of an early return to the gold standard, a cessation of Government borrowing, and a deflationary policy of dear money. This policy the Government accepted, and it was to this policy of deflation and an early return to the gold standard at the old level that Norman as Governor devoted himself. Unmoved by industrial booms or slumps, or the rise or fall of unemployment which drove others to second thoughts, he stuck to it through thick and thin. Having once made up his mind he did not easily move, perhaps because the illness from which he had by no means fully recovered, if he ever did, made such immobility of will an essential factor in his capacity to carry on. A man less inflexible might have accepted the need to pay regard to the internal as well as the external consequences of Bank policy. Such moderation was not for Norman: he could never be less than compulsively committed. When taxed, as at the Macmillan Committee, with paying insufficient regard to the effect of his actions on industry and employment he simply denied that they had any.

When he first became Governor he had been inclined to support the British Government's desire to relate inter-allied debts to Britain's debt to America, restricting its own claims on war debtors and Reparations to the net sum needed to meet payments to the United States. As soon, however, as he learned from Strong of the Federal Reserve Bank of New York and other friends in Wall Street that they were against treating the British war debt as part of a general settlement he abandoned the idea as likely to harm London's international position. This was to him the first priority. If it required the unilateral funding of the British war debt then funded it must be, whatever the cost to the national economy.

When he heard that despite his objections the Government intended to persist in its proposals for a general settlement he protested violently that the opinion of the City ought to be taken into account and provoked from Lloyd George the tart reply that the Cabinet knew all it needed to about the City's opinions and saw no reason to let them affect its own. But Lloyd George's rule was ending. With defeat by Bonar Law Baldwin came to the Treasury. Nothing could have suited Norman better. Baldwin had little interest in economic matters as Neville Chamberlain was to observe in 1931. But he was easily affected by references to national honour and very ready to accept the view that this was a matter that touched it closely.

So Baldwin and Norman set off to the States there to negotiate in a cloud of amity the terms of an American war loan settlement that was to collapse of its own inner contradictions within twelve years, after inflicting enormous damage on the economy. To Norman who played the major part in the negotiations the terms were pleasing.

'Once admit the Debt was binding and the result *is* good and will soon begin to bear fruit in Europe generally', he wrote to his friend Sir Basil Blackett, then Finance Member of the Viceroy of India's Council. And again: 'I think everyone at the Treasury and the Bank is really pleased and satisfied: I certainly am and I now seem to see a light at the end of the tunnel.'

Keynes's view that it was the debtor who had the last word in these matters and that we should have shown the Americans 'that they are at our mercy as we are at France's, France at Germany's' seemed to him to be heretical and immoral. As for the objections of Lord Beaverbrook and others of like mind, they were no more that the barking of dogs as the caravan moved on. To Norman the important thing was that London's position as a world money centre should not be affected by any suggestion of default.

Six months later on 7 July 1923 the Bank Rate was raised from three per cent to four per cent despite a Treasury warning less than a month before that such a rise in the Bank Rate might have serious effects on employment. It was, said Keynes, 'one of the most misguided movements of that indicator that has ever occurred'; for prices were falling and unemployment severe and dearer money was bound to worsen the internal situation. But it was a necessary first stage in Norman's campaign for a return to gold.

Nearly two years and a further rise in the Bank Rate to five per cent were needed to achieve his objective. But in April 1925 he could claim success. Britain returned to the gold standard at the prewar parity, thereby pricing many of her exports including coal out of export markets, provoking an attack on wages over a wide front and precipitating first a coal strike and then the only General Strike in Britain's history. The responsibility was not of course Norman's alone. He was supported by much orthodox economic opinion – Keynes was as usual the brilliant exception – and by politicians who obscurely felt that 'the pound must look the dollar in the face'. Yet when, in Sir Roy Harrod's words, we ask ourselves 'what would have been the economic fortunes of Britain had she not returned to the gold standard in 1925 thus saving herself from the Coal Strike and the General Strike and other consequential industrial troubles, had she shaped a policy for maintaining the sterling price level when the world slump came in 1929 and had she executed a thorough reconstruction of her public utilities and basic industries in the 'twenties when she had spare resources for the purpose?' it is difficult not to place a heavy responsibility upon the shoulders of the strange man who had so unexpectedly become the autocrat of national monetary and credit policy. His was the guiding spirit and motive power in these matters.

After April 1925 he engaged, in the words of his official biographer, 'in continuous struggle to maintain sterling on gold at the parity adopted against recurrent strains which he could not prevent' – although one cannot help but think that he might have been expected to foresee some of them. He was wholly dedicated to the effort, noble in conception if doomed in practice, to preserve the gold standard and by its means restore international stability and rehabilitate the credit structure of Europe. Compared with these purposes the shocks and tribulations inflicted on British industry seemed to him of little account. Even when he was forced to take cognizance of the plight of heavy industry because of the difficulties of the armament firm of Armstrong Whitworth and Co., a client of the Bank from prewar days when the business of commercial banking had been combined with that of a Central Bank, he did so reluctantly and with little or no show of appreciation of the relationship between monetary and industrial policy. His sole major contribution to the solving of Britain's industrial ills was to seek to promote 'rationalization' through the Bankers' Industrial Development Company. By this he meant the compulsory merging of firms into larger units and the closing down of 'redundant' shipyards, cotton factories and industrial plants without, it appeared, any regard for the effect on the workers in them – a policy that later reached its dramatic climax in the virtual murder of the shipbuilding town of Jarrow.

His contributions to European stability were more positive and at first seemed more beneficent. In a study of Norman's first decade at the Bank Dr Paul Einzig claimed for him 'a stronger influence upon the foreign policy of Great Britain than anyone else during the post-war years'; and certainly he went far beyond the nominal responsi-bilities of a central banker to pursue, in Einzig's words, 'the traditional balance of power in a political sense by economic and financial means'. To this end he consistently favoured Germany at the expense of France, irrespective of Foreign Office policy at any given time, and succeeded in antagonizing the French to such a degree, that by 1931, when Britain was sorely in need of French credits to help her meet a run on the pound, M. Moret, the Governor of the Bank of France, refused to speak to him at the Bank for International Settlements.

These were the days of Norman's paramountcy. He moved about

his world like a conqueror whose every word was wrung dry for its significance. To many, including one suspects himself, he seemed the most potent of all the forces making for the rehabilitation and unification of Europe. Like Chamberlain he built on conceptions as to the nature of power and the pattern of society that belonged to a pre-war age, and like Chamberlain refused to see what he did not want to see, clinging stubbornly to his conviction of prescience far beyond the point of no return.

This comes out markedly in his evidence before the Macmillan Committee on Finance and Industry of 1929-31 – one of the few occasions in his life when he was required to justify himself and his policies in public.

As had already been noted, Norman was not a good witness. Whether from disdain or because he had no aptitude for intellectual argument of a theoretical kind, he refused to be drawn into the discussions of principle in which Keynes, Reginald McKenna and Ernest Bevin sought to engage him. 'His negatives' when asked to do so were in Sir Roy Harrod's phrase, 'cold, aloof and relentless.'

Even when he may have wished to do so he found great difficulty in putting into words the principles that moved him. As he said to Bevin in a comparatively genial response to a question from one with whom in the main he made it clear he was out of sympathy: 'Of course you may complain, Mr Bevin, of me or of those bankers you have seen that the evidence they have given comes through their nose and is not sufficiently technical or expert. Of course that may in some measure be true; I plead guilty to it myself to some extent and it is a curious thing, that so many of those who inhabit the City find difficulty in stating the reasons for the faith that is in them.'

When he was asked to explain the movements of the Bank Rate his answer resembled that given by Pavlova when asked to describe her interpretation of Giselle: 'Why would I dance it, if I could put it into words.' He gave the impression of having given no thought whatever to reasons or consequences but of regarding intuition, the feel of things, as he put it, as enough.

So unaware of, or uninterested in, the internal effects of Bank Rate movements was he, that Keynes felt compelled to intervene at one stage in the Governor's evidence to say that although he had earlier described to the Committee what he believed to be the orthodox theory of the Bank Rate, 'the theory I thought all authorities would accept', he now found to his amazement that 'what you have been telling us today very nearly amounts to a repudiation of that theory'. As he understood it, Keynes continued, the accepted theory of the Bank Rate was that it worked two ways, internationally in attracting short-term funds from other centres, thus correcting pressures on the exchange rate, while at the same time the method of its operation on the internal situation is that the higher Bank Rate would mean curtailment of credit, that this curtailment of credit would diminish enterprise and cause unemployment and the unemployment would tend to bring down wages and costs of production generally. We should then be able to increase our exports with the result that the high Bank Rate which was to put on to check foreign lending would no longer be necessary....

To this Norman listened politely but without interest, commenting at the conclusion, 'I could not dispute it with you.'

'If that is so,' continued Keynes 'half the point of the Bank Rate is that it should have an effect on the internal situation.'

But Norman was not to be moved. He denied that it did so 'apart from the short money position'.

With Bevin he was even more off-hand. He refused to consider any possibility of a stiff rate for foreign borrowers with a lower one for domestic borrowers, an innovation for which Keynes had earlier argued with great brilliance before the Committee, and when Bevin said, 'Having regard to the fact that the workpeople at home have to suffer the biggest blow of unemployment and the depression of their standard of life, can you see any way to separate the national and international policies so that the effect of restoring the gold position internationally can be in some way modified in its effect upon British industry?', Norman replied briefly that he thought it impossible. Lord Macmillan, the Chairman, pressed the matter, 'Let us follow that,' he said. 'That is interesting; that is one of the problems – whether you can, so to speak, dissociate your national and external policies. Is it not possible that you can maintain your international policy outwards and by some of those devices which you have no doubt considered and others have considered mitigate the internal consequences of your outward policy?' 'I think not', replied Norman curtly.

Through all these exchanges he displayed complacency that would have been remarkable at any time and was truly extraordinary considering the state of the national economy and the critical problems of finance and industry which this very Committee had been appointed to explore.

Setting out before him the scope of the Committee's inquiry and the problems to which it felt it necessary to apply itself, Lord Macmillan explained that 'among the causes at work many minds apparently maintain that the deficiencies in our financial system are at least partly to blame and that some revisal of financial policy is necessary'.

Norman did not agree. He considered all that was needed was the 'rationalization' of industry.

Lord Macmillan persisted. 'We have always known,' he said dryly, 'that good organization and good management produce better results; in one sense there is nothing new in that; it is a new phrase, a new word and these long words become very attractive to popular imagination. Now rationalization means nothing more than putting businesses in order when they have got out of shape. But that does not seem to me to go to the root of the matter. It does not really deal with the kind of problems to which we have got to address ourselves, namely the presuppositions of the whole system on which we work, the control by the Bank of England of the Bank Rate as the main instrument of the policy.' After a further exposition of the basic problems affecting national industry and commerce Lord Macmillan concluded: 'It is the presuppositions of the financial structure of our country upon which our attention at the moment is concentrated and we are anxious to scrutinize it to see whether it is at that door that the present distress can be laid and then to see how far it can be aided by any financial expedient. You see how I am looking at it?'

To this Norman replied with fifteen bleak and arrogant words: 'I think it is not our financial system which is the cause of our difficulties.'

Again Lord Macmillan persisted. 'If a machine gets jammed,' he said, 'it will not work. May it not be that some of our troubles at the present moment are due to trying to deal with financial problems with an instrument which was designed to deal with other and more normal conditions?'

'I do not think the financial machine is at fault,' was Norman's response.

Nor was he interested in Bevin's experience as head of the largest trade union in the country – and the most outstanding labour leader of the time.

Cross-examining him on industrial 'rationalization', Bevin asked Norman whether he did not consider that consultations with labour were necessary to avoid vast upheavals of employment. That, he replied shortly, was none of the Bank's business. When Bevin went on that it had been his experience that two schemes of rationalization in which he had been directly involved had been rendered nugatory by lack of regard for the labour problem Norman replied coldly: 'It has not been mine.' That, it was plain, was that.

He was even less ready to consider opinions other than his own when it came to discussion of the gold standard. He refused to contemplate the possibility that the return to gold in 1925 might have had anything to do with what Bevin described as the jam in industry 'when we as industrialists were given a task of adjusting to the point of ten per cent without notice and without even considering the question'. The ills of industry, he replied sharply, had nothing to do with the return to gold but were due to 'certain misfortunes of one kind and another' which subsequently intervened.

This exchange then took place.

Bevin: But in view of the fact that it did involve facing the work-people of this country with a proportionate reduction of wages, did it not make the misfortunes that you describe absolutely inevitable?

Norman: No, I do not think so.

Bevin: That is what happened.

Norman: I do not think as a necessary consequence.

Bevin: How could it have been done? You are a Governor of the Bank of England. I am a Trade Union official. That is the point we had to face across the table. I am taking from 1921 up to the point of 1924. I am meeting the industrialists who do not know anything that is in the mind of the Bank of England on the financial policy of this country. They have no knowledge that you are going to interfere, that you are going to restore the gold standard, that you are going to do anything. We met morally the first period of deflation in 1921 when the first step to deflation was taken. We knew that we had to face a heavy reduction of money wages to get a postwar adjustment. We proceeded from 1921 onwards meeting employers across the table and getting that postwar adjustment to a new price. Contracts have been fixed on that new price, new standards have been worked out, men are becoming accustomed to that level of earning, to everything on the new basis. Suddenly the whole thing is upset by the steps taken in 1925 which throws every bit of work that the two parties in industry have done out of gear. We are faced with rising unemployment, bitter disputes and a new level of wages to be fixed without notice, without consideration, without guide, without any indication as to what its object is. I ask you, Mr Norman, if industry is placed in a position like that whether or not you do not think the misfortune of the jam is absolutely inevitable?

Norman: No, I do not, Sir.

At this stage Lord Macmillan made another effort to bring together these two irreconcilables. Might it not be, he asked, that the consequences of the return to gold had been aggravated 'by other conspiring causes', with the result 'that the timing of the return, which had seemed apposite enough in the conditions then thought to be ruling, had subsequently not turned out to be so', and that expectations had been falsified with serious results. 'If these circumstances which have supervened had been foreseen,' he continued, addressing Norman, 'it may be that you would not have reverted to the gold standard at the time you did.' But Norman was giving no ground. 'I will not say that,' he replied.

Even more remarkable than his disdain when asked to consider the effects of the return to gold on the welfare of industry, was the optimism he displayed regarding the international scene despite the clouds, so clearly discernible to other eyes.

He offered the Committee a sketch of what he had been trying to do over the past few years and the objectives he had set himself.

First was the stabilization of European currencies. The task had been 'long, tiresome and in some ways disappointing'. But despite the intransigence of those countries which had insisted on returning to gold on a lower level than he approved, it had been achieved. Second was the need to promote international cooperation through the machinery of the Central Banks of Europe and to bring them together in a common organization. This too had been difficult. Many personal questions had arisen. But here, too, success had crowned the day. With the establishment of the Bank for International Settlements, 'the climax of our efforts', those endeavours had, he claimed, in large measure been accomplished.

When he again appeared before the members of the Macmillan Committee towards the close of their deliberations he continued his evidence on the international situation. Speaking with a mastery, a lucidity, a passion even, quite different from the mood he had displayed when asked to discuss problems of industry and employment, he assured them that Reparations and other international debts were being taken out of 'the arena of politics' and 'put into a back room in the B.I.S.'

Yet it was all illusion. The magnificent edifice of international confidence and stability, for which the temporary distresses of industry were but a small and insignificant price to pay, was a house of cards which even as he was speaking had begun to shutter down around him, blown apart by the gales that swept the world but whose cause and strength he so resolutely refused to recognize.

He concluded his evidence to the Macmillan Committee on 18 February 1931. Within three months the closely integrated financial system of Western Europe had been shattered by the collapse of the Credit-Anstalt. Within five Germany, to the restoration of whose financial stability he had, with his friend Dr Schacht, devoted his first energies, had to meet a credit crisis so serious as to force the biggest German commercial bank, the Darmstädter and Nationalbank, to close its doors, and Reparations had broken out of their back room in the Bank for International Settlements and erupted on the world stage to such compelling effect that President Hoover felt it necessary to propose a year's moratorium on all Reparation and War Debt payments.

Yet even this was not all. Nothing that Norman pinned his faith to was safe. On 21 September, just 215 days after he completed his evidence to the Macmillan Committee, the Bank of England was compelled to ask for authority to suspend the gold standard. One by one the purposes Norman had worked for with such fanatical, such compulsive devotion were wrecked by the forces he had dismissed so off-handedly, so sharply refused to accept responsibility for, when Bevin, Keynes, McKenna and the others had the impertinence to ask him to argue.

He was not at the Bank when the decision to leave gold was reached. He collapsed at a meeting of the Committee of Treasury a week or two after the Hoover moratorium and was ordered to bed, to that same prison which had engulfed him nearly twenty years before. There he remained until 15 August when he was sent on a voyage to Canada in search of rest and health.

He returned on 23 September, two days after the decision to leave gold. He learned of it only as he stepped ashore at Liverpool. The Deputy Governor had tried to warn him in advance. But Norman had not taken a cable code with him and a message could only be sent in clear. 'Sorry to go off before you arrived', radioed the Deputy Governor and determinedly oblivious of what was happening around him, Norman took it as an apology for not being at the Bank to meet him when he got back. The real news shattered him. 'Nothing', his official biographer confesses, 'could have been a greater blow. He

"I like to believe that we shall meet here again next year and that then, as I believe is more than likely, we shall see clearly where we are going and be sensible of the rapid pace towards that goal at which we are proceeding." (CHEERS)

GOVERNOR NORMAN AT THE BANKERS DINNER.

BANK OF ENGLAND CELLARS

LOCKED-UP CAPITAL

"HERE WE GO ROUND THE MULBERRY BUSH"

Evening Standard, 24 October 1932

was profoundly depressed and for a time his temper showed it.'
It was the end for Norman. He stayed on as Governor for another
thirteen years doing valuable public service, although on a stage much
reduced. Inside the Bank he was still a despot. But outside his power
was ended except within now narrowly defined limits.

With the end of the gold standard the division between internal and
external credit policy advocated by Keynes and Bevin at the Macmillan
Committee and dismissed so contemptuously by Norman was made
effective by an Exchange Equalization Account which replaced the
rigid obligations of the gold standard by a technique of managed
currency. To the management of this account Norman loyally devoted
the resources of his technical skill. But he was a man under authority –
Treasury authority – and knew it.

He was slow to reconcile himself to the passing of his power. But
resistance was empty. When the imminence of war further extended
the limits imposed by politics on his management of the Exchange
Account in 1939 he declared with a flash of his old arrogance that he
'was not going to sit with his hands folded seeing his assets go and
sacrificing everything London stood for'. But it came to nothing. Nor
did his earlier attempt to block the decision to make no more than a
token payment on the American War Debt and finally to suspend it
altogether. Never, he confessed in a rare moment of intimacy to those
closest to him at the Bank, had he felt 'so confused and baffled and
unsure of himself'. Even his talent for cajolery no longer served him
now the power behind it was gone.

The weight of his presence was still tangible in every department of
the Bank. He was energetic and decisive in its affairs. But to most of
the world outside he had become an old gentleman complaining that
things were not what they were. The principles by which he had
guided his destiny had been set aside. The perils he had prophesied
should they be denied had not come. Now there were other and greater
perils to consider. In producing them his policies had had their part.
In meeting and overcoming them he had no real place.

Patrician, arrogant, still active, but increasingly conscious of relega-
tion to a subsidiary role in the great orchestra of Britain at war, he
stayed on at the Bank until January 1944. Then he resigned. Six years
later he died. The bank he had tried to preserve in his own image had
been nationalized four and a quarter years before with scarcely one
word of protest from within or without the City.

Lord Halifax

Edward Wood: born 1881; son of 2nd Viscount Halifax; educated at Eton and Christ Church, Oxford; Fellow of All Souls; Unionist M.P. for Ripon, 1910-25; Parliamentary Under-Secretary for the Colonies 1921-22; President of the Board of Education 1922-24; Minister of Agriculture 1924-25; created 1st Baron Irwin 1925; Viceroy of India 1926-31; President of the Board of Education 1932-35; Chancellor of University of Oxford 1933; Secretary of State for War 1935; Lord Privy Seal 1935-37; Leader of the House of Lords 1935-38 and 1940; Foreign Secretary 1938-40; British Ambassador in Washington 1941-46; created 1st Earl of Halifax 1944; died 1959.

1. Saint in Anger

IN the ruling pattern of the decades between the wars Lord Halifax's place was smaller than that of MacDonald, Baldwin, Chamberlain, or even Norman. He exercised influence rather than direct power and for this reason may seem a less appropriate subject than they for either praise or blame. But the prestige of his public personality gave him an atlantean role in much that happened; his public character provided a cloak for those with greater power than himself.

With his imposing presence and high principles Lord Halifax was ideally fitted to satisfy the British yearning for an aristocrat near the centre of their affairs, especially as to this aristocratic image he added one that seemed almost a saint's to earthier men. Great landowner, Fellow of All Souls, High Churchman and Master of Foxhounds, he had everything the English could wish for from those whom they like to persuade themselves are above the battle because they require from the world no material advantage it has not already given them at birth.

Nothing Lord Halifax actually did could affect the growth of the Halifax mystique: he was a man immune from the consequences of participation in disastrous acts. So great indeed was the protective power of his personal reputation that although no man was less fitted by nature than he for the role of war-leader it was only by the skin of their teeth that the British people were saved from the final disaster of having him instead of Winston Churchill as their Prime Minister at the lowest ebb of our military fortunes in 1940.

In 1918 there were few indications that he would come to enjoy such unique moral eminence.

He had behind him, it is true, a glittering family heritage; but no more so than several others who never came within hail of his popular stature. His family – the Woods of Hickleton – had been landowners in the West Riding of Yorkshire since the sixteenth century. He was a great grandson of the Whig leader Lord Grey; a grandson of that Charles Wood, First Viscount Halifax, who having fought for the Reform Bill on the very just assessment that it would prove to be 'an efficient, substantial, anti-democratic, pro-party measure' ended up as a most enlightened Secretary of State for India; a great-nephew of the Lord Durham who laid the foundations of the modern Commonwealth in Canada – and observed in passing that he 'supposed a man might jog along on £40,000 a year'. Through his mother he was linked with that fabulous family on whose singular fortunes and vast distinctions Gibbon meditated ('wearers of the purple of three Emperors who have reigned at Constantinople') – the Courtenays of Devon.

It was thus to a heritage rich in material fortune and assured in position that Edward Wood, later Lord Irwin, subsequently Viscount and Earl of Halifax, was born in April 1881. It was also one distinguished for religious sensibilities of a character at once humble and patrician. His father had so far put the claims of the world behind him as to renounce at an early age the glittering political ambitions to which his Whig ancestry, his territorial interests, the reputation of his father, the first Lord Halifax, and his own social eminence as a Groom of the Bedchamber and close personal friend of the Prince of Wales entitled him, to choose instead a lifetime's labour for the unity of the Catholic churches as President of the English Church Union, principal guardian of the Oxford Movement, and chief lay champion of Anglo-Catholicism, of the High against the Low in the Church of England. A man of remarkable and eccentric character, the second Viscount Halifax exercised, until he died at the age of ninety-two, an influence on the life and ideas of his son exceptional even among those made most conscious of their headship of a great family by birth and vast possessions.

Disease, however, shadowed this splendid family. Edward was born with a withered arm and both his elder brothers died of tuberculosis before he was ten, although there is no evidence that tragedy affected the family's serenity of character and certainly none that it touched its religious faith.

This faith was essentially sacramental, a fact that may offer some guide to much that is puzzling in Halifax's subsequent career, with its antinomy between what he was and what he was sometimes willing to do. It is a vulgar habit to link faith and works and, without, of course, going so far as to put the belief into practice, to imagine that true Christians ought to be governed by a code of ethics as applicable to the secular as the religious life. Edward Wood recognized more plainly than many of his admirers the distinction between the two.

His position is perhaps made clearest in a small, dull book on Keble which he wrote in his twenties for a series called 'Leaders of the Modern Church'. In it he noted 'the increased facility with which men nowadays have learnt to recognize conflicting rules of life and to allot to each the control of a certain sphere of action'. Earlier theologians had argued that man should yield 'an undivided allegiance to a single principle', but a distinction was now accepted between principles governing different departments of life: 'What is not possible for a man as a member of the Church is not impossible, may even be right, in his capacity as a citizen.' He recognized that this could, of course, be carried too far: 'Real liberty', he observed, turning a phrase, 'is not "licence" ', and added the clarification: 'Rather is it the attainment, by a regulated following of law, of that vantage ground from which the perspective of the lower plains may be discerned, and conflicting duties more easily harmonized.' From such a vantage point he conducted his own political life.

It was, however, the landed aristocrat rather than the Christian who in 1910 entered politics at the age of twenty-nine: choosing despite his Whig ancestry the Conservative not the Liberal side. To the lustre of his own lineage he had lately added alliance with an even greater family by his marriage to Lady Dorothy Evelyn Augusta, younger daughter of the fourth Earl of Onslow. It was therefore appropriate that defence of the House of Lords against the reforming excesses of a Welsh solicitor should be the trumpet to call him to political action. He had contemplated entering Parliament four years earlier but had refrained. Liberalism had become too vulgar and radical for a Whig, but Conservatism, especially as shown in some of the domestic policies of Joseph Chamberlain, did not then wholly appeal. Besides, to deter him there was the experience of his brother-in-law, Colonel Lane Fox, later Lord Bingley, who two years before had been ignominiously defeated in what had been considered until then a safe Conservative Yorkshire constituency. In 1910, however, it was very different. The Liberal tide in the constituencies was receding. Joe Chamberlain was out of politics and the Conservative flirtation with radicalism was over. It was a time for the great Whig families to declare themselves.

Standing for Ripon in the Conservative interest Edward Wood was returned to the House of Commons with a large majority, there to speak on behalf of Conservative amendments cunningly drafted (although not sufficiently so for debate with Asquith, Lloyd George *and* Winston Churchill) to suggest that the passing of power from the Lords to the Commons ought to be opposed in the interests of democracy. The new member interested himself, also, in imperial affairs. He spoke for firm government in Egypt, not, as he explained, out of any wish 'permanently to hold down the black races' but because 'if our position in these countries is to be maintained it can only be, as it is at the present moment, by maintaining the position and fulfilling the functions of a superior race'. He also spoke out very strongly indeed against the Welsh Disestablishment Bill.

A privileged, solemn, intellectual young man, towering above his contemporaries from the lanky height of six foot five inches, his withered arm almost ostentatiously disregarded, but modest in demeanour, respectful to his elders and with all the right connections and ideas, he had the additional advantage of knowing a little about the Empire. He had done a modern grand tour and had visited India, Australia and South Africa, lunching in this latter country with Milner and talking with his fellow Fellows of All Souls, Lionel Curtis, Geoffrey Robinson (later to be known as Geoffrey Dawson of *The Times*), the Hon. Robert Brand, and others of that potent and pervasive kindergarten who were later, in their influential way, to carry the ideas there learnt into so many ministerial anterooms – popping up in so many places at so many times that they often seemed in danger of running the world without having time to find out what was happening in it.

As he pursued his amiable, amateurish way through politics, aroused to emotion only by attacks on the landed interests or the Established Church, Edward Wood seemed the natural raw material of what would in due course become another Conservative Under-Secretary, and later, no doubt, a Conservative Minister of Agriculture or President of the Board of Education. Passion came in with the war. He served in the Yorkshire Dragoons with the distinction to be expected of one of his antecedents, but reserved his most militant emotions for those of his fellow Christians whose consciences differed from his own. In his religion there was, he made very plain, no place for conscientious objectors or peace makers. In a savage speech in the House of Commons he demanded the total disenfranchisement of all conscientious objectors not only during the war but for five years after. He had, he declared, 'absolutely no sympathy with the real conscientious objector' (whether he had with bogus ones he did not make clear), and urged that Britain should do what he alleged, on inadequate information, was being done in America, 'Where I am told they do not waste time passing special laws and legislation as to conscientious objectors but if they are quite sure they have got the right people they compel them to wear scarlet uniforms and walk the street' – a curious speech for the future saint of British politics to look back on. The Lansdowne letter arguing the case for a negotiated peace in 1917, which his friend Geoffrey Dawson refused to publish in *The Times*, threw him into an equal fury. For him, indeed, even Lloyd George was suspect as too soft on the enemy. He was a signatory to the notorious Lowther Petition demanding that the Prime Minister get tougher at Versailles.

Lord Halifax's rise, despite this inauspicious beginning, to an almost godlike stature as a voice of conscience between the wars provides one of the most impressive examples in our history of the influence of the myth in British politics. Of one such myth MacDonald, as has been seen, was the beneficiary and the victim, and of another, Baldwin, who in the end himself came to believe in his public myth so much that he almost lost touch with his own nature. The myth of Lord Halifax was different from either of these. He was not thought, as Baldwin was, to be more honest and simple than other men, nor did he, as happened with MacDonald, come to symbolize in the public mind ideas and attitudes to which he was in fact wholly antipathetic. It was rather that by a compound of the true and the false in the public understanding of his character he came to symbolize for many a quality of disinterested goodness that placed him above personal controversy and made him a shield for the policies of others, an embodiment of Christian principles so lofty as to put him beyond common judgment. Even his political opponents came to regard him as motivated in what he did by no ordinary considerations of political advantage or part loyalty but by moral imperatives beyond mundane analysis.

2. Patrician over Politics

THERE is no man more dangerous in politics than the man who is thought to be above them. Halifax came to be such a man. He gave tangible form to a self-deception to which the English are prone, the belief that if they look long enough among those socially above them they will find an abstract public virtue untainted by political or hereditary interest.

No man climbs to the top in politics without a liking for power. Such liking was concealed in Halifax's case – possibly even from himself – by an aloofness that appeared incapable of passion and a preference for the broad principles rather than the details of politics. He seemed so disinterested in those stratagems that necessarily concern men of less assured position that it was generally assumed that only a sense of duty had driven him into politics and that he would rather have lived the life of a country gentleman. Impressive in presence and manner he cast over everything he touched – even foxhunting – an ethical glow, and although capable in youth, as has been indicated, of the most extreme partisanship, he developed as he grew older so measured a tone that he came to be thought of as a man so moderate that he must be right. He seemed above the battle – perhaps because he had grown confident it would not touch him – a patrician guest at a plebeian party, his shoulders sagging a little beneath the weight of history.

For such a man with such connections political promotion in a predominantly Conservative House of Commons was unavoidable. He moved forward at a measured pace from a minor post under Sir Eric Geddes in the reconstituted Ministry of National Service from which his future friend and leader Neville Chamberlain had just been ignominiously dismissed, to an Under-Secretaryship at the Colonial Office where he did well, particularly during a tour to the West Indies carried out with almost Viceregal ceremony, and from there to his first senior Ministerial appointment as President of the Board of Education – a post then as now regarded by Conservative Governments as peculiarly fitted to Old Etonians. In this he demonstrated a talent for hopeful generalities which could not disguise that, whether willingly or unwillingly, he was an agent of contraction and economy. He moved to Agriculture of which his practical knowledge was greater although not, it soon began to appear, sufficiently so to be likely to save him from the fate common to most of his predecessors of digging the grave of his own political reputation in its unpromising soil.

From such disaster he was saved in 1925 by the invitation – astonishing at the time to everyone including himself – to succeed the Marquess of Reading, a man of infinitely greater stature and eminence than he was, as Viceroy of India. This invitation it appears from Sir Harold Nicolson's *Life of King George V* was initiated by the King, who with Queen Mary had been entertained at Hickleton shortly after his accession and knew the family well and whose interest may also have been aroused by the private recommendations of Geoffrey Dawson, who with other members of the Round Table and All Souls saw in Edward Wood a distillation of these virtues of rule by informed members of country house parties they spent so much of their time promoting. It was a recommendation that much commended itself to Stanley Baldwin. He found in this High Church member of the landed aristocracy a man of exactly the noble if vague aspirations and non-controversial turn of mind that most appealed to him: 'A man', as he once said, 'whose ideals and views in political life approximate most closely to my own.' ('Those who think that out', as Vansittart acidly remarked in *The Mist Procession*, 'will be instructed.') Not until he had gone to Yorkshire to discuss it with his eighty-six year old father and the two of them had together received guidance in prayer did the recipient of the invitation agree.

It was a fateful decision. It was as Viceroy that the future Lord Halifax came to establish in the public mind the particular image of himself that thereafter was to remain constant whatever he did and to make him so valuable a shield to the policies of others in later years. This image was by no means entirely due to his achievements in India. Indeed in the total perspective of India's struggle for independence these cannot be judged of permanent importance. Nor did it result from any decisions he made as Viceroy. On the greatest single issue that came before him, the decision as to the composition of the Simon Commission, he was wrong. He considered and so advised that it must be composed only of members of the two British Houses of Parliament and should not include representatives of either Hindus or Muslims, thus directly ensuring the boycott of the Commission by those in whose hands the future of India actually lay. And as head of the Government of India he filled its gaols with 60,000 political offenders, headed by Gandhi, Nehru and all the other major leaders of Congress.

He had, however, the great merit for the British ruling class at this period in their Indian relationship of habitually speaking in terms of high principle. They were not yet prepared to let India go but they had a great need to assure themselves, as they moved reluctantly towards the idea of Dominion status which was already both too little and too late for Indian nationalism, that in their attitude to this great imperial possession their motives were noble. He put down civil disobedience with a firm hand but always did so in the most liberal accents, and managed to combine in his person the viceregal splendours of Curzon with a spiritual humility that allowed him to speak to Gandhi as an equal.

If there was to be retreat from India, and almost everyone except Winston Churchill and his small band of opponents of imperial change accepted the fact that sooner or later there must be, he was the man to conduct it in the grand manner. He was also most fortunately a phenomenon the Indians themselves could understand. They were well used in their history to the combination of material splendour and holiness – or at least deference to it – that he presented to them. He respected Gandhi even while he imprisoned him and Gandhi in his turn showed every indication of respecting him.

This latter fact while of importance to India was even more so to Britain. Gandhi disturbed the conscience of the British. They did not like imprisoning a saint. It made them feel better when it was done by a man whose own saintliness, if not quite equal to Gandhi's, was at least superior, it was said, to anything they aspired to themselves. The Viceroy's character eased their sense of guilt. When he said 'I am not fighting Civil Disobedience because I lack sympathy with the genuine Nationalist feelings of India', they could feel they were getting the best of both worlds, and when he conducted Gandhi to the steps of his house and said 'Goodnight, Mr Gandhi, and my prayers go with you', could enjoy an obscure sense of moral equality with those they oppressed. Moreover the Viceroy had two immense advantages in terms of his future reputation: he was under constant and bitter attack from the imperialist wing of his own party and during the latter part of his time in India served under a Labour Government in London with the greatest amiability. His public image as a man superior to party was thus consolidated. It is true also, as his biographer Alan Campbell-Johnson claims, that his aristocratic origins were a source of strength in this much criticized office: 'They removed the terrors of personal failure, the lure of private ambition. If everything he stood for crashed in ruins around him he could, like Cincinnatus, return to his estates.... Although to some it seemed that India had demonstrated the triumph of his personality over the failure of his policy, there was no doubt as to where he stood in popular regard when he returned home.'

Back in England he slipped with becoming modesty into that life he most enjoyed: the life of great country houses which to his mind provided 'by far the best means that a society with some opportunity for leisure has to offer for the making of new acquaintances or for the renewing of old ones': Hatfield with the Salisburys where he could not doubt that 'the Holy Spirit had been among our little company as we worshipped together in the family chapel'; swimming, golf, tennis and talk, 'talk through the daylight hours without prejudice to further talk after dinner when night and day met' with the Astors at Cliveden, grouse shooting with the Bentincks at Underley, weekends at Welbeck with the Portlands, house parties at his own Garrowby, and long talks with William Temple on the place of suffering in the Christian religion and whether it would have been right for him as Viceroy to have answered Gandhi's fast by one of his own ('I can', said the Archbishop, 'conceive its being a justifiable as well as a heroic thing to do; but if so, it is because it was right that Civil Disobedience should be ended, and if so the Indians ought to have stopped it for that reason, their attention being called to it by your action; if they stopped it only to save you from suffering and death, that would be good so far as it goes, for it would be an expression of love, but it would not settle whether Civil Disobedience is inherently right or wise ...'). Almost best of all were long days with the Garrowby Harriers or the Middleton Hounds of which he was Master. In India his habit of hunting with the Delhi Hounds whatever the state of the crisis around him had struck some members of Congress as odd in a man so spiritual. In Yorkshire God and fox hunting were not thought of as antipathetical.

Spending his time in these delights he remained aloof from the 1931 crisis and the feuds that marked the birth of the National Government, just as he had earlier avoided taking sides in the intrigues that brought down Lloyd George. He had a genius for non-involvement in domestic controversy. Even when Baldwin summoned him to London on the formation of the National Government and with MacDonald's approval invited him to be Foreign Secretary, he persuaded them that since he was suspect among right-wing Conservatives for his India policy it would be unwise for him to come out of seclusion just yet.

Not until a year later, when the electorate had had time massively to show its support for the National Government, did he join it, and then in a comparatively non-contentious capacity – as President of the Board of Education once more. The rotund phrases of his sympathetic biographer do adequate justice to his term of office there, except that one may doubt whether he will be remembered in this capacity at all: 'On the whole he will probably be longest remembered as an Education Minister who gave notable expression to the broad principles on which British educational policy should be based. He said nothing new or startling but he gave fresh polish to old truths ...' Nor did he either say or do anything fresh during a brief spell as Secretary of State for War, although this was a time when a new mind at work on defence problems was badly needed.

None of this mattered. His public image was fixed. It could not be affected by comparative failure in any office. He was Chancellor of Oxford University, President of the Anglo-Catholic Congress to celebrate the centenary of the Oxford Movement, Master of the Middleton Hunt. It was not necessary that he should be a good Departmental Minister as well. He had become an elder statesman on his return from India at the age of fifty. He remained one for the rest of his life. It was what he had been born to be. Without effort on his part his career moved inexorably forward with each new Prime Minister. MacDonald, Baldwin, Chamberlain all found him indispensable, even Churchill, who regarded him as the chief instrument of retreat in India and to whom his record as an appeaser-in-chief under Chamberlain can scarcely have appealed, made him Ambassador to the United States when his day came.

But it is not so much the enigma of his success that stirs curiosity. There are men in every age – and in every political party – who gather to themselves, as he did, a reputation for disinterested wisdom and find themselves often for reason much less obvious than in his case, Public Figures in capital letters. What is harder to understand is how a man of his disposition and morality could come to take so lenient a view of some of the greatest criminals in history and shield with his support, not so much the policy of appeasement, for adhesion to that is perhaps understandable enough in a man of his kind, but the half-truths and deceptions that were used in its service.

Consider for example under the first heading his visit to Germany in November 1937 at the invitation of Goering. He was by now Lord President of the Council, a non-departmental post with vague frontiers

NAZI HUNTING EXHIBITION.

"Great Britain and every country owe a debt of gratitude - - for the encouragement given to sport by this exhibition —"
LORD HALIFAX

Evening Standard, 19 November 1937

Q

more suited to his capacity for high-minded advice without executive responsibility than either Education or the War Office, which also enabled him to keep a supervisory eye on Eden of whose less compromising attitude to the Fascist dictators Chamberlain was becoming suspicious. It was, however, ostensibly in his capacity as Master of the Middleton Hunt that he received in that month, through the medium of the Editor of *The Field*, an invitation from Goering to attend a hunting exhibition in Berlin to be followed by an opportunity to shoot foxes in East Prussia, Mecklenburg or Saxony, which struck him as amusing. He was urged to accept by Chamberlain and, according to his own account in *Fulness of Days*, by Eden also, although at the time the general impression among Eden's friends, including Churchill, was that the arrangement was made behind Eden's back and against his advice when he came to hear of it.

Be that as it may, he set off – not particularly sanguine of results but it would appear wholly unaware of, or else uninterested in, the effect of this friendly visit of one sportsman to another on the minds of those who were already feeling the weight of Nazi terror. A message from Ribbentrop preceded him, reporting that Halifax had expressed to him 'his pleasure at having an opportunity of becoming acquainted with the Führer ... whose work he admires'. After an enjoyable day at the hunting exhibition he was, therefore, conveyed by special train to Berchtesgaden and driven to Hitler's chalet. With true aristocratic unimpressionability he first mistook Hitler for a footman but, this corrected, they had a long and friendly talk in the course of which Halifax told his host that although there were things in the Nazi system that offended British opinion, 'I was not blind to what he had done for Germany and to the achievement from his point of view of keeping Communism out of his country'.

It had been assumed by many in Britain, possibly even by Halifax himself, that the man who had 'tamed Gandhi' would similarly be able to 'tame Hitler'. After all were they not, in the words of Arnold Toynbee, seeking to explain British attitudes at this time, 'two hardly distinguishable specimens of the same species of foreigner ... political "mad mullahs", non-smokers, non-drinkers of alcohol, non-eaters of meat, non-riders on horseback and non-practisers of blood sports in their cranky private lives. In the minds of his countrymen, peers and colleagues Lord Halifax was regarded with a certain pride and awe not unmingled with a spice of sceptical amusement as a characteristically English exponent of some simple but noble virtues who at the same

234

time had the gift of charming the most outlandish, un-English "wild men" by the unconsious exercise of an intuitive art which was capable of surpassing the Machiavellian triumphs of cleverer and less scrupulous politicians.'

It did not turn out quite like that. This 'Gandhi in jack-boots' was not interested in theology but power. He was not concerned to evoke the moral conscience of a nation but to command attention by naked force. Halifax did not make the mistake of underestimating the difference between the two of them. He was shrewder than Chamberlain. On this occasion at least he showed a perception that might have avoided future errors if he had stuck to it. 'One had', he recorded in notes after the meeting, 'the feeling all the time that we had a totally different sense of values and were speaking a different language. It was not only the difference between a totalitarian and democractic state. He gave me the impression of feeling that, whilst he had attained to power only after a hard struggle with present day realities, the British Government was still living comfortably in a world of its own making, a fairyland of strange, if respectable, illusions.' His final judgment was: 'While I think he wants to be on friendly terms with us he is not going to be in any hurry to consider the question of League of Nations return, regards disarmament as pretty hopeless and in short feels himself to be in a strong position and is not going to run after us.'

It has been hoped by many people that as a Churchman Halifax would seek an opportunity to protest against the Nazi persecution of the churches which had recently been the subject of a pamphlet with an introduction by the Bishop of Lichfield setting out the story of the persecutions of the previous four years. 'What will especially interest me to learn', wrote Tom Jones to Lady Grigg, 'will be what line Halifax takes on the religious issue which is as acute as ever.' But Halifax said nothing. He avoided contentious issues.

He was indeed in a singularly accommodating mood for a man of so spiritual a reputation. He was much taken with Goering, his comments on whom underline the enigma of the Halifax personality. 'I was', he recorded, and the choice of words is revealing, 'immensely entertained at meeting the man. One remembered all the time that he had been concerned with the "clean up" in Berlin on June 30, 1934 and I wondered how many people he had been responsible for getting killed. Like a great schoolboy, full of life and pride in all he was doing, showing it all off and talking high politics out of the setting of green jerkin and red dagger. A modern Robin Hood: producing in me a composite

impression of film star, gangster, great landowner interested in his property, Prime Minister, party manager, head gamekeeper at Chatsworth.'

He liked Goebbels, too, when he and his wife came to tea at the
British Embassy, although he was a little ashamed that he did. However,
he felt able to reconcile his actual feelings with those he had expected
of himself by finding in Goebbels's conversation confirmation of 'what
I had always been inclined to think about part of the Nazi attitude
arising from an inferiority complex'.

It was a pleasing assumption and well suited to support the British
ego. Indeed throughout his own record of this visit one catches the tone
of a visitor from a higher plane who, observing the habits of a lower
order of being, feels it unnecessary to make moral judgments since
these are creatures who do not come into the context of his own life.
There is a lack of any sense of personal involvement, a feeling not only
of intellectual but also of moral detachment.

This disengagement from the emotions which beset so many of his
fellow countrymen as they watched the unfolding panorama of
violence and horror across Europe is to be found in other matters also.
Thus he found it difficult not only to sympathize with but even to
understand the common reaction of many ordinary British people to
the Spanish Civil War, and later professed himself baffled by the long
continuance of the British 'reserve' towards Franco once he had proved
victorious, or why friendship with his régime should seem to so many
'something like disloyalty to the cause of free men'. He finally decided
that this was not to be accounted for by any process of reasoning but
must (surely one of the most tortuous explanations ever evolved to
explain away a direct human response to what seemed to so many the
first clear demonstration of the nature of Fascist tyranny) be due to
'some instinctive hang-over from past history, the Spanish danger of
the sixteenth and seventeenth centuries, the Armada, the Inquisition,
and the fires of Smithfield, an impression of the cruelty involved in
bull-fighting, all touching the British sub-conscious self at sensitive
points, and all uniting to leave an impression that Spain is something
to be kept as far away as possible'. One is tempted to say that a man
who could believe that would believe anything.

He was capable of a similar disengagement where his own direct
responsibility as a Minister comes into the matter. Thus seeking to
defend the Munich settlement in *Fulness of Days* nearly twenty years
later he could write that those who criticized it 'ought to have criticized
the failure of successive Governments and of all parties, to foresee the

necessity of rearming in the light of what was going on in Germany; and the right date on which criticism ought to have fastened was 1936 which had seen the German re-occupation of the Rhineland in defence of treaty provisions', without any acknowledgement of the fact that he was a prominent member of each of these successive Governments and War Minister in one of them. Indeed in 1936 he had but recently moved from this office to become Lord Privy Seal so that he could help the Prime Minister on foreign policy following Hoare's enforced resignation from the Foreign Office and the youthful Eden's appointment to the vacant chair in face of much right wing Tory suspicion. Although twenty years later he argued that if in 1936 we had 'told Hitler bluntly to go back, his power for future and larger mischief would have been broken' and that failure to do so lost 'the last effective chance of securing peace without war', there is no evidence that he used his massive influence in the Cabinet in support of such a policy at the time – or, which is even more curious, later acknowledged even to himself any share in the responsibility for failing to stop Hitler at the one moment when according to his own argument it could have been done. Stranger still is his reference to the attitude of the French at that time: 'But, leaving entirely aside the French, there was no section of British public opinion that would not have been directly opposed to such action in 1936.'

Leaving entirely aside the French! The obvious conclusion to be drawn from such a reference in such a context is that French opinion was even more opposed to action than British. Yet when Halifax and Eden arrived in Paris for urgent discussions ('Lord Halifax had been appointed to second Mr Eden who the British Cabinet feared might act recklessly if left to himself' observed Madame Tabouis voicing a general French suspicion) they found the French determined to demand an immediate general withdrawal from the Rhineland, and insistent that if this demand were not met sanctions should be applied. Indeed, Flandin went even further, offering to take military action alone if the other Locarno Powers would authorize him to do so. Only the refusal of Halifax and Eden – a refusal in which Halifax provided the main weight, for Eden was much nearer to the French view and argued for it in Cabinet when they returned – prevented the French from taking the very action that according to Halifax's later view could have secured 'peace without war', and failure to take which according to him justified Munich.

Such sophistry in *post hoc* reporting might just be forgivable in a lesser man, it is hard to reconcile with Halifax's private character and public image.

Yet one becomes accustomed to it as one studies his career.

Having defended sanctions against Italy and given his firm assurance as Leader of the House of Lords that the Government would remain true to 'a policy for which they have the overwhelming support of the mass of the people', he defended the Hoare–Laval Pact no less eloquently. The premature publication of the terms in Paris had surprised both Government and country. There had been questions as to why they had not been challenged at this stage. But that, he explained, would have been impossible. It might have suggested that they were preparing to repudiate the Foreign Secretary. Speaking with an emotion that deeply moved their Lordships, he proceeded: 'If we erred I venture to think we erred for motives that will be appreciated by all who know how close are the bonds of trust that bind colleagues and how essentially these bonds of comradeship are the foundation of all that is best in the political life of a free nation.' Yet when the crunch came and public indignation made it expedient that Hoare should go it was Halifax who led the Cabinet pack against him. To some, including Chamberlain, it was distasteful to use a colleague as scapegoat for a policy all had approved. Not so Halifax – 'Unless Sam went the moral force of the Government would be gone,' he said.

In such matters his taste was impeccable. When later it was a matter of dismissing another colleague, Hore-Belisha, from the War Office and Chamberlain toyed with the idea of offering him the Ministry of Information, this man of honour again intervened. To do so he objected, 'would have a bad effect on the neutrals both because H.B. was a Jew and because his methods would let down British prestige'. Belisha's career was destroyed.

Nor did he hesitate when another friend with whom he had had the closest association over several years, Anthony Eden, was sacrificed. With the 'greatest reluctance' he agreed to replace him as Foreign Secretary confessing even twenty years later that he found it hard to understand why he had resigned at all.

3. The Indestructible Man

HALIFAX'S acceptance of the Foreign Secretaryship in such circumstances was perhaps his greatest single contribution to the course of history in the 'thirties. His prestige and character deflected the public anxiety caused by Eden's resignation and the rumours of pressure from Mussolini that surrounded it. It thus checked the public demand for a reappraisal of Britain's foreign policy at the moment when it might have been most effective. Although there was some opposition to a Foreign Secretary in the House of Lords at this critical juncture in British and world affairs, it was universally felt that here was a man of integrity and moral principle who would be quick to guard British honour against any inroads appeasement might threaten. At the very least, it was assumed, he would not be content to be a cipher but would bring to bear, with more weight and influence than Eden had been able to mobilise, the full power of an independent and honourable character. Even Churchill, who had fought Halifax over India, welcomed his appointment with relief. 'The new British Foreign Secretary, Lord Halifax', he wrote, 'must not be dismissed as a pious devotee of "peace at any price". Hitherto he has wielded undue influence in the Cabinet as a vague sincere advocate of making friends with everybody. Now in the collar of a great Department he will be brought face to face with grim duties arising from the movement of events and I for one shall not assume he will be found unworthy of them.' And in the Commons debate on the appointment he summed up one who had so often differed from him as 'a man not only of integrity and high character but force and courage which, if ultimately provoked will be found at least as enduring as that on any man on either side of the House.'

These expectations were to be disappointed. Halifax was to prove not a brake on appeasement but its chief prop and support. Perhaps this was to be expected. He was by nature a quietist. His closest intimates, Lothian, Londonderry and Dawson, were appeasers to a man. He shared most of their attitudes. The sincerity of his readiness to grasp peace with Germany at almost any cost need not be doubted. On that there can be no charge against him except – and it is serious enough – of a misjudgment so extreme that in the end it closed his mind, as it did that of Chamberlain, to all the warning signs that were plain to see and that grew in force and clarity with every passing month.

What is more curious is that having accepted the Foreign Secretaryship with a full awareness – for he cannot have been ignorant of his own public standing and of the trust his private reputation and stature invoked – of the weight of public confidence he carried, he then willingly, or at any rate with no obvious struggle, allowed the office to be demoted to a subsidiary position. While carrying the title and the public image of one of the great Ministers of State he became in effect no more than a sort of supernumerary Permanent Secretary. He did not seek to mould policy but was content to be the interpreter and agent of the policy of others, a man whose vast prestige was used to immunize the British people, not so much from knowledge of the purpose of the policy that was being followed, for this he sympathized with, as from an understanding of some of the methods that were employed to further it. Not for him the independence of a Cranborne or even of those like Vansittart, Cadogan and Strang who, though public servants and as such committed in the ultimate to executing rather than forming policy, were prepared on occasion to protest. They were sometimes able to bring him to a show of firmness. But never for long. He was, as A. J. P. Taylor has said, a man 'fertile in negations', perfectly willing to be left on the periphery of great decisions and to abdicate the Foreign Secretary's proper place at the right hand of the Prime Minister in favour of that man of little experience and lesser judgment of international affairs, Sir Horace Wilson. There had perhaps been no previous time in history when the stature of Foreign Secretary and the Foreign Office was so reduced as during his occupation. He seemed perfectly prepared to conceive of it not as one of the great offices of the State but as an annexe to the Prime Minister's private office at 10 Downing Street.

As Viceroy of India there had been occasions when, as his biographer Alan Campbell-Johnson claimed in a passage already quoted, 'his aristocratic origins seemed a source of strength.... If everything he stood for crashed in ruins around him he could, like Cincinnatus, return to his estates.' It was no longer so. And now, too, the intellectual detachment that had previously seemed to be one of his great strengths revealed itself as a weakness. When one talked to him what struck one most was what seemed the absence of a capacity for passion. His lack of a sense of personal involvement appeared so complete that one could begin to understand why he was content to act as a man under authority rather than as a Minister holding great office. It was as though his emotions, like his left arm, had become atrophied. In pursuit of what he regarded as his public duty he seemed able to close his mind to all that was most menacing and ugly in the Nazi régime including those areas of religious persecution and racial intolerance where he might have been expected to have a particular concern. The Nazi treatment of the Jews touched the conscience of the whole world but his, so far as his actions reveal, it left unaffected. He was sometimes troubled by what it was necessary to do to compel Czechoslovakia to surrender. 'It was very clear', recorded Hugh Dalton after leading a deputation to protest against the treatment of Czechoslovakia after Berchtesgaden, 'that he was most unhappy. I am sure he shared our sense of shame.' But when George Dallas, one of the deputation erupted violently, 'Lord Halifax, listening to you we are ashamed to be Britishers', he retreated into imperturbability and sophistry, speaking of 'moralities and expediences. Morality knew no geography. There was no more case for us to go to war with Germany on behalf of Czechoslovakia, than with Japan on behalf of China. The French had a direct obligation to the Czechs but we had none.'

No doubt his attitude can in part be explained by his aversion to any alliance with Soviet Russia – even when such an alliance seemed the most likely method of checking Hitler. Like many less eminent peers he saw Communists under every bed. The strongest argument he offered to deter Hitler when an invasion of Czechoslovakia seemed imminent in May 1938 was that 'the parties concerned' must 'all be stronger than fate' for if they let the situation get out of hand 'the only ones to profit would be the Communists' and at the interview with the Labour deputation referred to he told Dalton with his usual detachment that he had seen no reason to instruct the British Ambassador in Moscow to ask the Soviet Government their intentions.

In private conversation he made no attempt to disguise his dislike of the Franco-Soviet Pact and his desire to see it ended, and found it much easier to contemplate friendship with dictators of the Right, with Franco, with Mussolini, with Hitler, than he did with a dictator of the Left, perhaps because they threatened less obviously the assumptions of privilege to which he had been born. Unlike Churchill he lacked the historical energy to divest himself of the pull of his aristocratic connections and take a world view when the foundations of national life were at issue. In this aversion to a Russian alliance and his preference for Fascism to Communism, he was, of course, at one with most of his own intimate circle and closest family friends and like many of them could not, as he had confided in that early visit to Berchtesgaden, withhold a certain admiration for Hitler's achievement in 'keeping Communism out of his country'. At times it seemed as though the desirability of making friends with Nazis rather than Communists was enough to justify any means.

Yet even so it is hard to understand how a man such as he was could behave as he did.

When the first German demands on Czechoslovakia started he used every pressure open to him to compel Beneš to go further in meeting them – only to admit to Bonnet (but not Beneš) when pressed, that even if Czechoslovakia offered concessions he thought reasonable and Hitler rejected them he would still be unwilling for Britain to join in her defence.

Thereafter the pressure, and the deception, mounted month by month, in the end almost day by day, in a frenzy of double talk which it is hard to justify in any man, and particularly so in one of Halifax's moral reputation. Thus when the French insisted on a communiqué that in view of the gravity of the situation Anglo-French staff talks would continue, he was within hours of its issue telling Kordt, the German Chargé d'Affaires, that it need not be taken seriously and that Britain's only desire was to continue 'fruitful collaboration' with Hitler. Although the British public were led to believe that Britain and France were acting in concert, indeed if there were any difficulties in the way of firm guarantees they were due to the French, he rejected a French proposal for a joint warning to Germany on 10 May and when the French Foreign Minister asked what Britain would do if there were a German attack on Czechoslovakia and France mobilized, gave the evasive reply that the British Government was 'unable to make precise statements of the character of their future actions'.

Even in September, when Britain was finally brought to the point of exchanging guarantees of mutual support with France and, following pressure by Churchill and senior Foreign Office officials, he agreed to issue an official statement that if Germany attacked Czechoslovakia France must come to her help and Great Britian and Russia would stand by France (he did not trouble to inform Russia that he was doing so), he at once took pains to counter the effect of this by privately informing Beneš that if he refused to accept the German demands and Hitler invaded, 'nothing that any other power can do will prevent this fate for your own country and people'.

It would be tedious to follow the various stages of intimidation and actual deception by which Czechoslovakia was brought to her sur-render – and the British people to acquiescence in it. But even at this distance of time it is surely hard to justify in a man of Halifax's delicate sense of honour the instructions he sent to Newton, the British Minister in Prague, telling him to call on the President of the Czech Republic with his French colleague in the middle of the night to demand that he should immediately withdraw his proposal that the German demands upon his country should be referred to arbitration under the German-Czechoslovak Treaty of October 1925 – a treaty that Hitler had only a short time previously acknowledged as still in force – and should instead submit unconditionally and without delay to German demands.

It is true that Halifax had a brief interval of firmness during Chamberlain's absence at Bad Godesberg for his second meeting with Hitler. As news of Hitler's intransigence arrived in London and reports of incursions by German troops across the Czech frontier into Egerland reached the Foreign Office he instructed his Under-Secretary, R. A. Butler, who was in Geneva, to contact Litvinov there and open conversations with the Russians at long last. And in the afternoon, despite telegraphed objections from Godesberg he acquiesced in Daladier's proposal that the Czech's should be given permission to mobilize. In this brief moment of independence he even found the resolution to voice the anxieties that now affected most of the Cabinet and wire Chamberlain that, 'While mistrustful of our plan [the Anglo-French plan for the orderly surrender of Czech territory Chamberlain had taken with him] but prepared perhaps to accept it with reluctance as alternative to war, great mass of public opinion [in Britain] seems to be hardening in sense of feeling that we have gone to limit of concession and that it is up to the Chancellor to make some contribution.'

This resolution did not last. When Chamberlain returned with terms so bad that even he had been moved to describe them as 'an ultimatum and not a negotiation' when Hitler presented them, and Nevile Henderson to interject 'Diktat', he fell in – reluctantly no doubt – with Chamberlain's view that they must nevertheless be accepted although other members of the Cabinet, notably Duff Cooper resisted.

All had now come down to the mere question of timing. A new British plan was produced giving Hitler all he wanted in return for an 'orderly' timetable of annexation, and Chamberlain with Halifax's anxious benediction sent the messages to Hitler and Mussolini that produced the Munich Conference. It remained for Halifax to go through the formality of getting Czech agreement to the British plan. Fighting for the last remnants of their national self-respect, although, indeed, it was not theirs that was in jeopardy, the Czechs made only one stipulation: that they should not be required to agree in advance of negotiation to any substantial divergence from the earlier Anglo-French plan forced upon them after so much pressure and so many threats. The only reply Halifax felt called on to make to this plea from the President of a country compelled to destroy itself at the insistence of its friends was that he looked to him 'not to render more difficult the Prime Minister's already delicate task' – surely a remarkable example of the insensitivity to which an honourable man can fall when driven to dishonourable courses.

Yet even this was not all. The Munich agreement – based not on the British plan but on one drawn up by Weizsäcker, Neurath and Goering, and approved by Hitler before being telephoned to Mussolini so that he could present it as his own – contained one small crumb of comfort for the Czechs: an Anglo-French undertaking to guarantee what was left of Czechoslovakia.

It remained for Halifax to draft the epilogue to betrayal. On 8 December he telegraphed to the British Minister in Prague:

'Question of guarantee of Czechoslovakia which Czech Government are understood to be anxious to see in force, was discussed with French Ministers in Paris, who were informed that His Majesty's Government were prepared to give a guarantee of the new Czech frontiers with France, Germany and Italy. In their view this guarantee would be against unprovoked aggression and would only come into operation when three of the four Munich Powers were prepared to implement it.... The French Ministers were disposed to argue that a guarantee which would not operate if Germany attacked Czechoslovakia and Italy stood aside could not be regarded as fulfilling the offer made in the Anglo-French proposals but it was pointed out to them that in such circumstances a guarantee by France and Great Britain alone could not be effective and might produce a situation in which the two powers would either have to go to war without any prospect of saving Czechoslovakia or to default on their guarantee. His Majesty's Government were not for their part prepared to put themselves in such a situation.'

In this way did Halifax preserve British honour and satisfy the last remaining pledge to Czechoslovakia: by a guarantee which as the French so properly pointed out could not be regarded as fulfilling the promise made at Munich and which, as both he and they knew, was not, in the form he insisted on, worth the paper it was written on since in no circumstances would Italy be likely to act if Germany attacked the Czechs.

He dismissed any question of Czechoslovakia being allowed to ask for or accept a guarantee from Russia on the grounds that this might well mean that Germany and Italy would refuse to join and 'if the matter came to one of clear choice between Germany and Russia [we] prefer the former at the price of exclusion of the latter'. And with what it is difficult not to describe as a remarkable example of hypocritical sophistry he explained that all this was really for the Czechs' own good: 'It might be that if Czechoslovakia thought herself able to count securely upon French and British help she might be tempted to adopt an attitude towards Germany which would only create the trouble we all wish to see avoided.'

Four months later Hitler swooped on Prague and Halifax could feel gratified that his drafting had saved Britain from the crime of formal default. She did nothing. She was legally excused.

In the light of all this it is surely one of the most curious features of these years that with the minor exception of Lord Dunglass (Sir Alec Douglas-Home), Chamberlain's P.P.S. and convinced disciple, Halifax alone among those responsible escaped the lash of public disillusion. (Possibly the cloak of aristocratic connection still so potent in British society sheltered both of them: the British dislike having to hate hereditary peers.) Even Butler who was no more than Halifax's Under-Secretary did not escape. His part in appeasement helped to deny him the Premiership in 1957.

None of this touched Halifax. The myth was beyond the erosion of reality. Yet he stuck to the course longer than most. Even as late as the afternoon of Saturday, 2 September 1939, when invading German troops had been fighting on Polish territory since 2 a.m. the previous day supported by air attacks on Polish cities, and even the most ardent supporters of appeasement had abandoned it, he was still seeking a means to avoid conflict with Hitler. True he asked for German withdrawal as a prerequisite of negotiations – the belatedly aroused Cabinet would agree to no less – but he set no time limit for withdrawal in his note to Germany and with Bonnet's connivance assured Ciano, who had been cast for the role of intermediary, that the British note should not be regarded as an ultimatum. Even when at its meeting at 4.30 in the afternoon the Cabinet agreed to send an ultimatum to the Germans to expire at midnight he did not send it. On the contrary he was still assuring Ciano at 6 o'clock that evening that the earlier British warning was not to be regarded as an ultimatum, and insisting that although the then state of British opinion made it impossible to hold a conference until troops were withdrawn if this were done they could look forward to 'fruitful negotiation' based on the premise that Danzig should go to Germany.

It was his belief that even at this late hour a deal with Hitler might yet be possible that caused Chamberlain to offer the House of Commons not the declaration of war it believed national honour to require but the bland statement that 'If the German Government should agree to withdraw their forces then His Majesty's Government would be willing to regard the position as being the same as it was before the German forces crossed the Polish frontier' and would be ready to associate itself with discussions between Germany and Poland.

'For two whole days', Amery wrote, 'the wretched Poles had been bombed and massacred and we were still considering within what time limit Hitler should be invited to tell us whether he felt like relinquishing his prey. And then these sheer irrelevancies about the terms of a hypothetical agreement between Germany and Poland . . . was all this havering the prelude to another Munich?' Members of the Cabinet who not three hours before had adjourned believing Halifax had gone off to send the ultimatum they had agreed on were, according to Hore-Belisha, 'completely aghast'. Even Simon was shocked. With Hore-Belisha, Anderson, Elliot and de la Warr he hurried to Chamberlain's room immediately the debate was over (following hard on the heels of Arthur Greenwood, the Acting Leader of the Labour Party) to protest that there could be no further equivocation. Only Halifax remained unmoved. Indeed to judge from his memoirs he found it hard to understand what all the fuss was about. Even a telegram from Kennard, our Ambassador in Warsaw, transmitting Beck's desperate request for 'some activity on the Western front' to draw off the planes that were bombing Polish men, women and children, and concluding, 'I trust I may be informed at the earliest possible moment of our declaration of war' left him unaffected. Indeed he did not even reply to it. Instead he telegraphed the text of Chamberlain's speech to Henderson in Berlin to pass on 'to certain quarters' and instructed him that he wanted the German Government given 'as much time as possible to consider their reply'.

Having done this he went off to have dinner with his wife. He was interrupted at his meal by a telephone call from the Prime Minister. 'I have never', he noted in *Fulness of Days*, 'known Chamberlain so disturbed.' Accordingly he went to No. 10 where Chamberlain gave him dinner: 'He told me that the statement had infuriated the House' (it had, Halifax had noted complacently, 'gone well' in the Lords), 'and that he did not believe, unless we could clear the position, the Government would be able to maintain itself when it met Parliament next day.' This surprised Halifax. He could not understand what made the Commons so emotional, why they should behave so differently from the Lords. Even when Count Raczyniski, the Polish Ambassador, waited on him on his return to the Foreign Office to advise him that the centre of Warsaw had been bombed that afternoon and that the Polish position was getting worse with every hour, he offered only the vague opiate that the British 'were fully alive both to the cruel strain to which his country was being subjected and to the urgent necessity of relieving it in any way that we could at the earliest possible moment'. Raczyniski did not conceal from him that 'the moral effect of this delay on Poland was devastating'. But without effect.

What Halifax himself was later to describe as 'of all evenings that I can remember the most miserable' concluded with a Cabinet meeting at 11 p.m. Hore-Belisha proposed a 2 a.m. ultimatum expiring at 6 a.m. Halifax and Chamberlain resisted. After two-and-a-half hours' acrimonious discussion they had their way. It was agreed that the ultimatum should not be sent until 9 a.m. and should not become effective until 11 a.m. – only one hour earlier than the time Halifax had previously asked for and been refused, although even he could no longer hold any expectation of a German withdrawal and every additional hour before Britain declared war was to Germany's advantage and Poland's disadvantage.

When the Cabinet ended Halifax walked across to the Foreign Office. His nerves, he confessed, had been somewhat frayed by the Cabinet discussions, but he was still as far as ever from understanding the emotions that now stirred most of the British people. 'So far as I was concerned', he wrote later, 'the last straw was when I went across to the Foreign Office after the Cabinet to send a final instruction to the Ambassador in Berlin and met a prominent member of the Labour Party coming out of the building.' (It was Hugh Dalton who had been asking Kirkpatrick and Strang for news.) 'As we passed in the passage he, still in the House of Commons atmosphere, said to me "Foreign Secretary, can you give me any hope?" to which I replied, "If you mean hope of a war I think I can promise you a certainty for tomorrow", to which in turn he replied "Thank God".' Indeed so far was he from understanding the shock of moral repugnance that had swept the Commons and the country that afternoon that twenty years later he could still describe those who had demanded an end of equivocation as 'mischief-makers' and confess that he still found it 'hard to forgive those in the Cabinet or outside it' who 'allowed excited feeling to run away with their judgment'. He was the last and most indomitable of the appeasers.

No doubt he felt justified in being so. Certainly he, who in the first world war had declared himself to have 'absolutely no sympathy with the real conscientious objectors' to war, was now prepared to go to almost any lengths to avoid war with Nazi Germany. He seemed then, as indeed he always did when one met him, astonishingly remote from the emotions that moved ordinary men, a detached patrician devoted to his friends and his concept of public service, but extraordinarily narrow in his understanding of the springs of popular action; a tall, ascetic, courteous yet curiously negative figure immunized against the passions and moral conflicts of the world by his position and perhaps by too long habitation in the House of Lords, a man of duty without energy, difficult to move from a course he had set himself not so much, as in some men, by reason of strong conviction as by an essential quietism that made change unwelcome and also perhaps by a conviction of superiority, an assumption more instinctive than intellectual, of his natural leadership among those born to public service.

Yet surely it remains one of the political curiosities of our age that not only should such a man have been prepared to close his eyes so completely to the moral nature of many of the issues that faced him and embrace without obvious discomfort the dubious diplomatic stratagems required of him, but that he alone of those involved in this tragic and disreputable episode in British political life should remain untouched either by self-doubt or the breath of public criticism. He was indestructible.

So indestructible that not only the Palace and Neville Chamberlain himself but a substantial body of public opinion also, including, most oddly of all, many leaders of the Labour Party were ready to see in him rather than Churchill Chamberlain's natural successor as Prime Minister after the disastrous Narvik retreat. 'Earlier that evening', Hugh Dalton records in the second volume of his *Memoirs* describing the scene in the House of Commons on 8 May 1939, 'I had told R. A. Butler that though I was not authorized to speak for my colleagues, in my view, provided Chamberlain, Simon and Hoare disappeared from the Government altogether, we should be prepared to discuss the possibility of coming in. I added that if I was asked who should succeed Chamberlain as P.M. I thought, and a number of others shared this view, that there was much to be said for Halifax.'

Halifax himself later disavowed any such ambition but this does not seem to have been entirely Churchill's impression at his meeting with

Chamberlain and Halifax. Indeed it was very possibly only Churchill's silence – a silence that as he records 'certainly seemed longer than the two minutes which one observes in the commemoration of Armistice day' – when Chamberlain indicated his preference at this interview, that compelled Halifax to retract such ambitions as he may have had and thus saved Britain from a disastrous decision. He remained as Foreign Secretary for another eight months until, somewhat regretfully, he went to the United States as Ambassador. He tried to persuade Eden to go instead but Eden had no intention of departing from the central places of power to which he had but recently returned, nor did Churchill wish him to do so.

It was a post that admirably suited the patina of patrician public service that had for so long characterized the public image of this curiously detached man and he enjoyed it greatly once he was there. The chapter in his memoirs dealing with this period of his life reveals his keen pleasure couched in prose reminiscent of the social gossip of a glossy weekly. One of the aspects of his responsibilities he rightly felt to be most important was that of presenting the British cause to the American people. In this he was a little hampered at first by the fact that many Americans were more critical of his complicity in appeasement than his own people had been, but he was so much what so many of them expected a British Ambassador to look like that in the end they forgave him. In this task of public relations he had, he confides with characteristic disdain for the professional efforts of the brilliant and dedicated group collected under the roofs of the British Information Services, none of whom he mentions in his memoirs, 'the invaluable help of my cousin Angus MacDonnell and I do not know what we could have done without him. His mother, a granddaughter of Lord Grey of the Reform Bill had married Lord Antrim a great character and a typical Irishman from whom Angus, no doubt, inherited his lively sense of the ridiculous.' There was indeed nearly always a cousin or an old family friend to be of help wherever he found himself. One other such friend, Major Lockhart, the biographer of his father, served him as private secretary and he, too, could, fortunately, see the funny side of things: 'One is sometimes told that people seldom recognize good fortune until it is no longer with them. I can truthfully say I did not realize all the time how lucky I was to have Jack Lockhart. Not the least rewarding thing about him was his alert sense of humour which ensured his collecting any gems that might be there to pick up' – as for example after a speech at a luncheon club at Des

Moines where 'Jack heard one member say to another "It's been fine
having the British Ambassador", "Yes", replied his friend, "we haven't
had a steak like that in the Club for twelve months".' 'The *agrément*
of life in Washington', to quote him yet again, 'was further increased
by the kindness of Mr and Mrs Ronald Tree in allowing us the full run
of their house at Mirador under the Blue Mountains just beyond
Charlottesville where is the lovely University of Virginia designed in
great part by Jefferson', and by the 'unique hospitality' of Mrs McLean,
the owner of the Hope diamond, whose dinner parties for one hundred
and fifty or more were for an Ambassador 'a wonderful means of
contact with many kinds of people whom he could never have met in
any other way'. Further afield there were days 'on the King ranch,
that estate like a Kingdom in Texas adjoining the Mexican border of
which the destiny is now controlled by Bob and Helen Kleberg. Who
ever could forget such friends . . . ?' Who indeed? Or those others, like
the Lamonts, 'who so constantly welcomed us as guests in their New
York home', or Mrs Traxton Beale who so enjoyed seeing 'her attractive house in Lafayette Square in Washington filled with her friends',
whose names are scattered through his innocent pages among the
somewhat scanty records of more arduous proceedings until loaded
with years and honorary degrees he said his farewell to them and the
Statue of Liberty: 'It had been an education and a privilege to be in
the United States at such a time and as the ship moved eastward one
was conscious both of the keen pleasure with which one looked forward to returning home and the real sorrow with which one bade
farewell to the United States.'

Of those whose impact on the tragic, wasted decades of the 'twenties
and 'thirties have been considered here he alone suffered no regression
in public approval. The legend lived on. As he looked back on his
life from the safe harbourage of Garrowby in *Fulness of Days*, his
memory imitated 'the sundial which only records the hours when
the sun shines'. No doubts disturbed him. 'Certainly', he recorded,
'the thought that dominates all other, as the moving picture of seventy
years travels across the screen is one of great thankfulness both to God
and man. My thanks go to Him for the home into which it was my
privilege to be born; for the early knowledge of Him to which this
home brought me; and for the countless opportunities He has given
me – alas! how sadly misused – of making this knowledge my invari-
able guide and counsellor; for the manifold blessings of life and health
and enjoyment of the world's best things'. He was the fortunate man.

The Age of Myth

'HUMBUG is part of politics, a convention of the "British way of life", something which the public expect the politicians to give them as their due. It often performs a valuable function for a party, a class, or the nation at large by enabling them not to see, or to pretend not to see, unwelcome changes in the real world until sentiment and habits have become sufficiently adapted to them. In this way it acts like the fluid which the snail exudes to mend its broken shell. But though healthy and preservative when applied at the right time and for the right purposes, humbug can become deleterious and even fatal if it is not shed when the time is past and those purposes fulfilled.'

So wrote 'A Conservative' in *The Times* of 2 April 1964. The observation was made in a context quite other than that of the events recorded in this book but it is not inappropriate to them. Humbug, sometimes conscious, sometimes, no doubt, unconscious, played its considerable part in the impact on their times of all the five public figures here considered. The quality of humbug was not the same in each instance, less artful or obvious in some than in others, indeed contrary, in the case of Chamberlain and Norman, to the general judgment of their characters: the humbug of action rather than words. But in each instance it was there. In each instance its power derived from the response it evoked, the wish of the British people to be deceived, their anxiety to be persuaded that things were other than they were, their desire to pretend that the first world war had not really altered anything.

In other less fortunate countries this war had released social forces capable of toppling thrones and standing the social structure on its head, providing, in Lenin's famous phrase, 'a great, mighty, all-powerful *régisseur* who was on the one hand in a position to accelerate the course of history on a grand scale and, on the other, to produce worldwide crisis of unheard-of intensity; economic, political, national and international'. None of this, the British wished to be persuaded, had affected, or could affect, the essential cosiness of British life, its capacity to broaden down from precedent to precedent, make revolutions and omelettes without breaking eggs, improve the lot of the dispossessed without inconvenience to the possessors. As so often before, the British people and especially the middle classes wanted to be moral. But they wanted even more to be comfortable.

It was an age of pretending that the deep conflicts in a society painfully emerging from the consequences of industrial capitalism at its most ruthless, and from the effects of a world war which had for ever destroyed the privileged national position on which this industrial capitalism had built, did not exist and that it was somehow un-British to think they did. In the soporifics of Baldwin and MacDonald, in the patrician spirituality of Halifax, in the compulsive certitudes of Chamberlain and Norman, the British found the tranquillizers they longed for, the excuse to sleep and postpone decision until, almost too late, they roused themselves at last to remember under different leaders that facts are better than dreams. At each stage of the sad procession between the wars there were, of course, some who never forgot this basic truth of history. But they were in a minority; fantasy and nostalgia held the majority firmly in their grip.

Like most of those who sustained, supported and advised them Baldwin, MacDonald, Chamberlain, Norman and Halifax were patriotic and honourable men. They enjoyed power, strove for it, and did not easily relax their hold on it, but they wished only to use it for the general good. They had many of the qualities desirable in politicians or bankers. They lacked the most necessary of all: the quality of living in their own time. Politics is the art of the possible and the possible is only made so if a sufficient number of people can be brought to believe that it is (a) necessary, (b) desirable, and (c) unlikely to harm them too much personally. It is also the art of timing, of knowing when a shift of emphasis that might have seemed difficult or even intolerable at an earlier stage has become acceptable or can be made so by a new tone of voice, an appeal to a different set of emotions, the awakening of hope or apprehension. To link the past and the present, to facilitate the transition from one age to another is thus one of the most important functions of the politician. If he is to serve his generation faithfully he needs to be adroit in persuading the electorate, emotionally as well as intellectually, that its future is linked harmoniously with its past, is, indeed, the natural and on the whole beneficent outcome of it.

Myth has its place in such a transition – the personal myth of a leader, the larger myth of a national situation or a national character. Nor does it matter if the myth does not coincide with reality in every particular, it is in the nature of myth that it should not, so long as it eases the transition to reality. The ability of a politician to deceive is not to be condemned. Practised in moderation it may be useful and even admirable. It becomes harmful only when the deceivers themselves become the victims of their own deceit, when the makers and beneficiaries of the myth come to put their trust in it themselves.

Those who ruled between the wars did so. They did so, one suspects, because the myths were even more important to them personally than to their supporters. Baldwin, so anxious to disguise neurosis behind a bland and equable exterior; MacDonald, so concerned to be accepted and invited inside; Chamberlain, so driven to free himself of early failure and rejection; Norman, hag-ridden by emotional instability and the fear of equals; Halifax with his atrophied left arm and commitment to perfection; each was the captive as well as the exploiter of the myths that surrounded him. If their histories have relevance to our own times it lies above all in the manifestation of the importance of avoiding the seduction of the national will by popular images. The enticement is great; the wish for a paragon no less profound than the need for a scapegoat. But there are no political saviours and to expect there to be so is a confession of popular failure. Democracy depends on a continuing dialogue. If the debate stops or is unheeded or comes to be regarded as unnecessary, impertinent or improper, the moment of danger has been reached. It is natural for party machines to seek to throw up public idols for to possess one is a hedge against defeat; but fatal if they are taken seriously by the country. The conviction that all Prime Ministers have feet of clay is the best preservative of the public interest. The only really dangerous man in politics is the one who enjoys general approval.

Looking back, Baldwin, MacDonald, Chamberlain, Halifax and Montagu Norman (although his appeal was always more esoterically based than that of the others) cannot help but seem a curiously muted collection to command the fatal fidelity they did. But they were creatures of the times they lived in. They grew in soil denuded of its proper measure of political manure. It was perhaps natural that in reaction to the nobilities and longueurs of war the British should turn to someone as unlike the man who had dominated their affairs during it as possible; their misfortune was that on this occasion they got a Baldwin rather than an Attlee. Yet Baldwin for all his inaptitude for practical decision and his liking for synthetic rural rhetoric might not have proved as calamitous as he did but for the political vacuum he found to fill. The Liberal Party died as a political force too soon for its own or the country's good. It left behind it nothing capable of taking its place. The Labour Party was still too young, too unformed, too unrepresentative of a major electoral interest to restore a proper balance to politics. It is the function of an opposition to hold up a reducing glass to Government; its job to make sure that power corrupts neither the man nor, which is no less important, the public view of the man. Labour had neither the experience, the parliamentary size nor, indeed, throughout most of the 'twenties the will, to do this. There was nothing MacDonald wanted less than to challenge the Baldwin myth of one-nation since his own strongest desire was to be accepted as a part of it; to prove, indeed, that, allowed office, he would behave just like him.

The National Government that emerged from the political love affair between these two can now be seen to have been the greatest political disaster of the interwar years. This 'extraordinary political disturbance' as Winston Churchill so correctly described it had prolonged and incalculable effects. This was not only, or primarily, because of its errors of commission and omission, serious though these were, but because it succeeded in deluding a majority of the British people into the belief that party politics were unrespectable and that to criticize those in charge was indecent.

For the earlier phase of the Baldwin–MacDonald saga it can perhaps be argued that although it drove a good deal of political activism into industrial courses and produced much misery and the General Strike it did at least make it possible for the British people to live through a potential civil war without recognizing it, thus making it less likely. Lulled by the cadences of the Baldwin–MacDonald substitute for philosophy they were, like sleepwalkers, able to walk along the edge of precipices without falling over.

The National Government extended this period of political somnambulism beyond the limit of safety. It established as respectable – indeed as alone worthy of respect – an a-political public mood that was the worst possible thing that could have happened to Britain at this stage in national and, even more, international affairs. Not only did it reduce opposition inside Parliament to a largely ineffective rump denied expectancy of power and therefore the practical means to rally counter-opinion in force behind it but also, by presenting the Government in office as national and all-party long after any vestige of its original right to be thought so had gone, it helped to create a general climate of opinion in which it seemed to very many honest and well-meaning people disloyal to express even the most moderate criticism of government policy. As the winds outside grew colder and the weather harsher the British built for themselves a cosy national hothouse in which the oddest blooms were able to grow to extravagant sizes. Only in such a climate would it have been possible for a well-meaning municipal bureaucrat like Chamberlain to come to be accepted as a world statesman or an evangelical country squire like Halifax to be regarded as a towering moral philosopher and keeper of the national conscience. Only in such a climate could the warnings of a Churchill have fallen on so many deaf ears; the economic arguments of a Keynes or an Ernest Bevin have made so little impact, the passion of those, not inconsiderable in prestige or numbers, who were awake to both the political and moral dangers of British policy, have gone so disregarded by so many. Aided and abetted by great organs of public opinion like *The Times*, faithless to its earlier and greater tradition of disclosure and dissent, the British put away their political instincts along with the pruning knife of party politics and left it all to the head gardener.

The British possess an aptitude for persuading themselves that leaders who seem modest and friendly and have the right social connections are superior persons who are doing them a favour by consenting to accept the tedium of governing them. The gentlemanly and amateur tradition in British politics which makes the clever or extreme man suspect, and should not be too lightly dismissed as safeguard against the excesses that can derive from too naked and professional a pursuit of power, can, when combined with the snobbery which is still so large an element in the British middle class and the very genuine and in many ways admirable sense of national cohesion in face of difficulties, actual or alleged, tip over into uncritical acceptance of the pretensions of those in authority. On such occasions the critic is likely to find himself confronted not only with the resistance of political interests but with the formidable weight of social disapproval for breaking the ranks. The British, it would seem, have a longing for heroes to worship. No doubt it is nurtured by their educational and social systems. It is all the stronger for being often unacknowledged and is missing in the American character whose heroes, on the whole more flamboyant than those of Britain, commonly evoke, except when they are victorious generals, a sharper reaction from contrary interests so that the very qualities that evoke passionate adulation on one side provoke an even more implacable hatred on the other, as many visitors to the United States found to their surprise during the Roosevelt administrations.

This British capacity for hero worship is normally kept in check by a strong tradition of political controversy. Those who believe in the importance of this tradition deceive themselves, however, if they believe it to be always universally approved. There is no more common reaction among those who are not themselves deeply involved in political affairs than that expressed in the frequently heard remark 'Why must the opposition always oppose? Why can't they all work together for the general good?' The longing for a respectable alternative to political conflict is deeply rooted in the British attitudes to public affairs, the desire for a universal panacea endemic.

Although the British were unfortunate in their leaders between the wars those leaders represented genuine tides of popular emotion. Baldwin with his eyes on a golden age of rural felicity that had never existed, his longing to persuade himself that neither the class struggle nor the decline in British world power had any permanent meaning and that England would become a Conservative Garden of Eden if only he closed his eyes tightly enough against the twentieth century, MacDonald with the deep need to persuade himself that he was on the same side as everybody else, both reflected a profound postwar inertia in the British people, a desire to escape the robust challenges to which leaders of more forthright character, whether of the right or left, called them, into the peace of a Nirvana created by and for the debilitated. At the Bank of England Norman reflected the comparable nostalgia for a departed golden age of those to whom the monetary theories of Keynes and the insistence of Bevin on the claims of the industrial workers were alike an impertinence. Between them these three created the context in which a National Government contrary to all the most deeply cherished principles of British political life could seem to be an appropriate instrument of parliamentary democracy. They were able to do so because a majority of the British people had already abdicated from the role of critical surveillance which political democracy requires of them.

It is of course an inherent feature of the British two-party system with its strongly imposed parliamentary discipline that a Cabinet with a clear majority in the House of Commons exercises a temporary dictatorship. What it decides shall be done is done. The danger of revolt sufficiently serious to jeopardize its position is minimal under normal conditions of party organization. It may or may not go some way to meet pressures from its back benchers. Whether it does so or not, in the last resort the majority votes as it decides. The curb on this dictatorship comes from the fact that it is temporary, leasehold not freehold, and must submit to the judgment of public opinion at periodic general elections. It therefore dare not altogether ignore such opinion in between, particularly as the two-party system provides, or should provide, an Opposition able and willing to offer itself as a successor and capable of keeping public opinion aware at every stage of the alternatives it offers. None of these curbs effectively operated during the nine years of National Government. The forms of parliamentary democracy were maintained but their reality was destroyed. The British people voluntarily handed over the management of their affairs to a dictatorship altogether more humane, respectable and circumspect than that to which the Germans voluntarily handed theirs, but not much less absolute in its political authority and ability to ignore – even although parliamentary forms required it to listen to – cricitism.

It is often assumed that when dictatorships condescend to hold general elections the practically unanimous support commonly shown for them in the voting figures is due to the polls being rigged. This is not necessarily entirely so. The fact is that where there is no strong parliamentary opposition the elector has no real opportunity to judge between contrasting personalities and policies and can have no confidence that there is any effective alternative to voting for the Government open to him. He votes for, with or without coercion, because there is no point in voting against. In similar circumstances, and for the same reasons, representative government can become virtually indistinguishable from dictatorship in so far as effective choice by the electorate is concerned.

The near destruction of the Labour Party as a parliamentary opposition produced such a situation. So far as practical politics were concerned it left the electorate with no opportunity for choosing even if it wished to do so. The little rump of a Labour opposition could criticize and protest – and no doubt it might have done both more effectively but for its own divisions – but it was in no position effectively to challenge the Government, still less to present itself as a feasible alternative. It simply had not the Parliamentary man-power. When a general election was fought in 1935 the sitting Government was thus bound to be confirmed in office even although it had by then ceased to be National in anything but name. It is remarkable that the Opposition succeeded in doing as well electorally as it did.

It was not, however, only the physical fact of the smallness, and therefore in any realistic power terms ineffectiveness, of the parliamentary opposition that eroded the principle of temporary dictatorship on which parliamentary democracy rests but the wilful abdication of political responsibility – the responsibility of criticism and choice – by a majority of public opinion. This made the dictatorship of the Cabinet – and above all of the Prime Minister, once that office was held by a man who enjoyed the exercise of power and was apt at it – absolute. Even MacDonald and Baldwin, neither of whom had any natural liking for decision, were able to shed most of those elements and persons who had given the Government's claim to be National and all-party such substance as it possessed – Snowden, Samuel, Sinclair, Reading, Sankey among them – without a tremor and ride the shock to the public conscience caused by the Hoare-Laval pact without serious damage to their position. When Neville Chamberlain, absolutionist in temper, authoritarian in administration, moved to the first place he was able to ignore with equal facility the warnings of the two greatest parliamentarians of the age, Lloyd George and Winston Churchill, and the anger of the most able and active of the younger members of his party such as Macmillan and Boothby. He could drive from office the most popular Foreign Secretary the country had known for years in Anthony Eden, sack an energetic and reforming War Minister, Belisha, for having a mind of his own and lose, at the height of a defence crisis, a popular and respected First Lord of the Admiralty, Duff Cooper, while he conducted the nation's foreign affairs according to his private whim against the opposition of most senior members of the Foreign Office. Until, almost too late, reverses in war stimulated public and parliamentary opinion to belated revolt his political authority was as absolute as that of any dictator, the practical checks on his egotism as minimal. In his biography of Hitler, Alan Bullock makes the valid but in some circles now unfashionable point that Hitler's hegemony of Europe 'could not have been won without a people and an army willing to serve him'. It is equally true that Neville Chamberlain could not have followed the courses that made this hegemony possible without a people willing to follow him wherever he led. Having abandoned their tradition of controversy and dissent the British slavishly followed a myth.

Independent political judgment – that capacity upon which political democracy most depends – was put aside. They were content to rely on a saviour.

The worst of the evils that sprang from this sequence of events might have been avoided had the Conservative Party, as the main political force in these years been capable of adjusting itself to what had in effect become a one-party system. But it was not. Party disciplines and party loyalties appropriate to survival in a two-party system were caried over into the new where it was not party but national survival that was at issue. Under the strong stimulus of their political and moral repugnance to what was afoot individuals were ready to embrace the need for internal party criticism and did not hesitate to provide it. They accepted a loyalty to the nation greater than that to the party machine. The vast mass of Conservative back-benchers remained, however, as loyal to the Whips as though they were members of a party with a narrow majority fighting for existence against a formidable and numerically powerful opposition. Even Eden, having resigned, felt himself constrained by the ties of party association to take no steps to make his protest effective in the country. He went not with a bang but a whimper, preferring loyal quietism to public protest – the greatest disservice he could have done his country.

Of course there was something to be said for Chamberlain. His policy was activated by a genuine longing for peace, a horror of the consequences of international conflict. If the price he was eventually prepared to pay seemed to many – and in the end to most – too high, yet the prize was great. In seeking it he expressed the natural longings of the British people. To examine every possibility of agreement with Germany was a sensible cause for British statesmanship. Moreover his freedom of manœuvre was restricted – although not so restricted as he allowed his prejudices to make it. He had to take into account – whatever his own share of responsibility for it – Britain's military weakness and the unwillingness of the British people of all political complexions to repair the gaps in their defences. He could not ignore the fact that successive French Governments were more ready to talk of resistance to Hitler than to look at their military establishment and their international alliances in the light of what it was practical to do – nor close his eyes to the defeatism that had eaten deep into French society. The French were prepared to protest, they were seldom ready to take the lead. They were anxious to keep their record clean but ready to fall in behind Britain as each new crisis came. Nor, with a necessary regard for prudence, could he properly do other than look each Soviet gift horse in the mouth.

He had a case. It was right for it to be heard. His tragedy and the world's was that he refused to listen to any other and that, driven by the compulsions of his own nature, he recoiled from the discipline of controversy and sought to smother that continuing dialogue on which the health of political democracy depends under the weight of cabinet and party discipline.

The pragmatic case for party discipline inside a parliamentary democracy is strong – indeed perhaps unanswerable – where two nearly equal parties confront each other. It rests not on party interest alone but on the national interest also, since without it firm cabinet rule would be impossible. The Government must govern. It can only do so if those elected to support it give it their votes even if they disagree with some aspects of what it does. Party discipline there must be. The dangers inherent in it, however, are great. They can be kept in check only if the party leadership is flexible and open to influence by alternative views accorded every facility for expressing themselves inside the party, and, above all, if it is, and knows itself to be, subject to the constant scrutiny of a public opinion able to judge the significance of major parliamentary debate not by the voting figures alone, for these are a foregone conclusion, but by the intellectual force and content of the argument. None of these conditions ruled during the 'thirties. The authority of the party Whips was accepted as final right to the end by all but a small group of Conservative M.P.s, the leadership was complacent and inflexible, the check of a critical public opinion was not there. Party discipline, so advantageous when the right conditions exist, became in these circumstances disruptive of the national interest. Those who belong to parties always have need to remember that party loyalty is not enough. In the 'thirties too many forgot.

Britain was unfortunate in the personalities of those who came to national leadership in the interwar years. But they were the product of the political conditions of their time; each reflected a public mood. The blame was not theirs alone. If there is anything to be learned from their rise and fall it is that there is no substitute for controversy and the clash of parties; no danger so great as that of promoting politicians to the status of gods and of suspending public judgment in the presence of myths.

Select Bibliography

General

CHURCHILL, WINSTON S., *The Second World War:* vol. I, *The Gathering Storm.* Cassell, 1948.

Documents Diplomatiques, 1935-39. French Yellow Book: Ministère des Affaires Étrangères, Paris.

Documents on British Foreign Policy, 1919-39. H.M.S.O., 1946-.

History of 'The Times': vol. IV. The Times Publishing Co., 1952.

JONES, THOMAS, *A Diary with Letters, 1931-50.* Oxford, 1954.

KEYNES, J. M., *The Economic Consequences of Mr Churchill.* Hogarth Press, 1925.

MACKINTOSH, JOHN P., *The British Cabinet.* Stevens & Sons, 1962.

NAMIER, L. B., *Diplomatic Prelude, 1938-39.* Macmillan, 1948.

NICOLSON, HAROLD, *King George V.* Constable, 1952.

TAYLOR, A. J. P., *The Origins of the Second World War.* Hamish Hamilton, 1961.

WRENCH, SIR EVELYN, *Geoffrey Dawson and Our Times.* Hutchinson, 1955.

Stanley Baldwin

BALDWIN, A. W., *My Father: The True Story.* Allen & Unwin, 1955.

BEAVERBROOK, LORD, *The Decline and Fall of Lloyd George.* Collins, 1963.

BULLOCK, ALAN, *The Life and Times of Ernest Bevin:* vol. I. Heinemann, 1960.

MARTIN, KINGSLEY, *The British Public and the General Strike.* Hogarth Press, 1926.

RAYMOND, JOHN (ed.), *The Baldwin Age.* Eyre & Spottiswoode, 1960.

ROBERTS, C. E. BECHHOFER, *Stanley Baldwin, Man or Miracle?* Robert Hale, 1936.

SYMONS, JULIAN, *The General Strike.* Cresset, 1957.

YOUNG, G. M., *Stanley Baldwin.* Rupert Hart-Davis, 1952.

Ramsay MacDonald

BASSETT, R., *1931: Political Crisis.* Macmillan, 1958.

COLE, G. D. H., *A Short History of the British Working Class Movement, 1789-1947.* Allen & Unwin, 1948.

ELTON, LORD, *The Life of James Ramsay MacDonald:* vol. I, *1866-1919.* Collins, 1939.

POSTGATE, RAYMOND, *The Life of George Lansbury.* Longmans, 1951.

SNOWDEN, PHILIP, VISCOUNT, *An Autobiography:* vol. II, *1919-34.* Nicholson & Watson, 1934.

THOMAS, J. H., *My Story.* Hutchinson, 1937.

WEBB, BEATRICE, *Diaries, 1924-32*. Longmans, 1956.

WEIR, L. MACNEILL, *The Tragedy of Ramsay MacDonald*. Secker & Warburg, 1938.

Neville Chamberlain

AMERY, L. S., *My Political Life:* vol. III. Hutchinson, 1955.

AVON, EARL OF, *The Eden Memoirs:* vol. II, *Facing the Dictators*. Cassell, 1962.

COOPER, DUFF, *Old Men Forget*. Rupert Hart-Davis, 1953.

DALTON, HUGH, *The Fateful Years, 1931-45*. Muller, 1957.

FEILING, KEITH, *The Life of Neville Chamberlain*. Macmillan, 1946.

GILBERT, MARTIN, and GOTT, RICHARD, *The Appeasers*. Weidenfeld & Nicolson, 1963.

HENDERSON, SIR NEVILE, *Failure of a Mission*. Hodder & Stoughton, 1940.

MACLEOD, IAIN, *Neville Chamberlain*. Muller, 1961.

MINNEY, R. J. (ed.), *The Private Papers of Hore-Belisha*. Collins, 1960.

ROTHSTEIN, ANDREW, *The Munich Conspiracy*. Lawrence & Wishart, 1958.

VANSITTART, LORD, *The Mist Procession*. Hutchinson, 1958.

Montagu Norman

CLAY, SIR HENRY, *Lord Norman*. Macmillan, 1957.

Committee on Finance and Industry, 1929-31 (Macmillan Committee): *Report and Evidence*. H.M.S.O., 1931.

EINZIG, PAUL, *Montagu Norman*. Kegan Paul, 1932.

— *World Finance Since 1914*. Kegan Paul, 1935.

SALTER, SIR ARTHUR, *Recovery: The Second Effort*. Bell, 1932.

League of Nations: *World Economic Survey*, 1931-32, 1932-33.

SCHACHT, HJALMAR, *My First Seventy-Six Years*. Allan Wingate, 1955.

Lord Halifax

HALIFAX, EARL OF (as E. F. L. Wood), *John Keble*. Mowbray, 1909.

— *Fulness of Days*. Collins, 1957.

JOHNSON, ALAN CAMPBELL-, *Viscount Halifax*. Robert Hale, 1941.

KIRKPATRICK, SIR IVONE, *The Inner Circle*. Macmillan, 1959.

POLAK, H. S. L., BRAILSFORD, H. N., and PETHICK-LAWRENCE, LORD, *Mahatma Gandhi*. Odhams, 1949.

ROWSE, A. L., *All Souls and Appeasement*. Macmillan, 1961.

STRANG, LORD, *Home and Abroad*. Deutsch, 1956.

TEMPLEWOOD, VISCOUNT, *Nine Troubled Years*. Collins, 1954.

Index

Abdication, the, Baldwin and, 43, 56, 134

Abyssinia, 50, 53, 132; invaded by Italy, 158

Agadir, 71

Aix-les-Bains, Baldwin and, 14-15, 110

Alexander, A. V. (later Earl) (1885-1965), 77, 114, 119, 123

American Loan Agreement, 27-8

Amery, Leopold Charles (1873-1955), 37; and a National Government, 122; and the invasion of Poland, 246

Amsterdam, and the 1931 financial crisis, 105, 106

Anglo-Russian Treaty, 86, 88, 90-2, 94-5

Appeasement, 1, 128; Chamberlain and, 163, 172-3, 180-2; political responsibility for, 182; Halifax and, 239, 245, 247-8

Asquith, Herbert Henry, Earl of Oxford and Asquith (1852-1928), 20, 96, 226; Liberal distrust of, 69, 71; and the War, 71; his last speech, 89-90

Astor, Nancy Viscountess (1879-1964), and Stalin, 190

Attlee, Clement, 1st Earl (1883-), 31, 180; first Oxford Labour M.P., 77; on Chamberlain, 135, 193

Auden, Wystan Hugh (1907-), 3

Austria, collapse of the Kreditanstalt, 105, 107, 219; invaded by Germany, 165

Baldwin, Alfred, father of Stanley, 5, 8-10, 11-12

Baldwin, Harold, on his cousin Stanley, 10

Baldwin (née Macdonald), Louisa, mother of Stanley, 8

Baldwin (née Ridsdale), Lucy, wife of Stanley, 10-11, 13, 51, 58; her death, 58

Baldwin, Arthur Windham, 3rd Earl (1899-), on his father, 33, 38

Baldwin, Stanley 1st Earl Baldwin of Bewdley (1867-1947), 63, 73, 84, 96, 124, 195, 258; biography, 5, 7, 8; at Harrow, 5-7, 9, 40; at Cambridge, 7, 10, 40; his character and pursuits, 6, 7, 10, 11, 16, 31, 32-3, 39, 40-2, 51-2, 55, 252, 253, 254, 256; and his mother and father, 8-9, 32, 40; in the family business, 9-10; his marriage, 10-11, 51, 58; efforts to enter Parliament, 11-12; returned for Bewdley, 12; his rapid rise, 12 ff.; and Beaverbrook, 13; at the Board of Trade, 14, 26; and Lloyd George's defeat, 15-25 passim, 41; his Conservatism, 16-17, 23, 24, 30, 42, 55, 78; and Bonar Law, 23, 24; his political talents, 24, 28, 41; becomes Prime Minister, 25, 28-9; his inexperience, 25, 26, 28, 42; as Chancellor of the Exchequer, 26-8, 211; and the American Loan Agreement, 27-8; and the Labour Party, 29, 31, 42, 52; and the Premiership, 29, 147; the issue with Curzon, 29-30; seeks an election, 30, 78; his hatred of Lloyd George, 30, 41, 55; foundations of his public image, 31-2, 40, 43, 48, 227; his profound egotism, 31, 41, 51; his conception of the English, 32-3, 42, 46, 48; his speeches and broadcasts, 33, 39, 41-2, 44-8, 54; and the General Strike, 33-5, 37-9; and India, 43; failure to deal with economic issues, 43-4, 50 ff.; and the possibility of war, 48-9; his disastrous foreign policy, 49-50, 101; and the Fulham by-election, 52, 54; last years, 56-9; public hatred of, 57-9; his death, 59; compared with MacDonald, 84, 94, 97, 115, 127; and the financial crisis, 110, 150; and MacDonald's last years, 130, 131-2, 132-3; succeeds MacDonald, 132, 134; and Chamberlain, 147; and Germany's rearmament, 159; succeeded by Chamberlain,

263

Baldwin, Stanley—*cont.*
159; and Halifax, 229, 231; product
of contemporary political conditions, 252, 253, 254, 256, 258
Balfour, Arthur James Balfour, Earl of
(1848-1930), 14, 16, 140; and Lloyd
George, 17, 18; and Curzon's passing
over, 28
Bank for International Settlements,
213, 218, 219
Bank of England, and the 1931 crisis,
106, 109, 219; and the Gold Standard, 111, 219; and the run on the
pound, 120; Montagu Norman's
unique position, 195, 205, 206;
method of promotion in, 205-7; its
nationalization, 221
Bank rate, alterations in, 106, 212;
Norman and, 214-18
Banks, Sir Reginald Mitchell, 89
Basset, R., *Political Crisis*, 99
Beaverbrook, William Maxwell
Aitken, Baron (1879-1964), 14, 27,
34, 111, 197; Baldwin and, 13, 51;
and Lloyd George's overthrow, 15,
16, 18; and Empire Free Trade, 16,
19-20, 23; his character, 19; and
Bonar Law, 20, 23-4; his fall from
political power, 23-4; and the
Munich crisis, 170; and Britain's war
debt, 212; *Decline and Fall of Lloyd
George*, 15, 20
Beck, Polish Foreign Minister, 187,
188, 246
Beneš, President, 171, 176, 185 242
Bevan, Aneurin (1897-1960), 28
Bevin, Ernest (1881-1951), 62, 255,
256; and the return to gold at pre-
war parity, 34, 111; and the
General Strike, 38; relations with
MacDonald, 86, 105; and the second
Labour Government, 104-5; and
Norman, 214, 215, 216-18
Birkenhead, Frederick Edwin Smith,
Earl of (1872-1930), 14, 16, 64; and
Lloyd George, 17, 18, 89; and the
General Strike, 35, 36, 37
Blake, Robert, *The Baldwin Age*, 38
Boardman, Harry, 2
Bondfield, Margaret, 123
Boothby, Sir Robert (later Baron)
(1900-), 258

Bottomley, Horatio (1860-1933), 64;
reveals MacDonald's illegitimacy in
John Bull, 62; slanders MacDonald,
74
British Expeditionary Force, plan for, 71
Burckhardt, League Commissioner in
Danzig, 174
Burne-Jones, Sir Edward (1833-98),
8, 9
Butler, Henry Montagu (1833-1918),
Headmaster of Harrow, 5-6, 7
Butler, R. A. (1902-), 243, 245

Cabinet Economy Committee, and
the financial crisis, 1931, 110-11
Campbell, J. R., his article in *Workers
Weekly*, 87; his arrest, etc., 87-90
passim, 92
Campbell-Johnson, Alan, biographer
of Halifax, 230-1, 232, 240
Carlton Club, Conservative meeting
at, 21-2, 23, 24, 146
Chamberlain, Arthur Neville (1869-
1940), 2, 35, 37, 85, 97, 124, 195; and
the financial crisis, 110; and
MacDonald, 113, 116, 122; biography, 135; his character and
personality, 135, 139, 140, 143, 147-
50, 160, 161, 166, 214, 251, 252;
birth and family relationships, 136,
146, 149; on Andros Island, 137-9;
his marriage, 140; early political
activities, 140, 141; Director of
National Service, 142-4, 149, 228;
hatred of Lloyd George, 144, 145-6;
Unionist M.P., 144; Postmaster-
General, 146; Minister of Health,
146-7; Chancellor of the Exchequer,
1931, 147, 150-2, 160; a natural
bureaucrat, 148; on the miners' lock-
out, 148; his nationalism, 152, 155;
Prime Minister, 152, 159, 258, 259;
attitude to Nazi aggression, 161-3;
inability to appreciate his opponents,
163-6, 176, 191; and the Czech
crisis, 166 ff.; his responsibility for
the War, 168; and Dawson's *Times*
leader, 170-2; at Berchtesgaden,
172-3; at Bad Godesberg, 176-7,
243; and Hitler's ultimatum, 177-9;
and the Munich Agreement, 180-1,
184; attitude to Russian proposals,

Chamberlain, Arthur Neville—*cont.*
184, 187-9; his post-Munich policy, 185-92, 246, 247; and the duration of the War, 191; succeeded by Churchill, 193; his death, 193; Cabinet protest to, 246; and his successor, 248, 249; his absolutism, 258; dismisses Eden, 258; product of contemporary political conditions, 252, 253, 254, 256, 258, 259, 260

Chamberlain, Sir (Joseph) Austen (1863-1937), 14, 16, 136; and Lloyd George, 17, 18, 20-1; calls for a vote of confidence, 21; his defeat, 25, 30, 259; early career, 136, 137, 140; and his brother, 145, 146; his death, 160

Chamberlain, Joseph (1836-1914), father of Neville, 136, 138, 225; and Beatrice Webb, 147

Chamberlain, Norman, 141

Churchill, Sir Winston (1874-1965), 14, 16, 86, 97, 111, 226, 258; and Lloyd George, 17, 18; on Baldwin, 24, 42, 50, 54, 55; Chancellor of the Exchequer, 34, 35; and the General Strike, 37; distrusted by Baldwin, 43; on the Government's failure in 1933, 50; and Baldwin's last years, 57; and the National Government, 117, 254; on MacDonald, 127, 128, 130; on Chamberlain, 140; black-balled by Chamberlain, 160; and the dangers of appeasement, 173; and Munich, 184, 185; and Russia's offer of a Triple Alliance, 188-90; becomes Prime Minister, 193; approves Halifax as Foreign Secretary, 239; *The Gathering Storm*, 42, 54, 130, 188

Citrine, Walter (later 1st Baron Citrine) (1887-   ), and the General Strike, 36, 38

City of London, and the 1931 crisis, 106, 109; and the Gold Standard, 111

Clay, Sir Henry, biographer of Norman, 201, 210, 213, 219-20

Clydesiders, and MacDonald, 75, 76, 77, 80, 96

Clynes, John Robert (1869-1949), 29, 85, 123; beaten by MacDonald, 75; and the second Labour Government, 113

Coalition Government, 74; calls for a vote of confidence in, 21; and the General Strike, 33, 34; its break up, 77

Cokayne, Brian (later Lord Cullen), Governor of the Bank of England, 204, 206

Collective Security, 53-4, 183

Collet, Sir Mark, 198

Communist International, and the Zinoviev letter, 92, 95

Communist Party, British, and Campbell's arrest, 87; and the Zinoviev letter, 92-3, 94

Conservative Party, Baldwin and, 16-17, 23, 24, 42, 55, 259; its distrust of Lloyd George, 17, 21; and Baldwin's success, 28-9; its vote of censure on Campbell's arrest, 88, 89, 90; and the Zinoviev letter, 96; and the 1929 election, 104; and the financial crisis, 110; distrust of a National Government, 122; and MacDonald's resignation, 131-2, 133; Chamberlain's influence on, 150; and the League of Nations, 157-8; and appeasement, 183; inability to adapt itself to a one-party system, 259

Conservative Reconstruction Committee, 145, 146

Conservative Research Department, 160

Cooper, Sir Alfred Duff (later Viscount Norwich) (1890-1956), and Hitler's ultimatum to Czechoslovakia, 177-8, 243; his dismissal, 258

Cripps, Sir Stafford (1889-1952), 129

Crowe, Sir Eyre (1864-1925), and the Zinoviev letter, 93, 94

Cunliffe, Lord, Governor of the Bank of England, 205-6

Cunliffe Committee, and the Gold Standard, 34, 210

Curzon, George Nathaniel Curzon, Marquis (1859-1925), 14, 16; and Lloyd George, 17; passed over for Baldwin, 28; as Foreign Secretary, 80

Czechoslovakia, Chamberlain and the German threat to, 166-70; Runciman sent as 'mediator', 169-70;

A PATTERN OF RULERS

Czechoslovakia—*cont.*
denounced by Hitler, 171; and *The Times* leader, 170-2; the Munich crisis, 172 ff., 180-2; Hitler's ultimatum to, 177, 179; starts to evacuate, 181; final German aggression against, 186; Halifax and, 241-5

Daily Express, and the Munich crisis, 170

Daily Herald, 86, 110; the author as financial editor, 111-12, 209; the author as Editor, 171

Daily Mail, 88, 102; and the General Strike, 36-7, 38; and the Zinoviev letter, 93, 94

Daily Telegraph, 186

Daladier, Edouard, 178-80, 243

Dallas, George, 241

Dalton, Hugh, Baron (1887-1962), 123, 188, 241, 247; and Halifax as P.M., 248

Davidson, J. C. C., 23, 29

Dawson, Geoffrey, Editor of *The Times*, his Leader on the Sudeten Germans, 170-2, 176; Halifax and, 226, 227, 229

Democracy, its inter-war failure to think as well as talk internationally, 153-5; its dependence on dialogue, 253

Derby, Edward George Villiers Stanley, Earl of (1865-1948), 18, 31

Dictatorships, remain despotic and nationalist, 155; comparable to an ineffective Opposition, 257-8

Dixon, Sir Pierson, 2

Dunglass, Lord (Sir Alec Douglas-Home) and Munich, 180, 245

Economist, and the 1931 election, 123

Eden, Anthony (later Lord Avon) (1897-), 184, 190; dismissed by Chamberlain, 166, 238, 258; Halifax and, 234, 237; his ineffective protest, 259

Edward VIII (1894-), his abdication, 1, 43, 56, 134

Einzig, Paul, 207, 213

Elton, Godfrey Elton, 1st Baron (1892-), biographer of MacDonald, 65, 66, 72

Fabian Society, MacDonald and, 64-5

Feiling, Sir Keith, biographer of Chamberlain, 139

First world war, 1914-18, 2; its political aftermath, 19; its effect on Baldwin's character, 40; MacDonald and, 68-72, 73; the Department of National Service and, 142-3; followed by an increase in internationalism, 153

Fisher, Sir Warren (1879-1948), and the Gold Standard, 111-12

Foreign Office, MacDonald and, 80; and the Zinoviev letter, 93-6; and *The Times* leader on Czechoslovakia, 171; and Chamberlain's post-Munich policy, 186

Four Power Pact, 127

France, and Hitler's entry into the Rhineland, 50, 237; Britain's commitment to, 1914, 71; MacDonald and, 84; and the 1931 crisis, 105, 109; Chamberlain and, 167, 176, 259; Norman's dislike of, 213; Halifax and, 237, 241, 242

Fulham, by-election of 1933, 52-4

Gandhi (1869-1948), 41, 230

Gee, Captain, V.C., defeats MacDonald, 74

General Strike, 1; Baldwin and, 33-9 *passim*; responsibility of the Administration for, 33-9 *passim*; Chamberlain and, 148; Norman and, 212

George V (1865-1936), 27; MacDonald and 82; and the formation of a National Government, 116, 150; and Chamberlain, 150; and Halifax's Viceroyship, 229

Germany, Baldwin and, 48, 50, 53, 54-6, 101; and the financial crisis, 1931, 105-6, 219; MacDonald and, 128; and National Socialism, 152; effect of the economic depression, 156; invades the Rhineland, 159; Chamberlain's attitude to, 160-1, 166, 169; invades Austria, 165; Norman's preference for, 213

Gladstone, Dr John Hall (1827-1902), 65

Gladstone, Margaret, her marriage to MacDonald, 65-7

Goebbels, Joseph, Halifax and, 236

Goering, Hermann, Halifax and, 232, 233, 235, 244

Gold Standard, the return to pre-war parity, 34, 155-6; and the 1931 financial crisis, 111, 120, 151, 219-21; a national myth, 111; Norman and, 210-13, 217 ff.; replaced by an Exchange Equalization Account, 221

Government of India Bill, 1935, 43

Graham, William, 114, 123; and the financial crisis, 110, 111; and MacDonald, 113

Grant, Sir Alexander, MacDonald and, 88-9

Great Britain, 1919-39, the Government's catastrophic policy, 1, 157, 251-60 passim; her commitment to France in 1914, 71; war debt to the U.S., 27, 211; foreign relations in 1929, 101; and the financial crisis, 1931, 105-7; her failure to act internationally, 153-5; and the return to the Gold Standard, 1925, 155, 157; and the invasion of Manchuria, 158; her attitude to Germany, 158; her unpreparedness for war, 183; and the gentleman amateur in politics, 255; capacity for hero-worship, 255-6; nature of her two-party system, 256-7

Greece, and Turkey, 16, 18

Greenwood, Arthur (1880-1954), 77, 114, 123, 191, 246

Gregory, J. D., 90

Gregory, Maundy, 64

Grey, Sir Edward, Viscount Grey of Falloden (1862-1933), MacDonald and, 69, 70, 71; public distrust of, 70; and the War, 71, 72

Griffith-Boscawen, Sir Arthur, 21

Hailsham, Douglas Hogg, Viscount, 126

Haldane, Richard Burdon, Viscount (1856-1928), 93; and the War, 71; MacDonald and, 85

Halifax, Charles Lindley Wood, Viscount (1839-1934), father of Edward, 224

Halifax, Edward Frederick Lindley Wood, 1st Earl of (1881-1959), 2; and the Czech crisis, 168, 169, 171,

174, 180, 241-5; and the invasion of Poland, 191, 245-7; biography, 223; his public image, 223, 227, 229, 232, 238; family background, 224-5; his character, 225, 228, 240, 248, 252, 253, 254, 256; enters Parliament, 225-6; his marriage, 225; and the war, 226-7; President of Board of Education, 228, 232; Viceroy of India, 229-30, 240; life in country houses, 231; and the National Government, 231-2; visits Germany, 233-6; and European atrocities, 236, 240; defends the Munich Agreement, 236; and France, 237, 241, 242; Foreign Secretary, 238 ff.; and appeasement, 239, 245, 247-8; and the Munich Conference, 243; escapes censure, 245, 250; and the declaration of war, 247-8; a possible successor to Chamberlain, 248-9; Ambassador to the U.S., 249-50; Fulness of Days, 234, 236-7, 246-7, 250

Hamilton, Mary Agnes, 124

Hardie, James Keir (1856-1915), 62, 69, 98

Harrod, Sir Roy, Life of Keynes, 151, 214; and the return to the Gold Standard, 212

Harrow School, Baldwin and, 5-7

Harvey, Colonel, American Ambassador, 27

Harvey, Sir Ernest, 109

Hastings, Sir Patrick (1880-1952), MacDonald and, 85, 87; and Campbell's arrest, 87-8, 89

Henderson, Arthur (1863-1935), 29, 38, 123; and the Labour Party, 74-5, 80; and MacDonald, 76, 85; as Foreign Secretary, 102, 108, 109; and the financial crisis, 110, 111, 114

Henderson, Sir Nevile (1882-1942), 167-8; fails to warn Hitler, 174-5

Henlein, Konrad, 170

Herriot, Edouard (1872-1957), 84

Hewart, Sir Gordon (later Viscount) (1870-1943), 89

Hitler, Adolf (1889-1945), 105, 128; and the Rhineland, 50, 158-9; invades Austria, 165; and Czechoslovakia, 166, 167 ff., 175 ff., 186, 187; his unplanned policy, 167; his

Hitler, Adolph—*cont.*
deception of Chamberlain, 168-9; firm action against advised, 174; his ultimatum, 177, 180; and Munich, 180-1; anti-Jewish atrocities, 185; takes Prague, 186, 245; and the Soviet Union, 189; meeting with Halifax, 234

Hoare, Sir Samuel (later 1st Viscount Templewood) (1880-1959), 31, 49, 132, 178, 238

Hoare/Laval Pact, 49, 132, 238, 258

Hoover, Herbert Clark (1874-1964), 49; proposes a moratorium on reparation payments, 105-6, 219

Hore-Belisha, Leslie, Baron (1893-1957), 246; on Chamberlain, 147; his dismissal, 192, 258

Horne, Robert Horne, Viscount (1871-1940), 14; and Lloyd George, 17; attacks MacDonald, 89

House of Lords, MacDonald and, 107; Halifax and, 225-6

Housman, Alfred Edward (1859-1936), 7

Independent Labour Party, MacDonald and, 65, 70, 72, 73, 74, 81; and the 1929 Government, 104

India, Baldwin's policy and, 43; Halifax as Viceroy, 229-31

Inskip, Sir Thomas (later Viscount Caldecote) (1876-1947), appointed Minister of Defence, 50, 160

Invergordon, Naval mutiny at, 119-20

Ireland, Lloyd George's Government and, 16; and Home Rule, 140

Isaacs, George, 36, 38

Italy, 49, 238; invades Abyssinia, 158

Japan, 49; and Manchuria, 53, 156, 158

Jarrow, 213

Jews, the, Hitler and, 185, 241

Johnston, Thomas, 77

Jones, Dr Thomas, 30, 98 235

Joynson-Hicks, William (later Viscount Brentford), 37

Jung, Carl (1875-), Norman and, 201

Kennard, Sir Howard, 191, 246

Keynes, John Maynard Keynes, Baron (1883-1946), 13, 27, 108, 255, 256; and the American Loan Agreement,

28; and the return to gold at pre-war parity, 34, 111; opposes a reduction in miners' wages, 34; condemns the National Government's measures, 119; and our war debt to America, 212; and Norman, 214-15; *General Theory of Employment*, 151

Kipling, Rudyard (1865-1936), 8, 9

Kirkwood, David, 77

Kordt, Theo, 172, 174, 242

Kuusinen, and the Zinoviev letter, 92

Labour Government, first (1924), its Administration, 80-6; marked by strikes, 86; its resignation and defeat, 86-7, 96-7; and the Zinoviev letter, 90-6; failure to relate economic and political actions, 157

Labour Government, second (1929), 101ff.; the crises facing, 104-6, 112; its responsibility for the financial crisis, 107, 108, 110, 112; its Budget deficit, 110; and the run on the pound, 112, 113-14; financial illiteracy of its Cabinet, 112-13; failure to relate political and economic actions, 157

Labour Monthly, 96

Labour Party, its weakness, 1, 254; its rise, 28; Baldwin and, 29, 31, 42, 52; and the General Strike, 38; and rearmament, 49; MacDonald and, 66, 67, 72, 74 ff.; its statements of policy, 74, 76; its needs in a leader, 75; MacDonald becomes its Parliamentary Leader, 74 ff.; its new membership, 76-7; and the 1922 election, 77; its need of a leader, 80; its dismay at MacDonald's Premiership, 81-3; disillusioned by his politics, 83, 89; and Campbell's arrest, 87; and the Zinoviev letter, 90-7 *passim*; its unreadiness for government, 100; and the 1929 election, 101; and MacDonald's defection, 115; and a National Government, 122, 123; and the Munich crisis, 172-3, 182; responsibility for the flowering of appeasement, 182-3; its near destruction, 257

Labour Representation Committee, 66

Lansbury, George (1859-1940), 70, 104, 114; member of the National Government, 123; and the Poor Law, 148

Law, Andrew Bonar (1858-1923), 13, 14, 147; and Lloyd George, 18, 22; Beaverbrook and, 20, 22-4; efforts to bring him back to leadership, 22-5; his illness, 23; Premiership and death, 25, 27, 146; and the American Loan Agreement, 27-8; and Chamberlain, 145, 146

League of Nations, Baldwin and, 49; the 'Peace Ballot', 53, 54; and disarmament, 101; embodiment of international justice, 152-3, 156; planned for a static society, 156; Government attitude to, 157; Chamberlain and, 165; the Labour Party and, 182

Lees-Smith, H. B., 77

Leicester, recruiting rally at, 1914, 68

Leicester Pioneer, 69

Lenin, Vladimir (1870-1924), 251

Liberal Party, 65; its disintegration, 1, 25, 28, 100, 254; defects to Labour, 77; and Campbell's arrest, 88, 89; and a National Government, 122

Lloyd George, David Lloyd George, 1st Earl (1863-1945), 77, 86, 89, 102, 226, 227; and Baldwin, 14; his overthrow, 15-25 *passim*; his foreign policy, 16; his personal life, 17; distrusted by the Conservative Party, 17 ff.; loss of prestige, 18; his defeat, 25; as Prime Minister, 82; his Emergency Powers Act, 86; and the dissolution of Parliament, 1931, 122; and Chamberlain, 142, 143, 144, 188, 258; on Bankers, 195; and the Bank of England, 206, 211

Lockhart, Major, Halifax and, 249-50

Lossiemouth, MacDonald and, 61, 62-4, 110, 134

Lough, Thomas, MacDonald and, 65, 66

MacDonald, George (1824-1905), his daughters, 8

MacDonald, James Ramsay (1866-1937), 2, 29, 195, 227; his political history, 25; biography, 61; his birth and upbringing, 61-2; effect of his illegitimacy, 62; his appearance and character, 62, 68, 70, 76, 79, 81, 85, 97, 98, 252, 253, 254, 256; his Socialism, 63-4, 67-8, 83, 100-1, 108; his need to be accepted, 64, 82-3, 117-18, 254; arrives in London, 64; and the Fabian Society, 64-5; his marriage, 65-7, 98; his social transformation, 65-6, 79, 81; and the Labour Movement and Party, 66, 67, 72, 74 ff., 99-100; M.P. for Leicester, 66; his speeches and writings, 67-8, 69, 70, 73, 76, 78, 79, 99, 107, 118, 127, 128-9; and the War, 68-72, 73; his public image, 68, 72, 75, 124; as a parliamentarian, 70, 74, 79; defeated at Leicester, 72, 73; returned for Aberavon, 74; leader of the Parliamentary Labour Party, 74-5, 76, 77; his ambitions for the Party, 78, 80; becomes Prime Minister, 78 ff.; as Foreign Secretary, 79, 83-5; his first Administration, 80-1; and social ceremony, 82-3, 98-9; his effect on political life, 83, 99; relations with his Cabinet, 85-6, 113, 116; and his Government's resignation and defeat, 86-7, 91-2, 96-7; accepts shares in McVitie and Price, 88-9; and the Campbell affair, 89; and the Zinoviev letter, 90, 92, 93-7; his intangibility, 97-8; and the 1929 Government, 101 ff.; and foreign affairs, 101-2, 127; and the financial crisis, 1931, 107-10 *passim*; his dislike of the T.U.C., 113; Prime Minister of a National Government, 115-22, 125-31, 258; results of his defection from Labour, 115-16, 128-9; and the 1931 general election, 122, 124; his increasing ambiguity, 129-31; his resignation, 131-2; returned for Scottish Universities, 132-3; last years and death, 134; a product of contemporary political conditions, 251-60 *passim*

MacDonald, John, father of Ramsay, 61

MacDonald, Malcolm (1901-), 116, 132

MacDonald (*née* Gladstone), Margaret, 65-7, 98

McKenna, Reginald (1863-1943), 214

Mackintosh, John P., *The British Cabinet*, 113
Macleod, Iain, 125; and MacDonald's defection, 117; and Chamberlain, 160
Macmanus, Arthur, and the Zinoviev letter, 92
Macmillan, Harold (1894-), 192, 258
Macmillan, Lord, and Norman, 215-17, 218
Macmillan Committee on Finance and Industry, 104, 106; Norman and, 209, 210, 214-19
Manchester Guardian, 122, 124
Marlowe, Thomas, Editor of the *Daily Mail*, and the General Strike, 36
Marxism, 63, 108
Masaryk, Jan (1886-1948), and Hitler's ultimatum, 178, 180
Masterman, Charles F. G. (1874-1927), 70
Maxton, James (1885-1946), 77, 88
May, Sir George, his Committee on Government Finance, 105, 107, 108, 110
Mining Industry, and the General Strike, 33, 34, 36; its Federation, 77
Morgan, J. P., and Britain's run on the pound, 114
Mosley, Sir Oswald (1896-), 104, 105
Munich Agreement, public reaction to the crisis, 170, 172, 183-4; events leading up to, 172-9; Chamberlain and, 180-2
Munro, Dr Hector, 68
Mussolini, Benito, 127, 166, 239; invades Abyssinia, 158; and Munich, 180

National Government, the, its formation, 1, 115-18; its solutions for the crisis, 118-19; and the run on the pound, 120; its election, 123-4; its popular appeal, 124, 152; a political disaster, 254-5, 256, 257
National Union of Conservative Associations, its 1922 Annual Conference, 21
Norman, Montagu, 1st Baron Norman (1871-1950), 2; and the drop in sterling exchange, 106, 109; and the Gold Standard, 111, 210-13, 217;

biography, 195; his rapid rise, 195-6, 204-6; his appearance, 196; background and education, 196-7; in the U.S., 197-8, 200; and the Boer War, 198; with Brown, Shipley, 198-9, 200-3, 207, 208; his character, 199, 200, 201, 203, 204, 251; consults psychoanalysts, 201-2; nature of his illness, 203; wartime employment, 204; enters the Bank of England, 204-5; Governor, 205; his despotic rule, 207-8; influence on monetary policy, 209; indifference to industry and trade unionism, 210, 213, 217-18; and Britain's war debt, 211-12; and European stability, 213-14, 218; examined by Macmillan Committee, 214-19; and the financial crisis, 1931, 219; last years and death, 221; product of the political conditions of his time, 251-60 *passim*
Norway, defeat in, 192

Observer, and the Munich crisis, 170
O'Neill, J. J., 89

Pacifism, 52-4, 68, 182-3
Parmoor, Charles Cripps, Baron (1852-1941), and MacDonald's defection, 116
Peacock, Edward, 109
Philadelphia Public Ledger, on Baldwin, 32
Poincaré, Jules (1854-1912), 84
Poland, Chamberlain and, 187-8, 190, 246; German attack on, 191, 245, 246-7; Halifax and, 245-7
Ponsonby, Arthur, Baron (1871-1946), 69, 93; MacDonald and, 85
Poynter, Sir Edward (1836-1919), 8, 9
Premiership, the, its flexibility, 26; a dictatorship without an effective Opposition, 258
Pugh, Arthur, and the General Strike, 35, 38

Quarterly Review, and the suspension of the Gold Standard, 121

Raczyniski, Count, Polish Ambassador, 247
Ramsay, Anne, mother of Ramsay MacDonald, 71; her death, 67

Reading, Rufus Isaacs, 1st Marquess of (1860-1935), 229, 258; on the Trades Disputes Act, 39-40
Repington, Colonel Charles à Court (1858-1925), 71
Roosevelt, Franklin Delano (1884-1945), 43, 108, 119; his offer of mediation, 184
Rothermere, Harold Harmsworth, 1st Viscount (1868-1940), 51
Roumania, Chamberlain and, 186-7, 188
Rowse, A. L., on Baldwin, 57
Royal Navy, mutiny in, 1, 111, 119-20
Runciman, Walter (later Viscount), 123; sent to Prague as a 'mediator', 169-70, 170-1
Russia, 69, 71, *see also* Soviet Union

Salter, Sir Arthur (1859-1928), on Chamberlain, 148
Samuel, Herbert (later Viscount) (1870-), and the National Government, 125, 126, 258
Samuel Report, on the Mining Industry, 36
Schacht, Dr, 219
Science, belief in as a liberating force, 63-4
Seaham, MacDonald and, 123, 124, 132
Shaw, George Bernard (1856-1950), 64
Shinwell, Emanuel (1884-), 123; and MacDonald, 76; M.P., in 1922, 77
Simon, John, 1st Viscount Simon (1873-1954), 49, 70, 88, 178, 188, 246
Simon Commission, 229
Sinclair, Sir Archibald (later 1st Viscount Thurso), 125, 180, 258
Snowden, Philip, Viscount (1864-1937), 69, 70, 104; distrust of MacDonald, 74, 76; his character, 76; and the first Labour Government, 81, 85-6; his Socialism, 108; and the financial crisis, 110-11; and the second Labour Government, 113, 114; and the National Government, 115, 125, 126, 258; vilifies his colleagues, 123, 124; his resignation, 126, 131; and Norman, 210
Social Democratic Foundation, 63, 64
Somervell, D. C., 7
Soviet Union, and the Zinoviev letter, 92, 95; signs the Kellogg Pact, 101;

Chamberlain and, 165, 187, 188; proposes a Triple Alliance against Germany, 188, 189-90; Halifax and, 241, 242-3
Spanish Civil War, 181, 236; British diplomacy and, 159
Sprigge, Cecil, and the Gold Standard, 111, 112
Stalin, Josef, 189; and Lady Astor, 190
Stamfordham, Arthur John Bigge, Baron (1849-1931), 29, 30
Steed, Henry Wickham (1871-1956), 13
Steel-Maitland, Sir Arthur (1876-1935), and the General Strike, 35
Strachey, Giles Lytton (1880-1932), *Eminent Victorians*, 3
Strang, William (later 1st Baron), 176, 180-1, 182, 240
Strong, Benjamin, and Norman, 203, 210, 211
Sudeten Germans, 170-1, 175
Sutherland, Millicent, Duchess of, 62-3, 83, 99
Switzerland, and the 1931 financial crisis, 106

Talbot, Lord Edmund, and Baldwin, 13
Taylor, A. J. P., 167, 240
Temple, William, Archbishop of Canterbury, 231
Thomas, James Henry (1874-1949), 29; and the General Strike, 35, 36; MacDonald and, 85; and the Zinoviev letter, 94; and the 1929 Labour Government, 104, 105, 113; and the financial crisis, 110; and the National Government, 115; his resignation, 132, 133
Thomson, Christopher Birdwood, Baron (1875-1930), MacDonald and, 85, 94
Times, The, 13, 185, 255; Baldwin's letter to ('F.S.T.'), 13-14; Bonar Law's letter to ('Colonial'), 27; reproved by Asquith, 71; and Sudeten Germans, 170 ff, 176; letter from 'A Conservative' (2.4.1964), 251
Trade Unions, and the General Strike, 35; their early demonstrations, 63; distrust of MacDonald, 74, 76, 86; the basis of the Labour Party, 77
Trades Disputes Act, 1927, 39-40

Trades Union Congress, and the General Strike, 35-9; MacDonald and, 86, 113; refuses a cut in unemployment benefit, 114; and Munich, 172-3

Trevelyan, Charles (later Sir) (1870-1958), 77; MacDonald and, 85

Trevor-Roper, Professor, 1, 127

Trotter, H. A., 206

Turkey, and Greece, 16, 18

Unemployment, 1; after the First World War, 15; basis of the 1929 election, 102; its subsequent rise, 104; and the 1931 financial crisis, 107, 108-9, 110; its world figures, 109; MacDonald and, 130

United States, Britain's war debt to, 27, 211; and MacDonald, 101; and the 1931 financial crisis, 105-6, 107, 109, 112; and Britain's run on the pound, 114; inter-war failure to accept its new responsibilities, 155; and the invasion of Manchuria, 158; emergence of New York as the most powerful banking centre, 206; its heroes, 255-6

Vansittart, Sir Robert (1881-1957), 240; and the appeasement of Germany, 173; The Mist Procession, 229

Versailles Treaty, ignored economics, 156; Britain's remorse for, 159, 182; the Lowther Petition and, 227

Vittoz, Dr Roger, Norman and, 202, 208

Warner, George, and the Munich crisis, 174

Waterhouse, Colonel, secretary to Baldwin, 37, 38

Webb, Beatrice (later Baroness Passfield) (1858-1943), and MacDonald's character, 64-5, 67, 75, 80-1, 96, 97, 98, 101-2; on Chamberlain, 147, 148

Webb, Mary (1881-1927), 8

Webb, Sydney (later Baron Passfield) (1859-1947), and the Labour Party, 74, 77; and MacDonald, 79; and the first Labour Government, 81, 86; his preoccupations, 108; and Chamberlain, 148

Weir, Macneill, private secretary to MacDonald, 129

Weizsäcker, Ernst, 173-4, 244

Welles, Sumner, 184

Wells, H. G. (1866-1946), 63, 64; Shape of Things to Come (film), 183

Westminster Bank Review, and the suspension of the Gold Standard, 121

Wheatley, John, 77, 80; MacDonald and, 85

Wiedemann, Captain, 168-9

Wigram, Sir Clive, private secretary to George V, 109

Wilmot, John (later Lord Wilmot), Labour victory at East Fulham, 52-3, 54

Wilson, Sir Henry (1864-1922), 71

Wilson, Sir Horace, Chamberlain and, 161-2, 166, 168; and the Czech crisis, 172, 174, 179, 180; and the invasion of Poland, 191; Halifax and, 240

Woolton, Lord (1883-1964), boycotts Germany, 168

Workers Weekly, 87

Wrench, Evelyn, Geoffrey Dawson, 171

Yorkshire Post, and the Munich crisis, 170

Young, George, 80

Young, G. M., biographer of Baldwin, 10-11, 23, 24-5, 39, 42, 54

Young, Plan for Reparations, 101, 105

Zaharoff, Sir Basil (1850-1936), 64

Zinoviev letter, 90-7; did it cause Labour's defeat, 90-1, 94-6; its arrival in London, 92-3; its publication, 94-5; denounced by the Soviet Union, 95-6; re-establishes MacDonald's leadership, 96-7